The Directors Guild of America
Oral History Series

Norman Lloyd,1988

Stages:
NORMAN LLOYD

Interviewed by
Francine Parker

The Directors Guild of America &
The Scarecrow Press, Inc.
Metuchen, N.J., & London, 1990

British Library Cataloguing-in-Publication data available

Library of Congress Cataloging-in-Publication data

Lloyd, Norman, 1914-
   Stages : Norman Lloyd / interviewed by Francine Parker.
      p.   cm. -- (The Directors Guild of America oral history
series ; 9)
   ISBN 0-8108-2290-3 (alk. paper)
   1. Lloyd, Norman, 1914- . 2. Actors--United States--Biography.
3. Television producers and directors--United States--Biography.
I. Parker, Francine. II. Title. III. Title: Norman Lloyd.
IV. Series.
PN2287.L53A3 1990
791.43'023'092--dc20
[B]

89-77810

For Peggy
this red rose

Table of Contents

Acknowledgments

A distinguished actor, director and producer in the theatre, television and motion pictures, Norman Lloyd participated in most of the seminal American theatre movements of the 1930's, including The Group Theatre, the Theatre of Action, the Federal Theatre, and the Mercury Theatre; guided the legendary *Alfred Hitchcock Presents* for eight years as both a producer and director; and worked on major films with, among others, Lewis Milestone, Charles Chaplin, Joseph Losey, and Jean Renoir. Norman Lloyd represents the finest traditions of American entertainment: his versatility, erudition and sheer talent were an invaluable asset to each production that he touched, and his standards of intelligence, wit, and taste were held without compromise. In this extensive review of his career, Norman Lloyd vividly recalls his colleagues and collaborators, his hopes and his accomplishments.

The interviews for Norman Lloyd's initial oral history were initiated by David Shepard and conducted by director Francine Parker between July 1981 and May 1983. The interviews were then put aside, while Mr. Lloyd continued to add credits to his distinguished career. Beginning in 1987, Mr. Lloyd extensively re-worked the initial series of interviews, adding further details to stories and memories so that the published version of this oral history is in fact a combination of interview and autobiography, as told in Norman Lloyd's always thoughtful and polished personal style. The Directors Guild of America is most grateful for the cooperation, good cheer, and patience evidenced by Norman Lloyd in bringing this work to its fruition. Beside him during the many drafts was his wife, Peggy, who made additional contributions. A special thanks to both of them.

The Directors Guild also wishes to extend its gratitude to Mr. James Bridges for his foreword; Woolsey Ackerman for carefully preparing the text for publication; Marian Barnett for assisting Mr. Lloyd; Nick Lovrovich, Leslie Weldon, Fritz Monsma, and Brian Rose of the DGA for checking the text and deciphering computer publishing programs; and especially to Mr. David Shepard, who initiated the project with the vision and historical knowledge for which he is so widely treasured. Photographs are from the collection of Mr. and Mrs. Norman Lloyd.

Deac Rossell
National Special Projects Officer
Directors Guild of America

Foreword

It never occurred to me when I first saw Norman Lloyd fall off the Statue of Liberty in Hitchcock's film — *Saboteur* that one day, many years later, that plummeting man (in one of the most startling special effects of all time) would give me my first professional writing job. At that time, in that dark theatre, in Paris, Arkansas I was only glad to see the villain get his due and the hero saved.

I recognized Norman immediately when he came backstage at the Beverly Hills Playhouse in 1961 where my first play, *The Days of the Dancing*, was having its world premiere. He was very enthusiastic about my writing and some months later when I was stage managing a play for John Houseman at the UCLA Theatre Group, I got a call from Norman who asked me if I would be interested in writing an episode of *The Alfred Hitchcock Hour* which he was producing. I was and I did. It starred Robert Redford and Zohra Lampert, and it was the official start of my career.

Although Norman was the first producer/director I ever worked for, he was and is the best. He knows how to develop a script, an ability not found very often in the motion picture business these days. He knows how to encourage a writer to do his or her best work and to make the process itself interesting and fun. We did eighteen shows on that series together in the space of three years, and later when he was producer/director of the Hollywood Television Theatre we worked on an adaptation of Jean Renoir's play *Carola* with the master Renoir himself. Those were easily my happiest years as a writer, and I've often wondered why. Was it because I was just starting out? Partly. But mainly, I think, it had to do with Norman who was so generous with his knowledge and friendship. It was truly a real education to work with someone who had had as much experience and who had done so much in the theatre, in film, in television and who understood the creative process and its ultimate relationship with the audience. Here is a man who started in vaudeville, worked with Le Gallienne as an apprentice, has been part of the Mercury Theatre, and has been a friend and a professional colleague of Welles, Chaplin, Hitchcock, Renoir, Milestone, Brecht, Houseman, and Laughton, to name a few.

Although I have known Norman and his lovely wife, Peg, since the early sixties and have had many wonderful evenings in their home (and heard many of Norman's amazing stories), I was not quite prepared for the scope of this oral history which you have in your hands. It is an important document from someone who was there, a very immediate and human history of a very exciting time. Is it still the same? No, of course not, and Norman offers some reasons why and lots of fascinating insights into the reasons why themselves.

Bravo.

James Bridges
Los Angeles, California

My Early Days

I started in the theatre. When I was six or seven, there was a great vogue for child actors, because of the enormous success of Jackie Coogan in *The Kid*. There was also another child by the name of Wesley Barry who was not as big a star but was very well known; later, he became an assistant director in the movies. With the enormous success of these two fellows and with the kind of vaudeville that existed in those days, I think that the mothers of the land all hoped that perhaps there was a fortune to be found in their children. In any case, I believe in retrospect that my mother, who had a good voice, sang very nicely and on occasion would appear as a singer for her ladies' club, had always fostered ambitions to be in the theatre. She got the idea that maybe I had some talent.

She started by taking me to what used to be called an elocution teacher and then later to dancing and singing lessons. This was not unusual; there were many children doing the same in those days. The professional Children's School didn't exist at the time; an organization called the Stage Children's Fund developed the song and dance talents of children. The Shuberts were interested in it, as were other established managers of the time.

FRANCINE PARKER: At a fee to the pupil?

LLOYD: For a modest fee you went to a large dance

1

studio on 57th Street near what was then 6th Avenue. The building is still there; whenever I am in New York I find myself walking past it and looking up to the fourth or fifth-floor studio of the Stage Children's Fund, where I started.

Well-known graduates were Milton Berle and Georgie Tapps. I remember Georgie Tapps, who was then Mortimer Becker. He was a brilliant dancer, far superior to any of us; he *should* have been named Georgie Tapps, because he was an incredible tap dancer. Berle was there a couple years ahead of me. We had various instructors; towards the end of my experience at the Stage Children's Fund, Adelaide and Hughes became the instructors. They were the foremost dance team in America at the time; before them, the Castles had been the greatest team. In vaudeville, there was almost always a dance team on the bill; the handsome man in tails, the lady in an evening gown. I remember one of the Bennett sisters, Barbara, dancing with a man named Maurice. Adelaide and Hughes would appear at the Palace. Mr. Hughes, my teacher, looked like Edward, the Prince of Wales. I took a couple of private lessons from him, much to his chagrin, because I could never really dance that well and could only do basic steps. He had a studio in Carnegie Hall, which seemed a little arty for a vaudeville team on the Keith circuit; nevertheless, that was where we children would go for private lessons.

I started to perform on occasion at benefits in theatres or in clubs like the ladies' clubs to which my mother belonged. One gained a reputation; people liked "kid acts." I would go out and do a song and dance. I stole most of my material from Al Jolson and Eddie Cantor, so I was always either listening to their records or going to see them. Jolson was a unique performer of extraordinary electricity; never mind the sentimentality, he was dynamite in the theatre. Alone, on stage, his hold on an audience was complete. Chaplin once told me he thought Jolson was the greatest performer of this kind he had seen. You listen to the songs, and they're sappy, sentimental, black-face, all that — except that he was amazing. Trying to imitate him and Cantor gave me a sense of the audience.

My mother would often take me to the matinee of a musical from which we would lift material to use in my act. If the musical starred Jolson or Cantor, so much the better. One afternoon, we went to the Imperial Theatre on 45th Street in New York. Through some oversight my mother had mistaken the matinee day for the Imperial. Thus we found ourselves in the lobby moving about in great disappointment. A very tall gentleman, some seven feet tall in my nine-year-old boy's eyes, dressed in a black overcoat and bowler, sensed our disappointment. After a few words, he learned of my aspiration. "So you want to be an actor?" "Yes," I replied. "Young man," he warned, "you'll end up with lumbago in Milwaukee."

I've carried his admonition with me all my days. I have never been to Milwaukee and have no intention of ever going there.

I appeared at vaudeville benefits, old actors' homes and such places until I was ten or eleven. Then one reaches that awkward stage where a "kid act" isn't really attractive anymore, unless you're brilliantly skillful, as Tapps was. So I gave it up for a while and finished school. But I kept a great love of theatre and performed in amateur dramatics, and at camp. What had developed was that by the time I was eight or nine, I was really a professional. Mr. Hughes pointed it out; I heard him remark to someone, "This boy is absolutely a professional actor in his attitude and in the way he works." I've been fortunate to have that attitude and I've always admired it in others. I find it all too rarely, but I have found in some fine actors a professionalism that is an attitude of getting the work done.

By the time I was eleven, I was a theatre buff. In

those days, in New York City, you went to Gray's, on the corner of 43rd Street and Broadway across from the Times Building. As you went in, it was a drug store; in the back was Joe Leblang's ticket agency. The great thing about the store was the basement, one of New York's subterranean stores, where you could get tickets for most shows for half price. The closest thing to it now is the ticket booth in Duffy Square, where you can see hundreds lined up before a matinee or evening performance. In the days of Gray's basement, for fifty cents, you could see a major star, so you didn't wait for hit shows. If there was an actor, a cast, a play or a writer that interested you, you paid fifty cents to sit in the balcony in a dollar seat — which was a very good seat, because some shows had a top of only $2.20. Many people remember Gray's basement fondly.

I graduated from high school at fifteen, and entered New York University, taking a general arts major. But my urge for theatre was growing in intensity. All around me I could see the way the Depression was affecting everyone; for my family, for people in business like my father, it was a terrible time. I just wasn't going to stay in college, paying tuition to get a degree to be a lawyer, when I could see lawyers that had become taxi-drivers. I had had great success as an actor with various amateur theatre groups, always thinking of myself as a person with professional experience, and shortly before the end of my sophomore year I read in the papers that Eva Le Gallienne was going to hold an audition for apprentices. Le Gallienne had a theatre adjoining the Armory on 14th Street, just west of 6th Avenue called the Civic Repertory Theatre. It was unique in its time and, in retrospect, unique in the history of the American theatre.

The Civic Repertory Theatre

It was May. I was coming to the end of my sophomore year at NYU and my restlessness was growing unmanageable. When I read about the audition, I decided to take it, just to see what would happen. I don't mean to imply that I was doubtful, for my confidence would have filled an entire theatre. I went over to 14th Street, which wasn't far from school, and into the theatre, which was built in the middle of the nineteenth century. It had boxes flush with the stage, pillars and gallery seating like pews, not individual seats. Next door, Le Gallienne had bought a store-front; down a few steps to the left as you went in was a little green room. Up the stairs on the 3rd or 4th floor were the offices, where I was interviewed by the vice-president, Helen Lohman.

I was startled when she told me it would cost five dollars. I had to figure out where I was going to get it. Anyone who auditioned had to pay this. You could not bring your own material; you were given four pieces, two that Le Gallienne classified as classical works and two modern pieces. Everyone was given the same material and chose one piece from each pair: The classical pieces were from *Romeo and Juliet*: the men chose between Romeo's speech ending with "thus with a kiss, I die" or Mercutio's Queen Mab speech. I think it's an insight into Le Gallienne's mind that in 1932 one modern piece was Quintero's play, *The Women Have Their Way* and the other was of like nature. Le Gallienne did very few new plays.

Those she staged were *Alison's House*, which won the
Pulitzer Prize, her adaptation with Florida Friebus of
Alice in Wonderland, and a new play for Josephine
Hutchinson called *Dear Jane*. By and large, she did the
classics. From her point-of-view, she was right; she
provided theatre at a dollar-and-a-half top for the best
seat in the house, and one could see Chekhov, Ibsen, and
Shakespeare played beautifully. For many people, that
theatre was their theatre education.

I borrowed the five dollars from a fellow student at
NYU and started to work on my material. Cocky as I
was, I thought I needed an ally; a director to direct me. I
thought of the great theatre star, Alfred Lunt.

On a Monday night, at about ten to eight, I presented
myself at the stage door of the Martin Beck Theatre,
where Alfred Lunt was playing. To the stage doorman,
whose job it was to keep out brash youngsters such as
myself, I showed my envelope full of material and mur-
mured Le Gallienne's name, which worked its magic. He
allowed me in, asked me to wait one moment, please, and
returned with the stage manager, Leonard Loan. Later
on, he was the stage manager for *Noah*, a play in which I
appeared. I explained to Loan that I was going to audition for Eva Le Gallienne's theatre, and that out of about
seven hundred people she was going to select only twenty-five boys and twenty-five girls. I wondered if I might
come in before a couple of matinees and have Mr. Lunt
work with me and direct me in my scenes.

When I look back at this kind of brashness, I'm sad
that it diminishes as you become wiser; I am not a convert
to wisdom at all. I would rather have retained the brashness.

Leonard Loan was charming. He explained that Mr.
Lunt was making up and couldn't see me at that time, but
said he would forward the information to Mr. Lunt and
let me know. So I left. I have in my files a note from
Alfred Lunt: sweetly, he expressed his regrets for not

having the time to work with me. "The only advice I can give you," he wrote, "is <u>mean</u> <u>every</u> <u>word</u> <u>you</u> <u>say</u>." The underlining is his. On stage, this was one of Alfred Lunt's secrets; he always had a total immersion, in an almost mad way. The Lunts' distinguishing characteristic was their gaiety, the joy they would experience on stage and project to the audience. To partake was like drinking at a mountain spring.

But whatever Lunt's answer was to be, a couple of days would pass and time was of the essence. I then thought of Leslie Howard, an actor I admired enormously and who had influenced me in my theatre work. I resembled him vaguely; he was blonde with an angular face and prominent nose; I had very red hair and a prominent nose. I found him the most graceful of actors and he was truly a matinee idol, with two enormous hits, *Berkeley Square* and *The Animal Kingdom*. It may seem surprising, but he was a revolutionary actor in this country; when he came here in the early twenties, he was one of the first to be completely natural on stage, to speak naturally instead of declaiming, to keep gesture to a minimum. His style was very influential and I suppose came from England, from Gerald du Maurier, the master of the drawing room, throw-away style performance. Du Maurier influenced every actor who came after, particularly Rex Harrison. I thought Leslie Howard would be a good man to direct me and so I went to the Empire Theatre where he was appearing in *The Animal Kingdom*.

As luck would have it, Howard had decided that as a major star he wanted long summer weekends, and instead of playing on Monday nights he did an extra matinee on Thursdays, which was very shrewd for the matinee draw. For me, it was unfortunate.

I wandered back to 45th Street and the Morosco Theatre, where Romney Brent was appearing. He was not a star, but he was a very successful actor, a Mexican who had, in fact, been to NYU. I felt he would be sympathetic to and familiar with my situation. I repeated my routine with the stage doorman, who pointed me to Brent's dressing room.

It was a rather hot evening, and the door to the dressing room was open. Brent was making up. There were two people beside him, also making up: the leading lady and another prominent actor in the cast, Colin Keith Johnson. I stared at the leading lady. I had never seen her work, but she was so beautiful, and she was wearing a bra and panties. I thought to myself, at seventeen, that if this was the theatre, where a beautiful lady makes up beside you in her bra and panties, I had to get into the theatre; I had to get into the theatre quickly. The lady was Katharine Hepburn, and this was the play in which she scored her first hit, *The Warrior's Husband*.

Brent was very nice; if I liked, he said, I could come back later, but now at 8:15, they were getting ready and he didn't have time. Looking back, I don't know why I wasn't thrown out on my ear.

As I walked up 45th Street, I came to the Bijou where *Springtime for Henry* was playing, which I thought was the best British farce I had ever seen. In it, there were two very good actors, Leslie Banks and Nigel Bruce.

I thought of asking Nigel Bruce to help me. I did not consider Leslie Banks, because he was a most formidable-looking man; he had been severely wounded in World War I and had a paralysis on one side of the face which gave him an expression that frightened me. In the play, he used it as a kind of mad anger. It was already 8:20 when I asked the doorman if I might see Mr. Bruce, and the curtain was at 8:40; Mr. Bruce had not yet arrived at the theatre however. The doorman allowed me to wait, and at 8:30 Nigel Bruce came down the alley.

I explained my audition to him and asked if, perhaps before a couple of matinees, he would coach me in my roles. He answered in a British mumble and I couldn't make out what he was saying. I took the mumbling for rejection, and I walked away talking to myself about man's inhumanity to man; here was I, a great talent wandering loose with no help from the profession; nobody really understood. I had crossed the street from the Bijou, and was under the 45th Street marquee of the Astor Hotel, now long gone, but then a famous New York landmark. I heard shouting behind me. Curious, I turned around and Bruce, now five minutes from curtain, was standing with the stage doorman, both calling to me to come back. I did so. Bruce would be delighted. "Delighted, old boy; come around Wednesday matinee, shortly before two." I now had my director.

I went for two sessions with Nigel. His dressing room was the size of the proverbial postage stamp; as Fred Allen used to say, "When I started in vaudeville, I lived in a room so small that I was afraid to stick out my tongue and hit the wall."

While Nigel made up for the matinee, I stood three feet away and did my piece. He would say a word here and there, very light and easy, let me know he was amused; it was the experience of having a professional actor give his stamp of approval. He approved. "You should do well, old boy," he mumbled cheerfully.

At my audition, I was accepted as one of the twenty-five young men in the company.

It was May, 1932; I had the final exams of my sophomore year at NYU. With my future assured, I indulged myself in playing out an enormously pleasurable fantasy. It was in geology.

It was the most boring of subjects to me, and I had used the geology class to read Bernard Shaw, while the teacher talked about the Pleistocene Age and layers of rock. Next to me sat a beautiful blonde who, mystified by my play-reading, offered to help me by lending me her index cards filled with geology notes. But I was not simply a poor student; I absolutely didn't know anything.

In Latin, I was having trouble, though I believe I ultimately passed. But in geology, I was pathetic.

As my last act in college, I went to the final exam. I sat down with the other students and received the booklet of questions. As everyone else set to work, I got up and walked to the proctor.

"Would you give these to Miss So-and-so?" I said, handing him the pile of index cards. "They are her notes." I walked out of the room and out of the college on my way to the Civic Repertory Theatre.

PARKER: How did your parents react?

LLOYD: My parents were shocked beyond measure. My father, who had wanted me to complete college and become a "professional man," was enormously disappointed that a serious person should become an actor. I promised, if it didn't work out, that I would try something else, but at that stage, nothing else could have worked. I prepared to join Le Gallienne at the end of August.

In the meantime, Nigel Bruce's play, *Springtime for Henry*, had moved to the Shubert Theatre. In his now-decent dressing room, where I went to thank him for his help, he had a framed postcard from the King of England, sent to the first troops who had gone into the trenches of France in World War I. As one of those troops, Nigel had been badly wounded in the leg, and always suffered a limp. When I arrived, he was combing his hair; he had a nice head of hair, of which he was very proud. He studied both sides in the mirror. Why had I chosen to ask him for help, he wondered. I had seen him in the play — I searched for words. He rescued me.

"Oh—thought I was a comedian, eh?" He made a friend for life.

By 1951, nineteen years later, Nigel had played the famous Dr. Watson in the Sherlock Holmes films. In the course of my activities, I had had the good fortune to become a friend of Charlie Chaplin, visiting with him several times a week. He was working on *Limelight*. He wanted me to play the choreographer, Bodalink, which I did. When Chaplin described another role to me, that of Postant, the manager of the theatre, I saw my opportunity. "I have just the man," I told him. "Nigel Bruce." I waited all those years to do something for Nigel, to find some way to repay him for his kindness to me. Charlie thought it was a good idea and cast Nigel, who gave a lovely performance in the film. Nigel, who lived out at Trancas, moved to a little house in town while the movie was being shot, and on the days we worked together I would call for him in my car and take him to the studio. By then, the Sherlock Holmes series of films had ended, so it was a good time for him to do *Limelight*.

The group of apprentices at Le Gallienne's was under the charge of May Sarton. I was the youngest apprentice, at seventeen; May was perhaps twenty-one. If she had aspirations to be a writer then, she kept them secret; she wanted to be an actress, a theatre manager and a director. She was following the footsteps of Le Gallienne.

PARKER: What was her background?

LLOYD: She came from the intellectual elite; her father was a distinguished professor of the history of science, a star of the Harvard faculty. George Sarton is today considered a seminal figure in the development of his field. They were Belgian and lived in a beautiful house in Cambridge. May spoke French like a native. I don't know that she went to school, but she was raised in a household of the highest cultural level.

May, who had joined the company herself as an apprentice two seasons earlier and was now an actress with the company, saw to it that we had our dance and diction

lessons, and prepared scenes. Once a month, Le Gallienne would look at the scenes May selected.

In the regular theatre productions, we were unpaid
walk-ons. I was taken out of the carnival scene at the
beginning of *Liliom* by Le Gallienne, because I drew too
much attention to myself. I was disappointed and angry.
Later on, she let me back into the show as the bearer of
the front end of the stretcher on which the dying Liliom
was carried. After I put down the stretcher, I would join
the other apprentices behind the fence, to watch Joseph
Schildkraut's death scene. I did try to build up the "front
end of the stretcher" part considerably, however. I was to
head through a gate to a certain mark on the stage and
lower the stretcher, placing it in the effectively dramatic
light for Le Gallienne and Schildkraut to play their beautiful scene. But I saw other lights as I led the way, and
worked my way along them. Instead of going directly to
my mark, I went by way of right field, maximizing the effect of light on my shock of red hair. Then I would put
down the stretcher and do a terrific reaction to the gory
scene before retiring behind the fence. I think the only
reason I got away with it was that Le Gallienne was so
concentrated on her role that she didn't notice what she
would ordinarily have seen.

She directed all the plays herself. Constance Collier
would come down on occasion just to give advice but
there was never an outside director, even when Le Gallienne played the lead. She was infatuated with Sarah
Bernhardt and Eleanora Duse. When she would walk out
of her dressing room and turn to the left, there was a nar-
row wall, on which was a picture of Duse — the last thing
she would see before she went on stage. As a young
actress she had made a vow that she would play all the
parts that Duse and Bernhardt had played. She did play
many, if not all of them. In 1930-31, two years before I
joined the apprentice program, she had an accident that
almost killed her, the results of which she had to live with

the rest of her life. She went down to inspect a faulty gas heater in the basement of her Westport home, and lit a match. The heater exploded. She was fortunate to come through the experience alive. She had several skin-graft operations. When I arrived in 1932, she often acted in a great deal of pain.

I don't remember her ever having the stage manager give direction. I've always resented stage managers doing that, as they do today when they go out and check the show. I didn't start out in the theatre that way; I've never been able to take it with good humor. Only the director had the right and I never took it in good spirit even from the producer.

PARKER: What was a typical day like for the apprentices of the Civic?

LLOYD: Dance classes began the day at nine in the morning. We took them at 66 Fifth Avenue, in a building which is still there, now looking quaint but in those days one of the most attractive buildings in the area. It contained the Fifth Avenue Playhouse, which was a foreign film theatre. Martha Graham had a studio in the building. We were taught by Ruth Wilton, a disciple of Mary Wigman and an ex-member of her company; Wigman was a major figure in dance in the twenties and early thirties. After the class, we walked back to the theatre at 14th Street where, during the day, we worked on our scenes, took make-up classes, fencing (should this be necessary in a production), and speech classes.

Donald Cameron, a Canadian, taught us speech, as did Sayre Crawley. Crawley was very English. He was rather small, with a shock of white hair, and he wore the most beautiful tweeds; he seemed straight out of the English countryside. He was married to Mary Ward, who also worked at the theatre. My speech was New York Brooklyn and Le Gallienne told me, "If you want to play in the repertory, and want to do the classics, then you must learn to speak properly." Cameron and Crawley gave me superb speech training.

At night, we were extras in the performance, and often we would rehearse again after the evening production. We were totally immersed in the work. Tonio Selwart, one of the actors in the company, told me that we didn't know how lucky we were to be in a situation so close to that of a European state theatre. Unlike drama school training today, ours was in a theatre where a professional show was performed every night, headed by major stars — Eva Le Gallienne, Joseph Schildkraut, and later Alla Nazimova. We were part of a theatre at work, taught and criticized by professional theatre people.

Joseph (Pepe) Schildkraut, whom I got to know very well in later years, came back from Europe to be in the company. He had just played Romeo for Max Reinhardt. He was a flamboyant star, unlike anyone I had ever met before. He was very European; wildly temperamental, and had to be the center of the stage at all times. Le Gallienne handled him well. He lived in slight fear of her; she could make him cry, though his tears were more from a secret faucet, turned on at will, and had little to do with his emotions. Eyeing the female apprentices one day, he informed Le Gallienne that he would like one of them to be his dresser. Le Gallienne told him to behave himself. He might have a dresser, but chosen from among the boys. Alexander Scourby and I were given the job at fifty cents a performance.

It was a fine opportunity, but I had no idea what a dresser was supposed to do. I was so curious about his make-up, his wardrobe, his shoes, that I was not really dressing him at all; I was just picking up things and examining them. Then I committed a grave faux pas. I gave him his shoes with a shoe horn. Horrors! He had a superstition against using shoe horns. I was promptly fired, and Al Scourby, who hadn't even begun the job, was fired with me. Pepe got a professional dresser.

In general, no money changed hands during our apprenticeship. We received our training free, in exchange for our unpaid appearances as extras in the productions.

PARKER: How were you supported?

LLOYD: I lived at home in Brooklyn, forty-five minutes away. Even though my father didn't approve of what I was doing, I had an allowance of three dollars a week. Subway fare was a nickel. At the Ideal Donut Shop next door to the theatre, coffee and a doughnut cost ten cents. This was the way everybody lived it seemed. We were just like everybody else during the Depression. We knew there were rich people but they were off somewhere beyond our contact, unconnected with the world we were living in. The glamourous people were all the stars of the theatre and movies, the fantasy world we really wanted to be a part of, as every actor does when he goes into the business.

Le Gallienne's was a wonderful experience for a young actor. In those days, one's ambition was to be in a repertory theatre, for two reasons: first, because it seemed to be a theatre of quality and second, the economics. Members of Le Gallienne's theatre, although not paid large salaries, were given the guarantee of a season of some thirty weeks, which was fantastic in those days of the Depression. Working for the Theatre Guild was another desirable job, for the same reason; they had a subscription list which guaranteed five weeks' work.

But for me, the attraction was not just the money. It was the classical theatre. It was a cultural world to which I aspired. I was cultivating a need I had been born with. At fourteen, I had read Chekhov, Dickens and Scott; going to the Civic and spending my days with people like Le Gallienne and May Sarton stimulated me further. My

introduction to Brahms's symphonies came from record-
ings May Sarton owned; I remember first hearing the
clarinet quintet of Mozart when I borrowed it from May.
It was May's copy of "The Four Quartets" that introduced
me to T. S. Eliot. Standards were set at The Civic Repertory and while one's taste and judgment change over the
years, the Civic was, for me, a foundation.

PARKER: Did you become a member of Le Gallienne's
Company?

LLOYD: It had been my dream to join Le Gallienne's
Civic Repertory company. But when the day came, and
she made her offer, I was already in Dublin, New
Hampshire, as a member of May Sarton's Apprentice
Theatre. I had given May my commitment; I was going
to act some interesting parts in plays which had not been
seen in this country. So I turned Le Gallienne down.
Not long ago, I came across her reply to me, written more
than a half a century ago on her lavender paper in
lavender ink. In her beautiful handwriting, she said she
understood; she wished me luck. It was a charming letter
and a measure of her stature.

In fact, the year I was with Le Gallienne proved to be
the last year of the Civic Repertory. We had moved up-
town to the New Amsterdam at 42nd and Times Square
with *Alice in Wonderland*, which had been a hit.
Nazimova did *The Cherry Orchard*, which alternated with
Alice. The theatre had been used by Dillingham and
Ziegfeld. On the seventh floor was the midnight roof,
where Fanny Brice had starred many times. But Le
Gallienne's two largest backers, Otto H. Kahn and Mrs.
Curtis Bok of *The Saturday Evening Post* family, could no
longer subsidize her; in the deepening Depression, Le
Gallienne had to close the repertory. Years later, she
formed the American Repertory Company.

In Dublin, near Peterborough, we all shared a house

together. The country was beautiful: hills, woods, Mt. Monadnock of *Our Town* fame and the Dublin Lake and Tennis Club. Mark Twain had lived in Dublin for a short time; so had William James, and painters George de Forest Brush, William Yarrow and Abbot Thayer.

We began by rehearsing three plays. Eventually we did ten. All were modern European pieces being performed for the first time in this country. The most important of them was *Fear*, translated from the Russian; it was a hit in Russia and became quite well known in this country. It strongly criticized the regime, which was then an unheard of thing to do. It was about Pavlov and his work with conditioned reflexes and I, at the age of eighteen or so, played Pavlov, the old man. I played the character without make-up or beard. Herman Shumlin, then one of the top producers and directors with a string of hits beginning with *The Children's Hour*, came to see it. He asked me to come to his office where he talked about my performance. When I knew him better, in later years, he often referred to that particular performance.

When the Apprentice Theatre began, in New Hampshire, we were not paid, but we were given room and board. From Dublin we went to Boston, and then back to New York, to the New School for Social Research; there we received $15 a week. It seemed like a great deal of money; I really felt like an actor. May Sarton, as the director, was intelligent, literate and had very good taste.

PARKER: How did their company come about?

LLOYD: Under the strong influence of Le Gallienne, she had wanted her own company; she felt it was the best way to express what she wanted to do in theatre, particularly in a literary sense.

May's actors were very young. We were not easy to control. I was rather arbitrary and filled with myself. I had amazing confidence and believed I was capable of anything. I was the greatest actor in the world. Consequently, it was not easy to direct me. In my opinion, formed during my vaudeville days, the vaudeville actors were the best, except for George Arliss and John Barrymore.

I believe it was a healthy learning process. I am happy that I didn't begin in a theatre working in the Method, before my confidence and opinions had been formed. When I first encountered the Method, I resisted much of it. Whether I was right or wrong was immaterial. I had a strong point-of-view and that meant I could not be, as many were, destroyed. For a time there was a sort of religious attitude about the Method. The people who were promulgating it were dictatorial and emotionally violent. It was threatening to the psyche.

Among the ten or twelve of us at the New School, the prevailing influence was Le Gallienne's. May reflected it, but to varying degrees we all did, in manner and speech. There were male actors who acted like Le Gallienne. I was less influenced. I chose to believe the British tinge in my speech came from studying George Arliss and Leslie Howard.

Social Theatre in the Thirties

I felt restless and in a state of rebellion against Sarton's company. Part of it was my own limitation: I could live with the intellectual qualities of May and Eleanor Flexner, her associate, for just so long and then my own innate show business rascality took over and I rebelled. Not that I was in the right; on the contrary, I think that their aspirations, along with Le Gallienne's, were the ones instilled in me; to this day I maintain them.

Nonetheless, I decided to take off. In the summer of 1934, I got a job as the drama director at the summer resort of the International Ladies Garment Workers Union in Forest Park, Pennsylvania. They had a big place there, just two miles away from Camp Taminent over a little country road.

Taminent's record for booking new talent was extraordinary: Danny Kaye, Jerome Robbins and many others of like fame played there.

I was brought out to the ILGWU by a friend of mine, Sy Bernhardt, who eventually became a drama and speech teacher in the high school system of New York. He was a good actor, but he was afraid to go into the theatre because of the economic risks; he was less foolhardy than I was. As a way of earning money for the summer, he was a waiter at Forest Park. He got me the job as head of the dramatic programs.

This was quite an experience because the entertainment was largely in Yiddish. David Dubinsky, one of the

founders of the union, was there every weekend. Morris
Novack, who ran the ILGWU radio station, WQED, was
in charge of the entertainment. Maurice Schwartz's Yiddish Art Theatre actors would visit. I remember meeting
Luther Adler there; he was not a member of Schwartz's
company. He was booked by Novack to give a one-man
performance, which he gave in Yiddish. He had an
animal magnetism. He was one of the finest actors I've
ever seen.

PARKER: How did you get the cast together?

LLOYD: My job entailed casting the plays in New
York. Only the set designer was permanent. One actor
came to see me, but turned me down, because a play he
had written, called *Hobbyhorses*, was receiving a try-out in
a theatre in New England. It was Cecil Holm; his *Hobbyhorses* went on to become *Three Men on a Horse*.
    I stayed for the summer and I would say, from a crea-
tive point-of-view, nothing was accomplished. I went
back to New York where May Sarton contacted me again
and invited me back to the company. I was delighted.
She had refined the operation, let some of the people go
and renamed the company The Associated Actors. In the
manner of the great companies — the Compagnie des
Quinze, the Moscow Art Theatre and the Group Theatre
— we went to the country to work. We rehearsed three
plays in Highview, New York. There again, as in Dublin,
New Hampshire, we lived in a house, were supported
financially, and I listened to music and read books.
    I went to Boston with May's company. We were seen
by some members of the Harvard Dramatic Club, which
was in the process of casting *A Bride for the Unicorn* by the
Irish writer, Denis Johnston. His *Moon Over the Yellow
River*, in which Claude Rains had appeared, had made a
major impression in New York; Denis Johnston was expected to be the next Sean O'Casey. He had also written

The Old Lady Says No, about Lady Gregory, who, with Yeats, ran the Abbey Theatre.

In search of a lead for *The Unicorn,* the Harvard Dramatic Club thought I should play the part. They contacted May through a friend of hers, Henry Wadsworth Longfellow Dana — the grandson of the poet — who lived in Longfellow's house in Cambridge. He was also the grandson of Richard Dana, the author of *Two Years Before the Mast.*

On being approached in this delicately correct way, I read the play and thought it would be a great adventure. The director was Joe Losey, a Dartmouth man. Most extraordinary was Virgil Thomson, who had just returned from Europe after living in France a long time. A Harvard alumnus, he wrote the incidental music. I'd never met anyone like Virgil. I was brought into the house where he was staying to meet him. He was sitting with his feet on the radiator, looking out at the Charles River on a blustery day, saying, "I don't know whether to wear a vestie-westie with my coatsie-woatsie." He was an eye-opener.

The two heads of the drama club were John Haggott, who became the production manager of the Theatre Guild, and John Cornell, who became a prominent production man in the New York theatre.

I felt that vistas were opening for me; I was seeing new worlds. Losey and I became very friendly on the show; we worked well together. Through Virgil, I learned about a world I had never seen or heard before. My appetite was sharpened for the kind of acting I wanted to do, and it has not changed since. I had a desire to work at a certain level, and I was riding high. I had started out with Le Gallienne and I was doing nothing but the finest kind of material at a high standard.

After *A Bride for the Unicorn,* I went back to May. Joe Losey joined us to direct a show; I was delighted to see him. The three plays we did in Boston were *Dr. Knock,*

Gallery Gods and *Gods of the Lightning*, which was directed by Losey. We played at the Peabody Playhouse, a small theatre on the Charles River.

Gods of the Lightning was about Sacco and Vanzetti; we had not realized the impact of the case on the city of Boston. It had happened seven years before, in 1927, and at my age, nineteen, it seemed to me to be ancient history; seven years was a very long time. Boston didn't feel that way. The city then had a section of the Police Department called The Red Squad, with the power to close any entertainment it considered inflammatory. They came to see the play, and there was a question of whether or not they would close us. We asked the officer in charge how he would determine the matter.

"Well," he told us, "If the audience leans forward during a play and watches it on the edge of their seat like this — I close it." They let us run.

Our worst mistake was to book, in Boston, in the heart of New England, a Thanksgiving Day matinee. When we looked out, there were six people in the audience and we were told that all of them were Sacco's relatives.

We went back to New York, but it was a losing battle trying to make a company out of The Associated Actors. I think it had been May's hope that either *Dr. Knock* or *Gallery Gods*, in which she played the lead, might make it to Broadway. Unfortunately, that did not happen, and she just gave up her idea of founding a company as Le Gallienne had done.

I went back home to Brooklyn, where I still lived, and started looking for work. When I asked Losey for suggestions, he sent me to Jerry Mayer, who was casting a play called *Noah* by Andre Obey.

Mayer cast me as Japhet, Noah's youngest son; this was to be my first Broadway play. The star was Pierre Fresnay, one of the great French actors of his time. The original production of *Noah* had been done by the Compagnie des Quinze, under the leadership of Jacques Copeau.

When the Compagnie des Quinze was living together in the country, the boys and girls fell in love with each other and had affairs. When they returned to the city, they fell out of love and everyone went his or her separate way. From this, Andre Obey, who was with the company, wrote *Noah*.

When the flood came, everyone was friendly — Noah and his wife and children and all the animals — because they all wanted to be saved together, on the ark. But after the forty days and nights, when the flood subsided and they landed on Mount Ararat, they all left Noah, even his wife.

Theatre is the memory of moments. Fresnay, as Noah, has left me with a succession of moments from this, my first Broadway play. At the end, Noah's children leave him, one by one, and then the animals do the same. The bear comes to him to embrace him, and he thinks, "Ah, the bear is going to stay." But the bear was embracing him to kill him, and as Noah extricated himself after this realization, it was heartbreaking. The play ended with Fresnay speaking to God, reprimanding Him for inflicting such an ordeal, but also telling God that he still had faith, and wasn't destroyed. In French, the line is "Je suis content" — "I am satisfied." He would then ask, "Are you satisfied, Lord?" And to Louis Horst's lovely music, a rainbow appeared over the stage to answer him. This ended the play.

The play also begins with Noah on stage alone, speaking to God, in a soliloquy which to my mind was lifted for the later *Fiddler on the Roof*. Noah is building his ark, measuring with a carpenter's square, which is one of the charming little anachronisms in the play.

"Lord," he would say. No answer. "Lord." Again, no answer.

"Lord — Oh, yes, lord, it's me. Me, Noah, Lord."
He'd get down on his knees as if he was going to pray,
and then get up again. "Oh, yes, Lord, you haven't time."

"Well, Lord, should I put a rudder on the boat? No,
Lord. Rudder. No, no ...R as in Robert, U as in Hubert,
D as in ...That's it Lord. Yes, Lord, I have confidence, oh
yes — ." And so on.

We, the young actors who were playing his children,
would stand in the wings every night to watch this soliloquy, and I remember it as the finest of this kind I have
ever seen; it was always magic.

The first act ended as the forty days and nights of rain
began, and the second act started with the flood having
subsided. As Japhet, the youngest child, I entered at the
beginning of the act to discover the sun. I ran to the top
of the ark to do a cock's crow and awaken everyone. All
the cries were in naval talk — "Avast, you landlubbers!"
and so forth. At rehearsal, it wasn't quite right. Fresnay
very politely said to me, "You know, if I may suggest, I
have an idea here," and he showed me a beautiful piece of
business. "But of course," he added, "I don't do it as well
as you."

Fresnay was the most elegant of actors at rehearsals.
He came dressed in a Saville Row suit, a beautifully cut
eggshell shirt, bespoke shoes, a derby, and an enormous
overcoat. This he wore for rehearsal like a cape, in
European fashion, with a scarf in a brilliant color flung
over his shoulder which reached his ankles. He liked to
rehearse the play, which he had already done in Paris,
from eleven in the morning to five, without a break.

He had not been a member of Copeau's company. As
one of the great French actors, he was a *sociétaire*, an
honored member of the Comédie Française. It was an in-
fraction of the rules to perform with another company,
and when he did so with the Compagnie des Quinze, he
became the second actor to be expelled from the Comédie
Française; the first was Sarah Bernhardt.

Fresnay, then in his early forties, was unconcerned. He was the greatest Cyrano of his time. He went to London to be with Yvonne Printemps, whom he later married. Printemps, who was married to Sacha Guitry, had left him for Fresnay. Either Fresnay had left his wife for Printemps, or Guitry had taken up with someone else — in any case, the grounds for divorce were "mutual adultery," a phrase which I found vivid in its accuracy.

Printemps stood in the wings almost every night when he worked, dressed in black with very pale make-up. At one performance, Fresnay said to me, "You know, it's getting close to April and she wants to go back to Paris. She stands there looking very pale and ill, you see, to remind me that we must go back to Paris."

Even offstage she was a star, and determined to have her way; she succeeded, because we closed after Fresnay's guaranteed four weeks and the two of them returned to France.

A *succès d'estime*, *Noah* did not sell tickets. It was a beautiful try. Actors and actresses played the animals, with masks by Remo Bufano, who was a puppeteer and mask-maker, one of the most prominent in his profession. It was a great loss when he was killed in a plane crash. I recall him vaguely as a little man with a sensitive face. Ludwig Bemelmans, who did the sets, had just come to this country from Germany. He loved good foods and wines and opened a restaurant, "The Hapsburg," which he decorated with his own drawings. He also wrote and illustrated charming children's books. Bemelmans was a unique artist. It was an inspiration to have him do the sets for *Noah*. He was not a member of the union, so Cleon Throckmorton was credited as set designer, with a separate credit indicating that they were realized from Bemelman's drawings, and under his personal supervision.

The music was written by Louis Horst, who was the music advisor to Martha Graham; together they ran the

Neighborhood Playhouse dance department. He was
reputed to be an important influence on Graham. When I
met him, he was an old man, stout in a Brahmsian way.
The dances in *Noah* were choreographed by Anna
Sokolow.

PARKER: Was Actor's Equity around at this time?

LLOYD: Actor's Equity existed then, in 1935, but in a
much more lenient form.   For example, there was no pay
for rehearsals.   There were two minimum scales: $25 for a
junior member, anyone of any age who had been an Equity member for less than two years; $40 for a senior mem-
ber, of more than two years standing.   But actors only
received pay when money was taken in at the box office,
which meant that in rehearsal time, during the last week
of which there was no limit to the number of hours one
could be required to work, we were paid nothing.   Paid
previews would have allowed the actors a salary, but at
that time, they were rare; they had not yet become the
custom.

A junior member, hired for a Broadway show, was
guaranteed two weeks pay, or $50. For this sum, you
might work five weeks: three weeks of rehearsal, two
weeks of playing.   It was recognized that Equity should
make two changes: the double minimum, which en-
couraged managers to hire the $25 actors and not the $40
ones, and that rehearsals should be paid.   Incredibly, at
meeting after meeting paid rehearsals were voted down.
The president, an actor of the nineteenth century named
Frank Gilmore, wanted us to consider ourselves a club,
not a union.   The leaders of the revolutionary movement
to get rehearsal pay were Sam Jaffe and Phil Loeb.

William Brady was a prominent manager married to a
major star, Grace George. He was also the father of
another star, Alice Brady.   He had been the manager of a
world champion prize fighter, James J. Corbett, and he

had backed the actors in the 1919 strike, for which he was awarded honorary membership in Equity for life. He took full advantage of this, and attended every meeting. As the motion for pay would come up, he would take the floor and issue a warning.

"It's tough enough to put on these plays. If you want us to pay for rehearsals, you will drive us all out of the business."

Grace George would follow, then Alice Brady, and Florence Reed, who made a great hit in *Shanghai Gesture*, as Mother Goddam. They were a breed of actresses; they all had marvelous voices and presences and they believed in the theatre and in being theatrical. They were stars in the grand manner, in great hats and white gloves, dressed magnificently. They had ways to make the actors feel it would be a terrible mistake if they voted themselves rehearsal pay. The battle went on for a couple of years, and finally we did get pay for rehearsals — $15 a week. It was the work of Jaffe and Loeb, whose careers were almost destroyed by their campaign (Jaffe also created the Equity Library Theatre, which still exists). Eventually, Equity did away with the double minimum.

Even with rehearsal pay, you couldn't make a living as an actor; I still lived at home, though I was on Broadway. To keep afloat, one had to do radio. The real actors were the Broadway actors, and radio actors were rich commercial actors. After a while that kind of snobbism changed, and we scrounged to get anything in radio. This was Equity during the Depression.

Within it, or perhaps contributing to it, was the sort of elegance Fresnay personified; actors dressed well to attend their unpaid rehearsals, wearing suits, ties and good shoes. The theatre was a holy place. There were actors who wouldn't smoke in the theatre. It was an attitude of the times.

PARKER: What did you do after the closing of *Noah*?

LLOYD: In the summer of 1935 I went to Peterborough, New Hampshire, to play summer stock:
Molière's *School for Wives*.

Other than the beauty of the place, my chief memory
is of one of the finest actors our theatre had in my time.
William Hansen was a little man, with an inherited dis-
ease which caused his bones to be very fragile, so that
they were always breaking. His repeated leg fractures
caused him to limp and he used a cane, but the beauty of
his acting never diminished. In the Group Theatre, he
was regarded as a pure actor who never made a wrong
move. He worked in Kazan's movies. He should be
remembered for his beautiful performances.

When I got back to New York in the fall, I was looking
for work. I would dress up every morning in my suit,
shirt and tie and visit all the agents and managers, starting around eleven. I visited Sarah Enright, Jane Broder,
Chamberlain Brown, and Dick Pittman. I sat and waited
for them to come out of their inner offices to ask them if
they would send me on the track of a job. I was getting
nowhere, and I said so to Joe Losey, with whom I had
done two plays and with whom I had a good working
relationship.

Joe knew of an acting collective, The Theatre of Action. They had a young director, Elia Kazan, who had
just done his first play, *The Young Go First*, about the CCC
camps. Joe told me they had a building down on East
27th Street near Lexington and that I should go down and
join them.

Most members of The Theatre of Action lived in a four
or five-story brownstone on East 27th Street. Downstairs
there was the kitchen and a main living-room; all the
living quarters were upstairs. In the group were
Nicholas Ray and Martin Ritt, who became directors; Earl
Robinson, the composer; Curt Conway; Will Lee; and Paul
Mann, who became an eminent teacher. There was one
young lady who did not live at the house. She was the

most beautiful girl I had ever seen. Her name was Peggy Craven and she became my wife. She lived with her parents, whose home was on Morningside Drive. There were other women in the company, but on the whole the others were not beautiful; one, Jane Kim, was striking, or startling, but did not continue her career. It was more realistic, the directors of social theatre felt, to have people who might be right out of the subway; it was their rebellion against the idea of the beautiful ingenue, like Dorothy McGuire and Jane Wyatt.

Al Sachs was the director and a teacher; he invited me to join them. It was my first experience of social theatre; I saw myself more as Alfred Lunt than as a part of the social movement. The Theatre of Action, of course, did not offer a salary.

They were preparing a play called *Crime*, by Michael Blankfort, directed by Elia Kazan. He was a good young actor with the Group Theatre; indeed, he had scored an enormous hit in *Paradise Lost*, Clifford Odets's second full-length play. Our teacher was Bobby Lewis, who was with The Group. We didn't study dance or speech; they didn't have time or need for that. We were, in a sense, a studio of The Group. In order to keep their theatre collective going, some of the men worked. But above all, they made an effort to get on WPA relief and the Federal Theatre.

PARKER: Do you mean that they wanted to be a group that might be funded by the Federal Theatre?

LLOYD: It was an individual effort. Each person applied for relief and contributed the money to the running of the house. To qualify for the Works Progress Administration, you had to be on relief, except that the program allowed for ten percent of its payroll to consist of non-relief personnel. The theory was that the arts projects — theatre, dance, and painters — could function

better with ten percent non-relief employees. It was how
I went, later, to the Federal Theatre.

The Theatre of Action was a most stimulating place.
It was there that I first learned about the Stanislavsky
Method, in the way we worked on plays and in the teach-
ings of Bobby Lewis. Though we took classes, the real
work was done in the rehearsal of *Crime.*

It was a long one-act play about an attempt to get a
union into the CIO, the Congress of Industrial Organizations, countering the AFL, which union members thought
had become old and ineffective, and about the corruption
preventing the formation of the CIO.

We did it for two nights at the Civic Repertory
Theatre, now leased not to Le Gallienne but to another
theatre collective, The Theatre Union. This was Albert
Maltz, George Sklar, and Paul Peters; they did plays like
Stevedore, Black Pit, and *Merry-Go-Round.*

PARKER: Didn't one of these groups put out a
magazine?

LLOYD: Besides the Theatre Union, whose plays were
exciting and good, there was the New Theatre League,
which published a magazine and did one-act plays on
Sunday evenings. It was under the New Theatre League
that Odets's *Waiting for Lefty* and Paul Green's *Hymn to
the Rising Sun* were first produced at the Civic Repertory.
Hanns Eisler, Bertolt Brecht's collaborator, came to The
Theatre of Action and brought a new kind of theatre
music with him.

Crime was my first experience with improvisation. I
resisted The Method, though now I realize I was resisting
it not on purely aesthetic terms; I was rather confused socially. From my middle-class Brooklyn point-of-view,
these fellows were low types who wanted to do things
with theatre that, to my mind, it wasn't meant for. I dis-
approved, and The Method was somehow tied up with all

these social ideas. Thus improvisations, as a part of The Method, were just indulgences, I felt.

On the other hand, some of these improvisations were really carried a bit far. In one of them, a black actor, Tommy Anderson, started putting matches to my feet. I broke out of the improvisation and said, "To hell with this — it has nothing to do with acting. It has to do with putting matches to someone's feet."

Al Sachs would start an improvisation by having us lie on the floor in pairs. We were the town asleep in the morning before the strike, before going out on the picket lines. This was to find relationships. Then Kazan would come in to run rehearsals, and he would supervise improvisations, too. I was attracted to The Method in the hands of Kazan; he was craftsman-like with it. Al Sachs, on the other hand, seemed to be prying into personal lives; he psychologized, which I resisted. In the abandoned factory loft where we rehearsed, we would pretend dawn was breaking on our improvisation as townspeople, lying in couples on the floor. "And did you *feel* anything for her, lying there?" Sachs would demand. Instinctively, I resisted, although I did feel something.

Kazan, however, got very good performances out of us when we did the play. Some of the members of The Theatre of Action joined the Federal Theatre.

Joe Losey had also joined the Federal Theatre. Far from being a relief case, he was part of the ten percent non-relief quota. He was living with Elizabeth Hawes, whom he later married. She was one of the two or three leading American clothes designers of the time. They lived very well indeed, in a townhouse where her salon was visited by New York's elegant ladies. Joe was even able, at that time, to visit Russia, and he had seen Meyerhold's and Stanislavsky's work there.

He was assigned to the Federal Theatre's Living Newspaper, which has proved since to have been one of the major events in the history of the American Theatre.

Plays in this distinct style are still done; a fairly recent example was *Zoot Suit*. When Joe was hired, the format still had to be evolved and he was significantly involved in developing it. He hired me, also as a ten-percent non-relief employee, to work again under his direction.

After *Crime*, I drifted away from The Theatre of Action. They continued to live as a collective in the brownstone for a while, until they broke down economically and couldn't support the enterprise. During their period of survival, they were very interesting. They were one of the first theatre groups to use The Method in a social way. They were a mobile theatre, going to picket lines, union halls, and all over town. They were very good at singing, dancing and cabaret, in a European tradition. Many distinguished people worked with them.

There were several different projects subsidized by the Federal Theatre. Besides the experimental, Yiddish and dance theatres, there was *Project 891*, which was Orson Welles's and John Houseman's. Before *891*, Houseman and Welles created a great stir with *Macbeth*, performed by the Negro Theatre of the WPA.

Orson and Jack also went on to do other projects for the Federal Theatre, including *Dr. Faustus* and *Horse Eats Hat*, with Joseph Cotten and Arlene Francis.

The idea of the Living Newspaper was conceived by Heywood Broun. He maintained that everyone in the arts was being helped by the Works Progress Administration, with the exception of the newspaperman. Broun was stagestruck; he had even produced shows, one of them being *Shoot the Works*, in which he also appeared. He was charismatic and charming, a big man; he was one of the best newspapermen we have ever had.

He prevailed upon the government to make a project for newsmen, with all the facilities of a newspaper, including reporters at work. Since he was so taken with the stage, he felt it should be a theatre — a living newspaper; the shows would change every night with the latest news, like our six o'clock TV news shows. The events would have to be dramatized, of course; there was not the technology to record the news on tape and to show it the same day. Scripts would have to be developed and slides and projections incorporated; it would all take time. A basic script would have to be evolved with space to accommodate news developments of any given day, which the actors would incorporate.

The entire Federal Theatre was in the charge of Hallie Flanagan, who was a Roosevelt appointee. In New York state, Hallie Flanagan chose Elmer Rice, the eminent playwright, to head the program. The administrative head of the Living Newspaper was Morris Watson, who had been with the Associated Press; the chief writer was Arthur Arent, who supervised a large group of newsmen writing our material. Joe Losey was the director of the show.

The first attempt was *Ethiopia*, which was about Mussolini's invasion. It was considered too controversial and political and the authorities stopped the production. Elmer Rice quickly resigned over what he felt was unreasonable government interference. The first full production was *Triple 'A' Plowed Under*. It was concerned with the Agricultural Administration — the farmer's struggle to survive, and the government's work to help the farmers. Between the drought and the Depression, the plight of the farmlands was severe. Stylistically, the show reflected what Losey had seen in Europe and Russia — the theatres of Piscator, Brecht and Meyerhold. Brecht had, in fact, arrived in America; his version of Gorky's *The Mother* had been produced at the Theatre Union, with Eisler's score for two pianos, played by Alex North and Jerome Moross.

Triple 'A' Plowed Under incorporated movies, projections, and a public address system speaking out to the actors and the audience. It had vaudeville sketches and a full orchestra. It was a mixture of elements, forty-five minutes long, and we gave two shows a night. Joe brought me in to play the leads in the vaudeville sketches, which had been giving him trouble. Many of the relief actors were unable to make the sketches work; they were often old and lacking energy, or they were too young and inexperienced.

The show was a smash. The audience, in any case, had never seen anything like it — and the audience, too, was new. The Federal Theatre's low prices, with a top of eighty-five cents, permitted a lot of people to go to the theatre who had never seen a legitimate show before; they had only seen movies. Whenever a scene provoked this new audience by its controversy or argument, they would hoot, howl and bring the show to a standstill with their vocal attack. It was exciting to play for these zippy new audiences when they became so involved.

In one scene of *Triple 'A,'* for example, four of us played a scene in silhouette, behind a projection of the Preamble of the Constitution which stretched the width of the stage. I played Louis Brandeis, the great Supreme Court Justice. Another figure was Al Smith, in his familiar derby. The fourth silhouette was that of the leader of the communist party at that time, Earl Browder.

Whenever Browder opened his mouth to speak, the audience started to yell and scream, so that the actor would have to wait to deliver his dialogue. The actor playing Browder — in effect, the shape of Browder — became convinced that this was a personal triumph; he went to the WPA authorities to ask for a raise, thinking he had proved himself the star of the show.

After this enormous success, Losey went to work on the next Living Newspaper, *Injunction Granted.* It was about the history of labor in the courts. When I saw the script, there was no role in the piece I particularly wanted to do; at first, I turned down Losey. But one day I went to the circus, which played under a tent on Nostrand Avenue, in Brooklyn. It occurred to me, as I was watching, that in *Injunction Granted* I could be a clown, commenting in pantomime on the action of the play. Losey liked the idea, and my part became the lead, though I never spoke a word.

Virgil Thomson wrote the score, making an orchestra of ratchets, sirens, trumpets, different kinds of kettle drums, ship's bells and trombones. The sound he achieved was marvelous; on opening night, the police burst into the theatre to investigate the apparent catastrophe.

One day, Peggy and I ran into Virgil on the 6th Avenue bus.

"Virgil," I accosted him. "You know I appear and reappear in this play all evening as a clown. Are you going to give me a theme for whenever I come on? A musical theme?"

"Certainly not," replied Virgil agreeably. "I'm going to write on the score, 'T.T.T.'"

"T.T.T.? What does T.T.T. mean?"

"Tunes Take Time," he said briskly.

He did write a tune for me, which I was to play on a toy piano of the kind given to two-year-olds. I carried it with me. Virgil taught me the correct fingering, insistent I should play it properly.

Nick Ray was the stage manager, and several of The Theatre of Action members were in the show. Losey designed his own set, which he first made in clay, with ramps, turrets and hiding places for me as the clown. His chief influences in this play were those of Meyerhold and the Russian Theatre—Okhlopkov's and Vakhtangov's styles, whose work he had seen. When he went to Russia, Losey was witness to one of the greatest theatre movements of the time, when all those talented directors were working simultaneously.

The Depression was crushing; good conservative men, Republicans like my father, who had been easy-going and had believed in all the right things, found it impossible to grasp what was happening to them and to millions of people like them. There was no Social Security; there was no way to recover and start again. But in spite of this, there was hope; there was a healthy rebellion against the difficult circumstances. Much unionizing was still to be done, not in today's terms of investment of pension funds, but in the basic union concepts of job conditions -- working hours, for example. We were down and poor, but everything in the world was before us, and we always managed to work, to be active, to be filled with ideas. Today, after another World War and subsequent wars, with high costs and with a technology which has pushed man to the point where he can so easily be wiped out, the moral climate is quite different. It seems to me a deterioration.

A young man today, wanting to make a lot of money, ought to go into politics. There, we see men taking jobs at sixty thousand a year, which is good — but they come out multi-millionaires; how does this happen? In our business, executives are convicted of embezzlement and then made heads of studios again, as if nothing had happened. The moral texture of this country must be affected; the young must conclude that this is the way to succeed.

The films of the thirties always convey the hope of the period. In *Modern Times*, as The Tramp goes down the road with the girl, he gives an image of hope. Today, this would be thought naive. Brecht, and many others, ridiculed hope; they believed it to be romantic, or antithetical to an aesthetic, realistic point-of-view. Bernard Shaw, on the other hand, said,"He will never know hope, who has not known despair." I feel that some bitterness was required.

In the actors of those days this quality appeared as an underlying humanity, even if the character being played was an evil one; there was a certain decency, even nobility, to the worst villain, as played by Cagney, Robinson or Muni. It was a sense that man will go on forever, a sense of the human race; it conveyed something universal.

Now, of course, we have no certainty that man will go on forever; we know that a little mistake can cause disaster, and today's acting reflects the times. Many modern actors, in spite of great skill and talent, have a neurotic, depressing edge. I find it adolescent, to present only the unpleasant side to a character. This is often taken for being real and true, but it may or may not be so. It presents an unpleasant person, without any sense of a wider vision — a character with whom you don't want to spend time.

It begins with the directing and producing, and in the choice of stories. It's a point-of-view. Hitchcock, for example, chose fantasies; no one was asked to think them real. We were asked only to believe them as tales he was telling. He was not saying, life is like this; he was ironic and amusing. Directors today have a different sense: that to plumb the lower depths is to be more real. But it isn't the case; one may or may not be real in that instance. The parts I played in the '30s were all infused with a vision of man in a difficult circumstance — but where life was still wonderful, and would be better. Even when the character was killed in the play, there was some way to say something positive and marvelous about the human race that affected the audience; then, the audience was affected by the death of the character.

In the thirties, I never had an awareness that so many people who knew nothing about the business were in charge; theatre managers had all done plays. There were no committee decisions, as there are now among network executives ruled by demographics. In the Federal Theatre, decisions were more personal.

After *Injunction Granted*, in 1936, Losey had a falling out with the Federal Theatre and left. I stayed on. The next play I did was *Power*, about the founding of the TVA.

It was the story of the struggle by the government — the Tennessee Valley Authority — to bring to the farmer the electricity he had been denied by the private company — Commonwealth and Southern, the head of which firm was Wendell Wilkie. When work on the TVA began, the private firm proceeded to make electricity available, but without telling anyone; they went onto the farmers' lands to build the lines. The farmers brought out their rifles to run off the the company men, telling them that they, the farmers, were now with the government. *Power* was the story of that conflict.

I played the leading role of Angus J. Buttoncooper, the little man — the consumer. Howard Bay was the designer and again used projections. Lee Wainer wrote the musical score. Brett Warren directed. He worked in the Epic Theatre style of Brecht and Piscator which Losey had used. He used projections, slides, stylized movements and levels; Losey was one of the first to use these devices in America.

My first scene was typical of the Living Newspaper. I began sitting alone on stage, in front of a rear projection of Howard Bay's line drawing of The Little Man; I had a shopping basket beside me. As I made a move to leave, the disembodied public address system stopped me and began to ask me questions.

P/A: Where are you going?

Angus: I'm going to pay my electric bill.

P/A: Your electric bill, how much is it?

Angus: Four dollars.

P/A: How did they arrive at that figure?

Angus: It's three cents a kilowatt hour.

P/A: What's a kilowatt hour?

Angus: Well—a kilo means a thousand, and a watt...?

I was speaking to the disembodied voice as if he were out front, in the audience. When, in our dialogue, I tried to explain a kilowatt hour, I got a warm laugh of recognition from the audience; like the character, they had no idea what a kilo or a watt was. Then I moved to stage left, where there were fruit and vegetable stands.

Angus: How much is this tomato?

Seller: Twenty-five cents a pound.

Angus: Too much, too high.

I moved to the next stand, which also sold tomatoes.

Angus: How much are these tomatoes?

Seller: Fifteen cents a pound.

Angus: I'll take them.

Next, I moved to the apple stands.

Angus: How much are these a pound?

Seller: Ten cents.

Angus: How much are these?

2nd Seller: Five cents a pound.

I'd buy the five-cent ones, making the point that I had a choice: I could buy either the twenty-five-cent tomatoes or the fifteen-cent ones. I would circle back to continue my dialogue with the public address system, noting that with foods, and other consumer items, I had a choice; in regard to electric power, I had none. I had to pay exactly what they said I was going to pay.

The Edison Company in New York issued a confidential inter-office memo about the show, which found its way to the Ritz Theatre. I was the villain of the memo: "There is an actor who makes out the case for the consumer to be worse that it is." I took it as a rave review.

The character of Angus J. Buttoncooper, the little Everyman-consumer, was so successful that he continued beyond the show. He reappeared in the Living Newspaper's *One Third of a Nation*, about housing; this show later became a movie. After the success of *Power*, however, I left the Federal Theatre. At the beginning of summer, I made an abortive visit to Green Mansions, one of the outstanding theatres of the summer borscht circuit. I stayed for a week, during which time I met John La-Touche who became a good friend, and with whom I later worked. But I didn't like Green Mansions, and I went back to New York.

Later that summer Peggy and I went to Deertrees Theatre in Harrison, Maine, to play summer stock. It was there that we first met Dorothy McGuire, who had come from Omaha, Nebraska, and was an apprentice. The stock repertoire was not remarkable; *The Queen's Husband*, by Robert Sherwood; *Officer 666*, which Douglas Fairbanks Sr. had done on Broadway; Edward Sheldon's *Romance*. When we returned to New York in the fall, I was asked to join the Mercury Theatre.

I believe it was John Houseman's idea that I should join the Mercury Theatre. I went to meet him and Orson Welles at their offices at the Empire, accompanied by my agent, Jane Broder. Jane was a matronly, stoutish lady, important in the New York theatre and very discriminating in her clients; they included Rosalind Russell and Bette Davis. She also cast the Theatre Guild shows, and it was an honor to be represented by her. We agreed that I should do Cinna, the poet, in *Julius Caesar*, and Hodges in *Shoemaker's Holiday*, the Mercury's first two productions, for forty dollars a week, or Equity minimum. Jane took no commissions, just as today an agent receives no commission from an actor for scale.

In my experience, Houseman and Welles were the most exciting duo in show business. As one looks back, it appears that Welles may have been in greater need of Houseman than vice versa. Orson did his best work in tandem with Jack: The Federal Theatre, The Mercury, the radio show, *Citizen Kane*, and *Native Son*. After their separation, Orson never quite managed to achieve that level of work again while Houseman developed his own abilities in several areas, indeed, flourished. So it would appear that Jack was Orson's catalyst, for while one saw a dropping off in Orson's work, Jack continued, with success, to produce in films, theatre and television, founded

The Juilliard School of Drama and six acting companies in addition to the Mercury.

Houseman has the gift of making things happen. Nowhere was this more evident than in the experience we shared in Pelican Productions at the Coronet Theatre in Los Angeles during the late 1940s. I will deal with that adventure later, but a certain digression is in order to make a point about Houseman and Welles.

I had come upon the Coronet Theatre just as the building was being completed. When the opportunity to lease it was presented to me, I went to Jack and suggested he might be interested in our going into partnership. Now it should be told that Jack cannot abide an empty theatre. He will immediately do something to fill it even if the monetary means are not at hand. Thus it was that Pelican Productions took over the Coronet with some money, but not enough. Eventually, the economics of the operation did us in. Truth to tell, I had cautioned Jack at the start that I didn't think that we were financially ready to go, although I had by this time been in contact with Brecht and Laughton to put the world premiere of *Galileo* in the theatre. Jack insisted on plunging ahead, to my great fear and admittedly to my great delight and admiration. And so it was that *Galileo*, starring Charles Laughton, was done in the theatre, thanks to T. Edward Hambleton, who produced it. In addition, *The Skin of Our Teeth*, *No Exit*, *Dark of the Moon*, and *The House of Bernarda Alba*, were seen for the first time on the West Coast. Had we been influenced by my caution rather than thrust into action by Jack's impetuosity, we would never have had the joy of that theatre. We would not have done *Galileo*, which justified the whole undertaking. Bankruptcy overtook us. It was bound to. But we had our day thanks to Jack's impecunious daring.

His standards to the end of his days remained unimpaired. He made things happen with an overlay of fun so that working with him was an adventure. It is to be noted that the passing of the years lessened his screaming somewhat. Nothing could match the screaming invective of Houseman vs. Welles. It got so monumental at The Mercury, so often, that one was not aware of hearing it. But it had its results. It galvanized. The whole record shouts louder than the screams.

What extraordinary good luck it was for me to have met with Jack Houseman that day in The Mercury offices in The Empire Theatre over fifty years ago. Our friendship grew over the years to where it became my closest one, filled with love and reveling in the joy of knowing him. Soldiers may wake reluctantly to bugles in the morning but I woke with delight at the telephone's ring, knowing it was Jack and the life he brought with him.

The Mercury company worked in a charming little theatre which had been known as the Comedy and was then renamed the Mercury by Houseman and Welles. It was between Sixth Avenue and Broadway, on 40th Street, and for the kind of theatre they intended to do, it was perfect. There were six hundred seats and a relatively large stage.

They had gathered a company of Geraldine Fitzgerald, Joseph Cotten, Hiram Sherman, George Coulouris, Vincent Price, Martin Gabel, Edith Barrett, Ruth Ford, Whitford Kane, John Hoyt and Mady Christians, among others. The Mercury drew hungry, talented young people who were in New York; for example, on the switchboard was a fifteen-year-old, Judy Holliday.

Julius Caesar was the first play. This was a modern dress version, set in contemporary Rome. This was in the fall of 1937. The play became a political melodrama about the Fascism of Mussolini, who had not then fallen under Hitler's shadow, but was still the florid megalomaniac making balcony speeches. Orson staged it absolutely marvelously and indeed reorganized the play in such a way that it was a thrilling telling of the story.

Marc Blitzstein used the Fascist anthem in his musical score. The citizens wore business suits; the officers were of the modern Fascist army in green uniforms with Sam Browne belts.

The play opened on a bare stage with a series of levels, irregularly spaced from a platform to the stage level. There were no flats; the back of the stage set was the theatre wall, painted blood red, like the set, and the stage entrance was visible to the audience. On occasion, a fireman would come in and stand next to the wall — his customary post. When the curtain went up, the fireman would discover himself to be in the show, and then had to find a way to get off the stage, trying to cover his embarrassment.

The lighting effects were brilliant. This was one of the first collaborations between Orson and Jean Rosenthal. The top level had what Orson called "Nuremberg Lights." They were lights such as Hitler used at Nuremberg, directed straight up from below. Holes were cut in the set and lights placed below, so that when the Fascists marched on with their flags, it was a tremendous effect. There was also what is called a "brute" in films — a great light which would roll forward and shine into the audience's faces. It was as if an airplane were coming at them. It was very difficult to get on stage and off. Eventually, Orson did away with some of the lighting effects; he rehearsed with them and felt they were too complicated.

We also had an enormous amount of sound; in lighting and sound, Orson was a master. The sound was supervised by a man who was in radio and considered one of the pioneer figures of radio drama, Irving Reis. He was director of the Columbia Workshop. For the play, he made records, just as he did for radio; the sound was all on acetates. He also used a thunder sheet. Before the show opened, Orson threw out all the sound. In the music, Marc Blitzstein used a trumpet and Hammond organ, and also the thunder sheet.

Before we reached the Mercury Theatre, however, we rehearsed for a couple of weeks in various rehearsal rooms in New York. Then we went to Fort Lee, across the river, to an old motion picture studio where the set was being built, so that we could rehearse on the set. Here, a fifteen-year-old boy named Arthur Anderson, who was playing Brutus's attendant, Lucius, stayed behind one day when we all went to lunch. A curious boy, he saw that squares were marked on the set where the holes for the Nuremberg lights were to be cut; he added a few more. If it hadn't been discovered, the set would have looked like Swiss cheese. Later, during the run of the play, he put a match to the Mercury's sprinkler system and flooded the stage during the matinee.

In the play as Shakespeare wrote it, Cinna the poet has about ten lines; very often, *Julius Caesar* is done without this scene. The film is without Cinna the poet. I think it is fair to say — and I have heard Orson say it publicly — that in this version, Cinna's scene became "the" scene of the play: the fulcrum around which the rest of the play swung. Orson saw the crowd in the scene actively threatening the poet; as written, the threat is implicit. He wanted the crowd to be chanting, and he took lines from the Capitol scene in *Coriolanus* for a mob chant to which he asked Blitzstein to write a rhythm accompaniment. As the scene opened, I would enter from the rear wall of the theatre, climb the ramp to the top level and deliver a four-line soliloquy. Then the citizens would enter — but at that point my rehearsal would stop, as Orson hadn't worked out the chanting. He didn't want to stage the scene until the crowd had mastered the chant, as that would affect the movement.

So day after day, the chant was rehearsed. Blitzstein asked me to help him by pounding a little drum and while the scene remained un-staged I banged the drum and the crowd chanted.

Discipline at rehearsal was not of a model nature — nor was it during performance, either. Orson might arrive at rehearsal and be amused to talk about something for two hours or do an imitation of Maurice Evans's Falstaff or of Guthrie McClintic, with whom he had worked. Or he told jokes. Finally, he would get around to the scene, which he would rehearse once over lightly before he left.

When we got to dress rehearsals with their technical demands, he'd work hours on end, until the stage hands dropped like flies, and the actors became punch drunk. He would have dinner for himself sent in from Longchamps, on the corner across from the Metropolitan Opera House. The actors, however, who were not eating, were angry and frustrated. He also had a trick of stealing away to sleep while making us believe that he could stay awake forever; perhaps he went off to a hotel nearby and then came back to the theatre. Meanwhile, the actors were falling apart. But this was only during the dress rehearsals; in the acting rehearsals while the scenes were being created, it was all fun and games.

For about three weeks, I pounded a drum and the previews were approaching. The audience was not a paying one, as it would be today — but it was an audience, nevertheless. As we came to the first preview, I informed Orson that I was not going on. He seemed surprised. I pointed out that apart from my entrance we had never rehearsed the scene; I could do the lines in a vague way, and probably get on and off, but in fact, there was no scene. I had spent time banging a drum. He accepted this calmly; if I didn't want to go on, that was all right.

In fact, it was only as Cinna that I did not appear; I, like most of the company, played several other parts. I opened the play in the dark as the Soothsayer, warning

Caesar to "Beware the Ides of March" in a drawn-out, wailing cry which rang around the theatre as the lights rose on Joseph Holland, as Caesar in uniform surrounded by his modern Fascist coterie. I was also a citizen leader. While Brutus and Antony delivered their orations from a pulpit, fully fourteen feet high and lit in white light, four bands of extras led by Hiram Sherman, Joe Cotten, John Hoyt and myself reacted down below. We were lit only by the spill of light, so that we were not recognizable as principal actors. But our leadership of the groups meant that their responses, which were all carefully scripted, had an unmechanical intensity; we were like animals responding to the orations. The first preview performance — without Cinna the poet, but with all the sound and light effects, and with a rather lengthy text — did not do well. When the curtain came down, not a single hand in the audience applauded; there was silence. I was in the wings, because I had decided not to take part in the curtain call; I was really very angry. But I looked out at the unforgettable sight of the company lined up to take its call, with Orson in the center, unable to raise the curtain again. The audience simply got up and walked out.

Hank Sember, of the publicity staff, raced backstage and confronted Orson, who was still standing there, stunned. "Jesus, Orson," said Hank Sember in fright. "We can't even get a call."

Orson cleared his throat, produced a large blob of phlegm and spat right in Hank's face. Orson was six feet two or three and weighed, in one of his thinner phases, some two hundred pounds. Hank Sember was a little fellow, about five foot three, but he reared back, ready to throw a punch straight to Orson's face. But Orson grabbed him by the arm. "Spit in my face!" begged Orson. "Please! Please! Spit in my face!"

Hank did so. The terrible moment passed and they were friends again.

It was decided that the performance had been an illuminating one and that certain things had to be done to the show. We postponed for five days. During this time, Orson took out all the sound, eliminated some of the lighting tricks, put in others and cut some of the text, adjusting it to well under two hours. He also set out to stage the Cinna the poet scene.

The scene is necessary in the making of the play; this is in the writing, and it surprises me when the scene is left out. In this production it was particularly important, because it brought the audience into the world of Fascism: the world of Mussolini and Hitler.

Cinna comes out on the street after having had a very disturbing dream about Caesar. He is accosted by a gang who have been roused by the oration of Antony to seek out conspirators. He tries to tell them that he is Cinna the poet, not Cinna the conspirator; in spite of his name, he is not the enemy. His attempts to convince them fail, and he is killed.

In my own work on the scene, I thought of Alfred Rosenberg, who was then an official high in the Nazi party. I thought of him facing a crowd who said he had a Jewish name, to which he replied,"Yes, but I'm not a Jewish Rosenberg." He could be killed for his name, even though he wasn't Jewish. This was one aspect of it, immediate to the scene. On the other hand, it seemed to me that the scene was of a liberal man who was an intellectual. I took my father-in-law, Simon Hirsdansky, as a model. I used his attitude. He was a school principal of a most beautiful tolerance, knowledgeable and well-educated and head of P.S. 4 in the Bronx for fifty years. He was the first to introduce school lunch, and a swimming pool to a public school in New York. At his funeral, several generations of pupils mourned him.

Cinna seemed to me that kind of figure — an intellectual liberal who thought that by reason and by explanation he could quiet the citizens though, of course, the opposite is true.

Orson, in our five-day rehearsal period, saw him differently. I visualized Cinna as a man dressed in a dark suit with a stiff collar, almost like Herbert Hoover, with a knit tie and black shoes: a little clerk. Orson saw him with a romantic Byronic collar, flowing tie and dress to suit. After everyone had gone home from rehearsal, I sat in the front row of the Mercury Theatre to tell Orson that I really didn't see the character his way. I saw him as a man who wrote letters to *The New York Times* and thought that that attitude would do the trick and cause the violence to subside. I also wanted to incorporate another person into the character — a down-and-out poet named Maxwell Bodenheim, whom I used to see in Washington Square in my NYU days. He wrote poems to order on yellow foolscap for twenty-five cents. When he had enough quarters, he would go and get drunk on wood alcohol.

Orson was unimpressed and the situation was very tense, made more so by the fact that he was eating a sumptuous steak. I left the theatre and called Peggy, telling her I thought we were out of work again. In those days, being out of work was quite a normal circumstance.

When I went to work next day, Orson was prepared to try it my way. He told me to go ahead and show him what I wanted to do.

After my opening soliloquy, I proceeded with a pantomimic beat, reacting to the citizens who came on from all corners of the stage. I had stuffed my pockets with many pieces of paper, for my Bodenheim idea, without telling the other actors. When I said I was Cinna the poet, not Cinna the conspirator, I took the papers out as evidence. I played a very gentle, diffident man with a great deal of pantomimic comedy; the terror came out of comedy, which becomes very moving in the theatre. All of it came from pantomime.

In this way, Orson was great: when you brought him a character he was able to stage it in a way that was hair-raising. He took my characterization and gave it fantastic staging. He had the citizens come out singly, or in threes or fours; they were very threatening. To the audience, the poet's reaction was funny. I played as if they were making a silly mistake: as if I were well-known and they just didn't recognize me. When they didn't react, the poet began to realize his words were falling on deaf ears; he produced the poems as proof. Orson had them take the poems and crumple them and throw them at me.

As I made a large semi-circle up and around to stage right, I became aware they were closing in on me, and I returned to the center where the poems had been thrown, increasingly apprehensive that the outcome could be terrible. As the gang surrounded me, I disappeared from the view of the audience save for one raised hand, with one last scream, "The Poet!" The mob rushed me down the ramp at the back of the set out of sight of the audience, as if I were being devoured by an animal.

The scene stopped the show. After the speeches of Brutus and Antony, the audience needed this physical manifestation to illustrate what Antony had been talking about; it gave a strong meaning to the play.

There are people who to this day, fifty years later, talk to me about the scene. Twenty years after it was played, Jacob Landau did a painting of it which is in the Museum of Modern Art in New York.

After five days of rehearsing this scene and making the other changes, we gave a matinee preview before opening night. We didn't know what we had — but a remarkable thing occurred.

The eminent New York critic, John Mason Brown, asked if he could come to the matinee to review the show as he was going on a lecture tour and would not be able to attend the opening. After the preview, John Mason Brown came onto the stage, dropped his overcoat and began to act the whole play with great enthusiasm. As he went over it, scene by scene, in rapture, it gave us the confidence we needed; if John Mason Brown, the critic, felt this way, we really had something.

That night, we played with great confidence and it was a triumph. New York had never seen Shakespeare like that. I think that to this day, it remains the most exciting Shakespearean production I have ever seen. It was as immediate and accessible as a column from *The Daily News*. I learned a lot about playing Shakespeare. I learned that in all classics where the language is difficult and remote to most audiences, you must make it immediate. You must forget reverence, speak well and find the ideas in it that are immediate to the audience and not rest on historical tradition.

We were the toast of New York; it was a great feeling. Orson began *Shoemaker's Holiday*. We had a sense that we were going to have another great success; we felt ourselves to be the darlings of the town, particularly of the theatre critics. So we rehearsed in the most relaxed and informal fashion. The new play would go into repertory with *Julius Caesar*.

Before previews, when the costumes, sets and lights were ready, Orson came to us during a performance of *Caesar* and asked if, right after the performance, we would be interested in doing *Shoemaker's Holiday* for the audience. We all agreed, and when the curtain fell on *Julius Caesar*, Orson stepped forward and addressed the audience.

"Ladies and gentlemen — we are going to give you a full performance, with lights, scenery and costumes, of *Shoemaker's Holiday*. You are all welcome to stay, free of charge. There's a coffee and donut shop across the way, or there's Longchamps down the street. We'll leave the curtain up and show you how we change the set; perhaps some of the actors will come out and talk to you."

It was already ten-thirty in the evening, and half the audience left because of work the next morning. But the news spread quickly up and down Broadway; by the time the lighting and sets were changed and we had changed our costumes and make-up — which was shortly after one o'clock in the morning — the theatre was packed to the rafters. People were standing everywhere — in the boxes, the balcony — and sitting in the aisles. Others were still struggling to get in. Richard Watts, the critic, was there.

With the curtain still up, we began to act our costume change; Chubby Sherman walked across putting together his costume and eating an apple. I crossed, putting on a shoe. We put on a great show of preparing for the show.

When the curtain was let in, Orson, Chubby Sherman and I kicked it, as we used to see in vaudeville; when someone was working behind the curtain, putting up a set, they didn't care if they accidently bumped the curtain and the audience saw it. But we did it deliberately, to create the effect of great activity on stage.

The curtain finally rose on the performance at 1:15, to the wildest triumph imaginable. The show was a smash during its run — but never again did we have a performance like that one. Most notable, in *Shoemaker's Holiday*, was the performance of Chubby Sherman as Firk. He was very relaxed and real; it was a classic, superb comic performance of great ease and understatement, such as one seldom sees. Most comics work too hard.

We were now a repertory with two smash hits, and really the cock of the walk, especially Orson. The Mercury had its share of adventures: Joe Holland was stabbed during a performance of *Caesar* — but this and other stories have been told before.

Orson added *Heartbreak House* to the repertory. He brought Geraldine Fitzgerald, a lady of refreshing brilliance, over from Ireland to be in it. This was her first performance in America. He also added Mady Chris-

tians. We moved *Caesar* and *Shoemaker's Holiday* to the
National Theatre on 40th Street, while *Heartbreak House*
went into the Mercury. In addition, Orson had done
Marc Blitzstein's *The Cradle Will Rock* for three Sunday
nights and it was so successful that he moved it into the
48th Street Theatre for a run. They hadn't been allowed
to do it on the Federal Theatre Program. John Houseman
has told the story brilliantly of the night *The Cradle* was
banned by the powers-that-be of the Federal Theatre.

I did a radio show for the Columbia Workshop called
I've Got the Tune, a half-hour opera in which Blitzstein
played a composer who had a tune, but he didn't know
where it belonged. Shirley Booth played a secretary;
Lotte Lenya was a woman who wanted to commit
suicide; I played Private Schnook who was being initiated
into the Nazi Bund by Kenny Delmar, who later was
Senator Klaghorn on *The Fred Allen Show.* Chubby Sherman played the leader of the children with whom the
tune finally found its place. It was a beautiful little work
of Marc's. In the booth at CBS while we did it sat Orson
Welles, John Houseman and Kurt Weill. Irving Reis
directed it. There were always exciting people around —
people who became legends, but in those days we were
all just working.

During this season at the Mercury, there was an attempt to do a production of *The Duchess of Malfi* and to
bring Aline McMahon into the company to play it. Orson
called a rehearsal for midnight; we found ourselves sitting in the Mercury along with eighty or ninety actors,
looking at each other and wondering what was going on;
there were only eight parts in the show.

Orson came on stage, fingering the gardenia he was
wearing and carrying a large dollar cigar. He had just arrived from Tony's, a former speakeasy, which had become
a very chic eating club. He said, "This is only going to
please a few friends and myself," and called eight of us
up on the stage to read the play, leaving all the others

who had been told they might be in *The Duchess of Malfi* sitting in the audience.

Hiram Sherman and I, having both scored something of a hit at the Mercury, found ourselves cast along with Whitford Kane as the three madmen, each with about three lines. Still trying to fathom what Orson was up to, we read the play, but it didn't go very well; there were about five actors sitting ready to play each part, should Orson want to make changes.

George Coulouris was particularly upset. He had been a fine Antony, and also did well in *Shoemaker*. He was an established actor who, in coming to the Mercury, had sacrificed a great deal of money because he was already playing major roles in Broadway productions while the rest of us were struggling to get Broadway roles. Suddenly he found himself on trial. After he left at the end of the reading, they called his home. He had a considerable drive to Riverdale, so at two o'clock in the morning his pregnant wife answered the telephone and heard, "Just tell George when he arrives that he's on probation." It was presented as a joke, but there was some seriousness behind it.

The result was that there was quite a hullabaloo about the reading and such a bad feeling was created in the company that it was the first and last rehearsal of the play, which was never done.

At the end of the season, I had a meeting with Orson and Jack Houseman. They asked me to come back in the company for the next season. I had made up my mind that I wasn't going to do it. It was partly because of *The Duchess of Malfi* experience and, in retrospect, I think it was partly to get out from under Orson's fantastic personal success which had resulted in the theatre's total identification with him. He *was* the theatre.

When Orson spoke at a testimonial given to him by the Hollywood foreign correspondents in 1981, he said that the biggest mistake of his career was in not going back to the theatre after his first film. He stayed with films because of their mystery, their seduction: he was captured by films and didn't want to give them up. But in the long run it had been a mistake. His masterpiece was his first film, though later he did make other remarkable ones. Later, he did go back to the theatre, doing *Native Son* and the Cole Porter show, *Around the World in Eighty Days*.

Looking back, I realize that without Orson's great success the Mercury would have been less. But then I felt he had become the major figure at the expense of the theatre, and I wanted out. Others were leaving too; Chubby Sherman didn't like the way *Shoemaker's Holiday* was handled, and he wanted to go.

I went back to see *Danton's Death*, and Orson again asked me to rejoin the company. But *Danton's Death* was virtually the end of the Mercury. This theatre, which has gone down in history as one of the truly exciting American theatres, really lasted only one season, followed by an abortive season of only one show. Though it was not successful, *Danton's Death* had many brilliant ideas. Orson devised a cyclorama made of ten thousand Halloween masks, on which the lights played; it looked like a Daumier, with all those heads staring. He also cut up the stage and made it into a hollow, with an elevator in the middle carrying tableaux up and down. Unfortunately this was disastrous, as it kept collapsing into the cellar.

The company went on to do radio, and then films. But the theatre was over with this first show of the second season.

My next experience was a curious one. Hallie Flanagan had had a Federal Theatre show in rehearsal for over a year which she couldn't seem to get off the ground. It was called *Sing for Your Supper*. Hallie felt that if someone came in from outside the Federal Theatre to be the comic and play in the sketches, the show might be saved. Some good people were working on it. There was one fine song, "Ballad for Americans," by Earl Robinson and John LaTouche. Harold Hecht, who later became a prominent film producer, was the director-producer. Anna Sokolow choreographed the dances. I agreed to perform in it and Hallie hired me on the ten-percent quota.

I went into rehearsal and started learning my songs, dances and sketches. Suddenly, one day, I was asked to leave the show.

I had been offered a role in a revue, *Sing Out the News*, which George S. Kaufman was directing. It was written by Harold Rome — his first revue after *Pins and Needles* — and produced by Max Gordon, the most successful producer of the time. They offered me a contract which was standard for revues. I would play anything I was required to play, because most of the sketches hadn't been written. They would be written during the summer and even during rehearsals. I turned them down, because I had promised Hallie I would do *Sing for Your Supper*.

At the racetrack near Washington D.C., Max Gordon ran into Harry Hopkins, of the Roosevelt administration. Max asked him, "What kind of theatre are you running there?" Hopkins wanted to know what he meant. "The Federal Theatre. You know Norman Lloyd? I offered him a job at two hundred and fifty dollars a week and he insists on staying at the Federal Theatre at twenty-three eighty-seven." Hopkins replied with the line that became famous, and for which he is well known: "That's how we run things. Tax, tax, spend, spend, elect, elect." I heard about it many years later from his son, David Hopkins.

It was a rule that you could not stay on the Federal Theatre if you turned down a job for equal money or more in private industry. Hopkins saw the possibility of bad publicity, and instructed Hallie to ask me to leave.

After I was removed from *Sing for Your Supper*, Herman Shumlin called one day and asked me to come visit him and Max Reinhardt. Shumlin knew my work, particularly my portrayal of the aged Pavlov when I was nineteen, and he liked it. He was producing a play called *The Merchant of Yonkers*, which Thornton Wilder had adapted from an Austrian comedy. Max Reinhardt had done the play in Europe with great success. Jane Cowl was to be the star. Later, this play became *The Matchmaker*, and in another metamorphosis, *Hello, Dolly!* They had been in rehearsal for about a week and someone was not pleased with one of the actors, Tom Ewell. I never knew who wanted him replaced; he was a good actor, one of the leading character actors on Broadway, but for some reason, there was a problem. I met Reinhardt at the Essex House, where he had a suite.

PARKER: What was Reinhardt like to work with?

LLOYD: He was a charming man, rather short but impressive looking. He was well-dressed, most polite and courteous. He and Shumlin told me the situation and gave me the script; they asked me to look it over in the adjacent room, which was the bedroom. My memory of sitting in the room, studying the script, includes my noticing a photograph, in a small silver frame beside the bed; it was of Max Reinhardt as a young man. I was interested that he carried it with him. At that time, he was probably in his sixties.

They liked my reading and asked me to come to the theatre. I can never understand why they made that decision without Thornton Wilder, considering his rights as the playwright. He was one of the best-known American writers, and must have had a lot to say about the casting of his own play.

I arrived at the theatre, met the company and went into rehearsal; we rehearsed for two days. But Thornton Wilder was insistent that he didn't want me to play the part; he would not let Reinhardt alone on this. Finally, I was asked, with profuse apologies, if I would mind stepping down, and Tommy Ewell was put back in the part. When I saw the show, I thought he was very good; I never understood why they took him out. As luck would have it, on the very same day, I had an offer of another part in a play called *Everywhere I Roam,* the first that Marc Connelly and Robert Edmond Jones were doing after *Green Pastures.* So I did not hold Shumlin to the run-of-the-play contract he had given me.

I enjoyed working with Reinhardt, who had been, in his time, the most famous director in the world. His way of working was to insert between each of the pages of his script a blank sheet, and to write on the blank pages every move of the production. He made these plans before coming to rehearsal. Every gesture, every eye-blink, every inflection of the performance was there, not just the attitudes and physical line, but the internal life of the play also. There was no room for the actor to improvise or invent. He gave instructions as one worked; he was very polite and gentle about it.

It was a German style, as I found when I subsequently worked with other German directors; whether Reinhardt originated it or followed it, I don't know. But where he was kind, others were not. When working with an unkind director one simply closed up, as an actor, and couldn't work at all. Reinhardt was a very good actor; he could get up and show what it was he wanted. He didn't speak English. An attractive blonde sat next to him at a table on-stage; he spoke to the actors in German and she conveyed it in English. I remember one phrase: "Keine pause, keine pause." "No pauses, no pauses." I was still carrying the sides of my part, and I hadn't even read the play; I was not thinking about pauses, just trying to make sense of the rehearsal. But he threw you into performance right away; you were not to think about it. He wanted the tempo, the pace; he wanted movement, immediately.

He could not get started in America. This was 1939; he had done the film of *A Midsummer Night's Dream* in Hollywood in 1935, and a play, *The Eternal Road*, but his career in this country had not been successful. He eventually did another play, *Sons and Soldiers*. The Reinhardt story in America is a sad one.

Jane Cowl's attitude during rehearsal was very regal. Her secretary stood at the ready. Jane would use hand-signals for whatever she needed; at her demand, the secretary appeared onstage with a lighted cigarette and placed it on the table of the set. Or, at some discreet sign, pineapple juice would appear.

Poor Jane; she ended up a pauper. Her body lay in the mausoleum of a famous scenario-writer of the silent days, Jane Murfin, for thirty days and was finally buried there; there was no one to claim her.

According to Gottfried Reinhardt, Jane Cowl made life tough for his father in that show. But for many actors, his way of work was very difficult. They were specifically directed in the length of a laugh, and the degree of a turn. German actors—Elizabeth Bergner, for example—flourished under Reinhardt's methods. Bergner seemed very natural, and that was the trick; the specifics he gave you were naturalistic, though arbitrary. We weren't trained that way, and it wasn't easy. During rehearsal, we realized Reinhardt was the star.

Today, particularly in pictures, directors let the actors do much of their own work; sometimes, too much. One often feels that the improvisations in films are allowed by the director to continue past any point of interest to an audience. The casting director of a Martin Scorsese picture once talked to me about possibly playing a role in a film. She told me that there would be a meeting with Scorsese and Robert DeNiro at which the three of us would improvise, so that Scorsese could see what I could do. In fact, she went on, the script had not yet been delivered — but they had material to suggest what the scene would be, so that I could improvise with the director.

I said nothing, and was given some drafts of scenes. I went back to my agent and announced that there was absolutely no chance of my accepting the conditions of my audition. I pointed out that I had often been very well paid to work on story development; if I improvised a scene and contributed to it, it would have a story value. Should I be in the picture, this was well and good; if I were not, why would I freely give them story ideas, for which writers are paid?

I believe there should be a ruling on this from the Screen Actors Guild; in improvisations, one contributes much that is of use.

But by the same token, improvisations are sometimes allowed to go far beyond the point the storyline needs, and they become boring and embarrassing. This is the opposite of Reinhardt's technique. His achievement in films was not comparable to his success in the theatre, although he had a strong visual gift. Besides being skilled with actors, he was a director who affected the style of a play; he imposed upon it, so that it was a Reinhardt production. Orson Welles was in this tradition, but he had the gift of carrying it over into film. There was a production scheme, a look to the show. The show created a certain world which they had envisioned and which they were able to realize. There was no happenstance.

Next, I played the role of Johnny Appleseed in *Everywhere I Roam*. Marc Connelly directed, and Robert Edmond Jones did the sets. The play had been written by Arnold Sundgard; Marc Connelly had come in as play-doctor. Dean Jagger and Katherine Emery were in it; Mel Ferrer was one of the dancers; another was Lew Christensen, who later ran the San Francisco Ballet. It was a lovely experience, although the play failed. For me, it was a success; in those days, before the Tony Awards, the critics' Ten Best Performers list at the end of the year was the

greatest recognition. For my performance, I was selected
to be on the list by the critics.

Marc Connelly was an energetic director. Because he
was bald, he would wear his hat during rehearsals. To
reduce the chill on his scalp, no doubt, and, additionally,
to prevent the work light from shining in his eyes. Marc
preferred to act out the scene for the actors, playing both
male and female roles.

In the man's role, Marc would read a speech, then
turn at the same time pulling off his hat to denote that
without hat was feminine, then read the lady's speech.
His bald pate thus exposed was somewhat disconcerting
at first but one soon got used to this method of direction.

I was offered another role as a result of my performance in *Everywhere I Roam,* and because of my earlier
work with The Theatre of Action. I was cast in a play by
Irwin Shaw that the Group Theatre was doing, called
Quiet City.

Quiet City had a fine cast. Sandy Meisner and I
played the leads; Frances Farmer was the leading lady.
In it were Morris Carnovsky, J. Edward Bromberg, Karl
Malden, Marty Ritt, Ruth Nelson, Leif Erickson, Curt
Conway, and Roman Bohnen. Lee Cobb was not in it; he
thought he should have been playing Carnovsky's part —
but he always felt that way. Kazan was the director.
Aaron Copland did the score.

It played three Sunday nights at the Belasco Theatre.
Mordecai Gorelik did the set, adjusting the one he had
done for *Gentle People* — which was one of the most successful of Irwin Shaw's plays.

Quiet City didn't work. Shaw gave up on it.

The score survives, as "Quiet City," a fantasia for orchestra, and is often played. I find it moving because I
was the trumpeter in the play; the part was that of a kid
wandering around New York, wanting to be a trumpet
player like Bix Beiderbecke.

I was given the role partly because of my performances; it was also because John Garfield and Franchot Tone had left The Group to go to Hollywood. They had become stars, but they were to have come back; they were always coming back. They never, all their lives, really left — though when they were with The Group they always seemed to want to leave. In their absence I played the part that Garfield was to have done and Sandy Meisner did the role first thought of for Tone. They were clearly quite different; Tone was a romantic figure, while Sandy, though brilliant, was a nervous, neurotic actor; both were valid for the part. But the combination of Frances Farmer and Franchot Tone might have been one of the great romantic teams of the time.

The Group was impressed by my work in the show, and I was invited to go with them to Lake Grove, Long Island, where they had taken a school for the summer. Winwood School, a Christian Science establishment, was very large with dormitories, school rooms, mess hall, baseball diamond, gym, and tennis courts. The entire Group went; Clifford Odets came back for the summer. There were others who had not been in *Quiet City* — Stella and Luther Adler, for example. Kermit Bloomgarden was the company manager.

Harold Clurman has written about this summer in his superb book, *The Fervent Years* — one of the best books ever written about the American theatre. It was the last summer The Group spent together.

It was a summer of disappointments. They had expected to get a play out of it, but were not able to; Irwin Shaw was to write one, but it never arrived. Clifford had a play called *The Silent Partner*, but he couldn't solve it; it remains the only play of his that has not been produced. It was the story of a New England family of factory-owners under the siege of a strike, and how they dealt with it.

It was also a difficult summer emotionally: the break-ups included the marriage of Frances Farmer and Leif Erickson.

There was discussion of a Chekhov play, either *The Three Sisters* or *The Seagull*. But these preparations didn't work out, either. We had speech classes, and there were dance classes — ballet with Piscator's wife, and modern dance with Anna Sokolow.

Most memorable, to me, were Clurman's lectures. The Group's affectionate nickname for him, in 1939 at the height of Hitler's power, was Der Fury, after Der Fuehrer. Clurman was, in his way, a wildly dictatorial man, with wild the operative word. He had a great intellectual commitment to the theatre; he was indeed fervent and a true leader. He established an aesthetic for his company, who were prepared to go to hell and back for him; they fought with him but always knew they were working on a level equivalent to the Moscow Art Theatre — or any other great theatre in the world that did have an aesthetic. I don't know of one of the many theatres in this country today which has this. In Harold's schoolroom lectures, which I marvelled at but rejected, subjectively, many of the actors took notes; Carnovsky and even Odets took notes as if they were at the feet of some great professor.

In one of his lectures, I remember Harold holding his stomach and saying urgently, "I am a Monist! I am a Monist!" I reminded him of it some thirty or forty years later; did he remember it? "Monism?" he said. "I haven't the faintest idea what it means." Then he smiled and added, "But of course, that is when I am my most eloquent."

On another occasion, he said: "I'm not an idealist. I'm against idealism. An idealist is a schmuck!"

Though he spoke to us at great length about *Quiet City*, particularly after it closed, I never had the good fortune to work with Harold Clurman on a play. I heard that his technique was to spend the first week or ten days of rehearsal talking about the play, and that these would be ten brilliant days as he talked about the characters. I may be doing him an injustice in believing that he seemed to lose interest when it came to putting the play on its feet, and deal with the technical aspects. His was an outstanding record in the theatre, particularly for doing new plays; he championed Odets. He dealt with the psychological and the subjective.

He directed one film, which Odets wrote and which starred Cary Grant. But clearly Harold was not a man who was able to handle film; the mechanics of the cinema bored him.

The summer wore on, and I had no money. The Group fed and boarded us; that was it. We couldn't even afford to go to the movies. Out of the blue, I received an offer from Orson Welles and John Houseman in Hollywood — to join the Mercury Theatre there to do a picture called *The Heart of Darkness.*

A Trip to Hollywood

I couldn't believe my good fortune. They were offering me five hundred dollars a week, which seemed at that time like untold wealth. After the night's lecture, I informed Clurman of my offer, that I had accepted it and was leaving the next day. "I give you permission to leave," he said to me, which I loved. Peggy and I got on the Super Chief, which is how one traveled to Hollywood, and rode in great luxury to Los Angeles.

For a poor actor who was always on the brink of economic disaster, to find himself on the Super Chief was something unbelievable.

At Union Station we thought ourselves in fantasyland. The quality of sunlight and the clear sky of those days was, for the two of us from New York, dazzling; like nothing we had experienced before.

It had been suggested that we stay at the Villa Carlotta, an apartment hotel on Franklin Avenue where many actors lived. It was across the street from the Chateau Elysee, an elegant apartment hotel. Now, the Villa Carlotta is rundown and sad and the Chateau Elysee is a home for elderly people. At that time, Walter Huston lived at the Elysee, and Bill Tilden taught on the tennis court.

The Mercury Theatre company was a union of both the theatre and radio companies. Some were missing: Hiram Sherman and Whitford Kane both had fallen out with Orson and were not there; Joe Cotten was on tour

65

with *The Philadelphia Story*. Vincent Price was missing, but George Coulouris was there. From the radio company were Paul Stewart, Everett Sloane, Ray Collins and Agnes Moorehead. Stefan Schnabel was in both the theatre and radio companies; Richard Wilson and William Alland were Orson's assistants.

We sat down together at RKO and read the script for the first time. Orson's treatment of the Joseph Conrad story was quite faithful; in *Apocalypse Now*, the same story was adapted to different circumstances. In his version, Orson played the camera. He was the narrator, Marlowe, telling the story as they went up the river. It was a new concept, and it gave Orson great freedom with the camera.

Strangely, this was the last reading of *Heart Of Darkness*. We heard that RKO did not approve of the script. I couldn't understand it; after all, Orson had brought out an entire company.

The actors had a six-week guarantee. The Mercury company remained in Los Angeles for this time, and I played tennis every day. We had been brought out by Columbia Artists Bureau, an agency which was a branch of CBS, and they were responsible for paying us. George Coulouris and I would dash up to the office every Thursday, looking for our checks. We were delighted to be playing tennis and being paid; the innate corruption of actors.

At the end of six weeks, we were called to Orson's office at RKO and we all crowded inside. Orson was smoking his pipe, using Royal Yacht tobacco; back in the theatre days, he had smoked Barking Dog. He had risen economically. He delivered a speech to us about his failure to get the studio to approve the script, and therefore he was abandoning it. He did have other ideas he was submitting; he asked us if we would mind staying around a few weeks in Hollywood, while he tried to arrange a deal around a new property. He mentioned several; the first was a suspense novel called *The Smiler with a Knife*.

I returned to the Villa Carlotta not knowing what to do, whether to stay or not. Then one of the radio actors telephoned. He was highly successful, and even then he was making between fifty and seventy-five thousand dollars a year — a fabulous sum. He said, rather authoritatively, that Orson's request was unfair; we should not be asked to stay in Hollywood without pay. He urged me to go back to New York. The impression he gave me was that this was the general feeling of the company and, naively and impulsively, I went back to New York. Those who stayed did *Citizen Kane*.

I guess Orson took it as a rejection on my part and in retrospect I feel I handled it badly. I was not skilled in weighing decisions. I was a Broadway actor who moved on impulse. I should have asked the opinion of Al Taylor, the agent who was close to Orson; I should have asked George Coulouris, who stayed. But I didn't — and Orson was right not to use me in *Kane*. I over-zealously believed one should be paid for what one does, and there are times when this should be forgotten. I have always regretted it.

We returned to New York. Peggy was pregnant and in May of 1940, our first child, Susanna, named after Shakespeare's daughter, was born. I plunged into various theatrical endeavors on Broadway.

The first of these was *Medicine Show*, an attempt to do a Living Newspaper in the commercial theatre. It was about medicine, which hadn't been treated as a subject by the Living Newspaper of the Federal Theatre. The director was Jules Dassin and the leads were played by Dorothy McGuire, Martin Gabel and myself. The score was by Hanns Eisler and the orchestra was conducted by Jascha Horenstein. Horenstein was a refugee and was very highly thought of in Europe. I was the song-and-dance man in the show; my singing was rather wavery, and Jascha would stop the rehearsal and in a German accent he'd say, "Every note must be like iron!" I always referred to him thereafter as "Jascha-every-note-must-be-like-iron-Horenstein." After the war, he was able to go back to Europe, where he had an outstanding career as a conductor with major symphony orchestras. I think he looked back at this time as the low point in his career.

Medicine Show was not successful. Back in the Federal Theatre we had a real newspaper room with a morgue and a staff of newspaper writers and reporters, a background for material; here two men did the writing and did not have these resources. It closed after about four weeks.

Another show I did at that time was *Village Green*, which was a modest Broadway play, starring one of the best actors I've ever worked with, Frank Craven. He was not only an actor, he was a well-known playwright and author of *The First Year* and *That's Gratitude*.

Frank Craven, who had been in the theatre many years by the time I worked with him in *Village Green*, had created the role of the stage manager in *Our Town*. His acting was of the most naturalistic sort; sometimes at rehearsal it was difficult to determine if he was doing the text or speaking to someone. His ability to talk and listen on stage was extraordinary, so much so that when he was working in England he would throw people in the cast; they would think he'd ad libbed, which he had not.

When we were trying out the show in Baltimore, he, Matt Briggs and I were on stage. The two of them went up in the scene. Matt Briggs got nervous and froze. He wasn't on top of the play yet, as we were still trying it out. Frank Craven began to ad lib, and it was beautiful, better than the original text. Matt Briggs interrupted him and Frank Craven said, "Wait a minute, let me finish, will you?" He completed the ad lib and brought the whole play back into line, and on we went with the story.

We did the play at the Henry Miller Theatre, which is now torn down. It was exquisite, like a music box — one of New York's most beautiful theatres.

I also did a Philip Barry play, *Liberty Jones,* for the Theatre Guild, which flopped and nearly put the Theatre Guild out of business. Fortunately, their next production was *Oklahoma!* I think they did *Liberty Jones* because of the success they had had with Barry's *Philadelphia Story.*

The most interesting aspect of *Liberty Jones* was its score by Paul Bowles, who later became a novelist. He was then one of the leading theatre composers in New York. With Virgil Thomson, he was responsible for the best musical criticism of the time; they wrote for the *Herald Tribune.*

Alfred Hitchcock
and *Saboteur*

It was 1941, and Alfred Hitchcock had a picture about to be released called *Suspicion*, with Cary Grant and Joan Fontaine. He came to New York for the premiere of the picture at Radio City Music Hall, which was the most desirable place to open. He had been brought to America and put under contract by David O. Selznick, and was preparing a picture called *Saboteur*, with a script by Dorothy Parker, Alan Campbell, Joan Harrison and Peter Viertel. Hitchcock was looking for someone to play the title role of the saboteur; he wanted an unknown because of the nature of the story. He mentioned this to John Houseman, who was also working for Selznick, and Houseman suggested to him that I might be right for the part. Houseman also got in touch with me, telling me to call Hitchcock at the St. Regis, which I did, using Houseman's name to get through to Hitch.

He was very kind and polite and suggested I come to see him.

I did so, and it was the start of a relationship that went on for over thirty-five years. Hitchcock had made only two pictures in America — *Suspicion* and *Rebecca* — after his English work, but it impressed me, as I came into his presence, that he was the definition, in one's imagination, of an international motion picture director. I don't mean in the cliché Hollywood style, or as in a George S.

Kaufman comedy, but in the sense of a director one felt to be a major figure in the contemporary entertainment world. It was more than that; it was an international aura of St. Moritz, trains, the best food, cigars, rare wines — all the fantasies that you saw on the screen, he seemed to embody in the way he lived. Actually, only part of that was true. He had a great sense of that world but he lived very quietly, like a bourgeois. He projected a professionalism, a big-league quality, immediately, and he was very much at ease. He was then in his early forties. He told me what he had in mind and said that he would have me tested; he didn't do the tests, because he had to go back to Los Angeles. I was to select a scene with a character who was like the character in the film, which he described to me. We had a chat about Houseman and Hitch's new picture, *Suspicion*, and the fact that I had also seen his English work. I had seen the first of his films to be released in America, including *The Man Who Knew Too Much*, during the run of *Noah*, because Pierre Fresnay was in it. Then came *The Thirty-Nine Steps*, and *The Girl Was Young*. He was considered an arty director then; these were released as art films.

I selected a scene from *Blind Alley*, a successful play of which variations have since been made — *Desperate Hours* and *Detective Story*: people held hostage by the criminal. I played the criminal in a short scene — less than two minutes. It was a single shot, with cues thrown to me from off-stage. There were also other actors testing.

The film was sent off to Hitchcock and he selected me. I was overwhelmed. I was paid three hundred dollars a week to play a title role in a film and was guaranteed four weeks. I had to pay a commission and living expenses out of this. They also had me stay on two extra days, for which they did not pay me, but gave me twenty-five dollars a day for expenses. I was given round-trip transportation by plane. That was my first trip to California by air, which in those days was a journey of about twenty-one hours. You slept in a berth on the plane. There were several stops.

Hitch never referred to the test again although he had hired me on the basis of it. The producer, Jack Skirball, did. He was then a theatre exhibitor, financier and in partnership with Bruce Manning. Together, they were producing the film independently at old Universal. Hitchcock was on loan-out from Selznick. Jack Skirball was very kind and hospitable. One day he took me out to dinner and told me, "You know that test? I thought you overdid it." He was probably right. Theatre acting was then a lot more florid than it is today, and it could well have been that I did a lot of "acting" to make the character of the psychopathic killer convince Hitchcock that I could be a deranged saboteur. In fact, that part was written quite differently.

Saboteur starred Robert Cummings, Priscilla Lane and some very good character actors like Otto Kruger, Egon Brecher, Alma Kruger, Alan Baxter and Ian Wolfe. Hitch was shooting when I arrived. I came on the set and he greeted me most charmingly. I waited. The shooting day was almost over and he invited me for a drink. This was my first experience drinking with Hitchcock; from then on, I was on my guard.

We went across the street from the lovely old Universal lot to a bar and restaurant run by one of the prop men, Eddie Keyes. Hitch ordered a martini, and I said I would have the same. When Hitch's "usual" arrived, it was in a goblet the size of those used to serve grapefruit, when the grapefruit is surrounded by ice. Mine, of course, was the same. I looked at it with fear. At no time in my life have I been much of a drinker; I was also not accustomed to driving, having learned when I was in Hollywood in 1939 with Orson, and not having driven in New York since. The drink made me fear for my safety; on the other hand, I was afraid that if I didn't drink it, I might lose the part.

I just sipped while Hitch drank one, then another. He never got drunk; it was his normal appetite.

Before I came to Hollywood, I had done some second unit work on the picture in New York. Once I was cast in the part, Hitch sent John Fulton to New York to direct the unit. He was the foremost trick cameraman in Hollywood; if you needed effects shot, he was the best man in town and, in his own way, a star.

The Statue of Liberty sequence has become one of the most famous Hitchcock ever made, and in the years since *Saboteur* I have often been asked how it was done. Audiences seem to know more about technical matters these days, perhaps because of the proliferation of all kinds of cameras. But at that time, audiences couldn't understand how the sequence was shot. That was precisely the effect that Hitchcock desired because as a director, as a man of great visual power, he looked for a style that would not only give the audience the emotional kick that he hoped for but would also leave them puzzled. I will get to the specifics of that as I lay out the sequence, which is probably my claim to fame, for people always say, "Oh yes — you fell off the Statue of Liberty."

In the story of *Saboteur*, my character commits the crime at the beginning of the film and the entire picture is a chase. Bob Cummings, the hero, tries to find and capture me. Two or three reels from the end, he finds me just as I'm about to blow up a boat — a Liberty ship carrying goods for the war.

At one point I run into Radio City Music Hall. I find my way onto the stage, and behind me a picture is playing on an enormous screen. A gunfight ensues between Bob Cummings, the detectives, and me. They are shooting from the audience; I'm shooting from the stage. At the same time, a gun-fight is in progress on the screen, so it is never clear where the sound of revolvers is coming from; you're not sure if it's from the screen, my revolver, or Cummings's. A man in the audience falls over dead, clearly shot by me from the stage, with only the woman next to him aware of it.

The essence of the Hitchcock touch in that sequence was not only the intermingling of reality, so to speak, with film, but also the humor of the situation, in which the audience continued to think all the shots being fired were on the screen; they were laughing. They were never aware of the real gun battle.

From there — in the continuity of the story, not in the order in which the film was shot (the Radio City Music Hall sequence was done in Hollywood) — I take a cab going down the West Side Highway. This, too, was done in Hollywood as a process shot. While we were shooting in California, news reached us that the Normandie was burning. This French ship was at that time the largest in the world; it was being prepared for the troops to use when it was sabotaged. In flames, the ship had keeled over. Hitch asked Universal Newsreel division, which existed at that time, to get some footage of the boat burning. He also had them shoot plates of a car going down the West Side Highway — an elevated structure which bordered the west side of Manhattan along the docks. He put me in a mock-up of a taxi and said, "When I cue you, look to your right as if you see the Normandie." He wanted a look that would be used as a cut — the juxtaposition of going down the highway, then a turn of the head with a slight smile, and the cut of the boat burning; it all tied together, indicating I had something to do with the burning boat. It is remembered as a chilling moment.

From a directorial point of view, it shows a man who was really on his toes and aware of any opportunity to create something for his film: to take history at the moment and incorporate it into a script — in character, story and action. Hitch always claimed the contrary: "I lay out the script shot for shot. It's boring to shoot a picture because I've done it all in the script." But that was an ex-

ample of his not having done this. It was history and absolutely memorable.

The cab arrived at the Battery at the tip of Manhattan.
In those days an aquarium was there, and the docks from
which boats left for the Statue of Liberty, on Bedloe's Island.

When we shot there with John Fulton's second unit, it
was December 15th, 1941, a few days after Pearl Harbor,
but it was supposed to be spring. It was very cold, but I
could not wear my hat and coat for the scene. I went into
the warmth of the little office where tickets for the Statue
of Liberty boats were sold. Thirty-five extras were waiting. Coffee and doughnuts were being served while the
first shots of my arriving at the ticket office, then ascend-
ing the gangplank of the boat, were being prepared. John
Fulton was also going to shoot plates to be used on Stage
12 at Universal when we went to California.

We had a big problem that day with clouds; it was
overcast, so John did not have the light that he wanted
much of the time. We did a lot of waiting; we would do
two or three takes and wait again. After the scene at the
gangplank, which we did two or three times, we did the
scene on the boat, going across the water. I went out on
deck to the railing at the front of the boat to look at Priscilla Lane, whom I was trying to pick up, at the opposite
railing. Fulton also had to shoot plates for Priscilla Lane,
who wasn't there, as well as my plates and shots of me
looking into the bay.

The extras were in these scenes, which we shot several
times. Next, we landed on Bedloe's Island where we shot
coming off the boat four times, again waiting for the right
light. From there, we did a shot walking from the landing up to the base of the Statue of Liberty, also requiring
several takes. It was then time to eat, and box lunches arrived.

One little old lady who was obediently repeating all
these actions with the extras finally turned to one of them

and said, "Do you have to do this every time you want to see the Statue of Liberty?" She had come from Virginia and had decided to see the statue the first thing in the morning. Wandering into the nice group of people who were having coffee and doughnuts, she had thought, "My goodness, what are all of these terrible stories I hear about New York? They've made me feel welcome with coffee and doughnuts, although they have this curious way of making you repeat all these things to see the statue."

It was explained to her that she was actually in the middle of thirty extras making pictures. She disappeared; to this day the mystery has never been solved. It's my own conclusion that she jumped in the bay, though they tell me that's not the case. Whatever happened to her, no one knows, because they were looking for her to sign a release. This was needed for anyone who was going to be seen on film — which she was.

Finally, we did the scene going into the base of the Statue of Liberty. This was it for the day; Fulton had his plates and live-action of me. John then went to the top of the statue, to shoot plates from there to the base, the bay, the harbor and so on. This done, I went to California to perform in the picture.

Saboteur is remembered chiefly for the Statue of Liberty sequence. In the story, after my character has gone into the base of the statue, Bob Cummings and the FBI men arrive. Priscilla Lane had been on the boat with me. I go up to the crown of the statue and she follows me. Her job is to detain me long enough for the FBI to reach me. I have a scene with her in which I go on the make and she goes along with it to hold me there. At the end of the scene, she speaks my name and I realize that I have been trapped. I look out and see speedboats arriving, which would not normally happen at Bedloe's Island. I move out of the inside of the crown and onto its balcony.

I did not do this on the real Statue of Liberty, of course. Hitchcock had the hand, torch and balcony built to scale on stage twelve of Universal. It was enormous. Parallels had been built out to the balcony with mattresses.

The inside of the crown was also built to scale, as all the dialogue scenes were done by Hitch at Universal.

Bob Cummings came out onto the balcony, following me. As we moved around, he pulled a gun and made a gesture towards me with it. I panicked and went over the balcony railing onto the parallel covered with mattresses, where I was caught by a grip named Scotty who was stationed to make sure I wouldn't go off the parapet.

At this point, Hitch switched to doubles. For the long shot, Davey Sharp, one of the greatest of stuntmen, repeated my fall backwards over the railing, through the air. He then caught the crotch of the thumb and forefinger on the statue and held on with both hands. Bob Cummings's stunt double, also in long shot, climbed down the forefinger to try to rescue me; Fry, the character I played, had to be taken alive to be persuaded to talk.

When Hitch returned to close-ups, he disassembled the torch piece. He put the thumb and forefinger piece of the torch, and the crotch of the thumb and the forefinger, down on the floor of the stage. The camera was angled at me lying on my stomach on the set piece, and I did all the close-up reactions there. Bob Cummings came down the forefinger, but could only reach the sleeve of my jacket. There were then intercuts between my close-up, Bob Cummings's close-up and the seam where the sleeve was stitched to the jacket, which began to tear.

Bob tried to get my hand to prevent me from falling, pulling the sleeve to bring me closer to him. But my hand was clinging to the statue, and he couldn't get a grip on me.

Eventually the sleeve came off and I fell, from a big close-up. I fell without a cut to the base of the statue, one continuous scream all the way down. That is what Hitch was building up to; that is the problem he had set for himself. The fall had to be done without a cut from a close-up.

People have wondered how we did that to this day. When Ben Hecht saw the sequence — referring to the sleeve that parted from my jacket — he told Hitchcock he thought I should have had a better tailor. Hitch himself decided that the only problem with the sequence, which is technically supreme, was that the story had the wrong man in jeopardy. It should have been the hero, he thought. He concluded that the scene on the hand of the statue, with all the technical and cinematic wizardry to hype up the audience, would have been more affecting had Bob Cummings been in jeopardy. John Fulton designed the falling scene in consultation with Hitch. Hitch knew a great deal about art direction; he had worked as an art director in silent films in London when he was young. He also knew more about trick photography than most people, so he could talk to Johnny Fulton as a peer.

This is how they did it. The removable piece of the statue — the thumb and forefinger — was taken to another stage and attached to a platform six feet high. The platform was on counterweights and rigged to the top of the stage. A hole was cut in the platform, with a camera placed to shoot down through the hole, towards the set piece fixed below it. Underneath the whole thing was a saddle-like affair on which I sat, on a pipe about four-and-a-half feet high, based on a black cloth. On a cue, the camera, on the counterweight system, starting from a close-up of me, would go up in the air to the grid, together with the set piece of the thumb and forefinger, leaving me behind; thus giving the effect of falling.

This was shot at different speeds, while I did movements of falling rather slowly and balletically. By the time the camera got to the top of its move, it had gone from an extreme close-up to a very long shot of my apparently falling figure. The small saddle was not visible;

the pipe and black cloth, which were seen, were later painted out in a traveling matte shot. Hitch succeeded in achieving what he wanted, which was to do the fall in one cut.

I was so fortunate to make my first picture with Hitchcock. I started at the top, and was introduced to a way of picture-making, a way of conducting oneself on the set—a way of life regarding a picture—that of an international star director. Not only was he an artist, but there was a very special world which he projected. Hitch always dressed in a black suit, white shirt and black tie. He looked like either a banker or an undertaker. He actually had twenty-eight of these suits, all the same. The coats and trousers were marked with corresponding numbers, so they wouldn't get matched in the wrong way; this was done for dry cleaning purposes. It was characteristic of his mind — so well organized. He would walk on the set and conduct it as if it were a fine banking firm in England — very quiet and masterful. But he had great humor and a sense of fun. He still had remnants of his gift for practical jokes at that time, and sometimes played them; they were always very funny. He left an indelible mark on me of what it means to be a director and how to conduct oneself on the set.

Chaplin and Renoir, with whom I worked later, each had a unique genius. Chaplin was a nineteenth-century romantic; he still had the flavor of silent pictures which caused him to work the way he did in my experience on *Limelight*. Renoir was a man of enormous personal charm, a humanist, erudite and witty. He was a prince of the human race. My friendship with Jean was a very loving and close one quite apart from pictures.

Hitch was really what you dreamed about when you picked up chic magazines — *Vanity Fair, Harper's Bazaar* or *Vogue,* and saw international salons with motion picture directors. He was St. Moritz and the Orient Express

— all the fantasies a New York actor without any money would savor.

PARKER: Why was *Saboteur* made as an independent production?

LLOYD: Jack Skirball had bought the property. He had done a few pictures previously, and went on to do *Shadow of a Doubt* with Hitchcock later. Hitch actually developed *Saboteur*. I don't know whether or not Selznick turned down the story, but he loaned Hitch to Skirball for this production.

As a director, Hitch often used the phrase "camera logic." He believed in a simple camera: it is exactly in the right place at the right time to tell the story. Joe Valentine, one of the top cameramen in Hollywood, shot *Saboteur* in black and white. Early on he asked Hitch if he would like to look at a shot through the camera. Hitch told him no, thank you; he had looked through a camera before. He never looked through the camera. He knew exactly the image that he wanted; he would ask the cameraman what lens he was using and where he was cutting the actor, at the knees or at the chest, etc. Upon receiving this information, he was ready to shoot. His chair was put alongside the camera.

I began to learn about the camera from Hitch — then, and also later, when we worked together on the television series. It was a source of pride that major directors seldom moved the camera, and would only move it if there was a real motivation for doing so, in the case of an actor moving — from a sofa to a chair across the room. If a character was going away from you, you had to follow him, or perhaps you were setting up a scene and needed a large panoramic shot on a crane. But for the most part, movement was kept to a minimum by the major directors. All that changed with the introduction of zoom lenses and other sophisticated equipment, such as the crab dolly and its variations.

Hitchcock sparked the invention of the crab dolly because of his demand for it; he wanted a camera that could not only dolly but could also move the way a crab moved — backward, forward, sideways and all the ways in between.

With the sophisticated technical improvements, and particularly with the expansion of television and its new techniques, many directors arrived from film schools, where they had become proficient with the equipment. They had become so enamored of the zoom that it became a thing in itself after a while. It can dilute staging and staging skill and result in the actor being ignored. It reached its zenith with the directors of commercials, who are full of tricks because they have to be; they have thirty seconds to catch the eye of the audience with zooms, tricks, dissolves, fast pans and curious dollies. All this moved into story-telling from commercials, which it must be admitted, did produce some good directors, particularly in England; they come into pictures with a strong visual sense, but for the most part, the effect becomes an end in itself.

In the final analysis, one must remember the director is the storyteller. He may not be the creator of it, but he is telling it, and it is his gifts as a storyteller that hold the audience. I remember Bertolt Brecht telling me, "Even a poem must have a story." What distinguishes people in this business, one from another, is the story he or she has to tell. An actor walking on stage, whether it be theatre or film, should carry a story with him — a personal story. To the extent to which that story is attractive or unique is the extent to which an audience will be interested in him.

John Ford always subscribed to the idea of telling a story and was very good at it. He used very little film; there are tales of his coming back after completing a day's work and not having used up one reel of film. He'd got everything he'd wanted. Hitch would shoot a scene and say, "Cut — that's all you need." It was a phrase of his, when he had all he wanted; he was seeing it as a piece of the story. Renoir said, later, that the most important element is the actor and what he is doing. What is important is what is happening in front of the camera and not behind it. When directors became enamored of the technical razzle-dazzle they became enamored with what was happening behind the camera, not in front of it. I think this is being tempered again. We are seeing simple, good camera work, and beautiful lighting and a great sense of visual strength.

After *Saboteur*, I left California; I would have loved to have stayed and to this day I don't know if I did the right thing. Peggy had remained in New York with our daughter, who was age two. I could have brought them to Hollywood. My agent, the William Morris office, wanted me to go back to New York. I have always believed it was because they didn't want another actor on their hands. It's true I didn't have the prospect of immediate work, and the picture was not due to come out until May, when it would open at Radio City Music Hall, so there would be a few months to wait. That would mean that the William Morris office would have to find me work to bridge that time, and it was in their interest, since I was not known as a picture actor but was known back on Broadway, to have me return there.

PARKER: Why would William Morris want you to go back to the East Coast when you had just starred in a film under a major director? It doesn't seem to be a smart move.

LLOYD: I wish I could answer that; I can't, not from a creative and positive point of view. From a negative point of view, as I explained, they were really interested in people who got immediate work or who were offered things immediately. They had no way of selling me until the picture came out. I always thought that if I had been in Hollywood when the picture was released, things might have been a little better. But I was in New York and nothing really happened as a result of *Saboteur*. I made the lists of best performances and a list of the ten future stars in the business in magazines, but I was not on the scene to take advantage of it.

There was another element: in those days, Broadway was the thing. I was a New Yorker — an actor, and New York was my city. I was raised there. Those of us who were serious actors, and I believed myself a serious actor, were truly committed to being New York actors — Broadway actors.

We had an inner confusion; we all really wanted to go out and do Hollywood movies. We all really wanted to be picture stars. We would never admit it to anyone, because we also wanted to be artists in the theatre — to be in the Mercury, the Group, the Federal Theatre— and later on I did the first production, as a co-director and actor, with the Phoenix. In 1942, one felt curiously guilty about not working in the theatre.

On the other hand, I was terribly drawn to staying in Hollywood. For one thing, I was a good tennis player, and tennis was not so common as it is now. While playing tennis at the homes of people in the business, I thought, "What a marvelous way to live, with tennis courts and swimming pools." Back at 123rd Street around Morningside Drive it was dreary.

I returned and did a few undistinguished plays, among them a musical for the CIO called *Marching with Johnny*. It was directed by Phil Loeb. Zero Mostel was around, because he was a friend of both Phil's and mine. I didn't want to do many of the comedy sketches; I attempted to get Zero to do them. While we were trying it out in Newark, he kept saying, "This stuff is so funny, Norman, you're all wrong about it." Phil Loeb said the same thing. Finally, I quit. I said to Zero, "If it's so funny, you do it." Zero said, "Oh, no. It's no good." Phil finally went into the show himself, because he couldn't find anyone else to do it; they went on to Philadelphia, where they closed.

It was typical of the shows I did in 1942 and 1943. Then in 1944 I got an offer from John Houseman, who was producing at Paramount Pictures, to come to Hollywood to do a film called *The Unseen*, with Joel McCrea, Gail Russell and Herbert Marshall. It was a sequel to a successful ghost picture called *The Uninvited* with Ray Milland; Lewis Allen directed both of them.

I had come out alone, while Peggy and Susanna stayed in New York. When shooting was over, I decided to see if I could get work in Hollywood as an actor.

A few weeks later, Hitchcock offered me a part, in *Spellbound*. It was a scene early in the film, with Ingrid Bergman; it established her as a psychiatrist, and I would be her first patient. Hitchcock wanted a certain quality, though it was a very small part; today it would be called a cameo. It was an honor to do it for him; I enjoyed it, and I played in the first scene that Hitchcock ever directed with Ingrid.

Ingrid was a woman of great strength and charm. I worked with her later, over a longer period of time, on *Arch of Triumph* as Lewis Milestone's associate. At the time of *Spellbound*, she was still rising to the top of her profession. She was a very well-known actress and was about to become the top star in the business. She was under contract to Selznick, as was Hitchcock; Selznick was making *Spellbound*.

Hitch laid out this first scene in a certain way, though Ingrid had other ideas — something to do with the movement, I think; it was not to do with character or interpretation. But Hitch had a definite concept of the shot and I assume that what Ingrid wanted would have altered it. Hitch, having made up his mind, would not alter anything — that was not his way. He had a great sense of himself and he was a vain man; he wasn't going to change a shot because an actor or actress had something else in mind.

It was certainly true then, and perhaps to a certain extent it still is, that the director had to give off an air of infallibility. Today, there is a little more give and take, though we still have directors who are God figures. Then, directors ruled by fear, by command, by their position. With John Ford, you took your life in your hands if you suggested anything. Betty Field once told me that when she did *Cheyenne Autumn* with Ford, she made a suggestion about what kind of dress she would wear. It was just an ordinary house dress. He said, "You really think so?" On the set, he always addressed her as "the wardrobe mistress," because she had the effrontery to suggest what she would wear.

Jean Renoir

After *Spellbound*, I stayed in Hollywood to give it a try. Nothing was happening, and it started to be a little dangerous. I was running out of money. The war was on and though it was not as bad as it had been in the Depression days, I now had two households.

I have no memory of how it came about that I met Renoir and was given the chance to do *The Southerner*. But I met him at the General Service Studio, and I had never encountered a man like him. First of all, he looked like a large Idaho potato farmer. He dressed informally, in chinos, an ordinary shirt open at the neck and a wonderful kind of hat (a Stetson, I think). He limped because of a World War I wound. In his last days it opened up again and gave him much pain. In his book, *Renoir, My Father*, he describes not only his father but also his own life, how he was wounded and how he began to make pictures. His mother saved his life by not permitting an amputation. While he was recuperating, he had nowhere to go, so he went to the movies; he would watch them all day long, holding his leg up so that it would heal. It never really did.

He was electric, a man of enormous energy. He was prototypically French, and so are his pictures. They are a history of France in the 1920s and '30s in the way they look, the way the people behave, and the way they dress.

At an interview, Renoir told me he had very little of the character in the script; he was rewriting it, and he

wanted to improvise much of it. He permitted me to take
the script and read it. When I returned, I talked to him
about concepts and how to do this strange character, who
was one of the heavies, somewhat retarded. The character lived on a farm and ran like an animal through the
crops — he was dangerous. We agreed that we wanted
something poetic about him. I talked about what I
wanted to do, and also about how I saw him dressed: I
saw him in WWI army breeches and a strange-looking
jacket. None of this was used in the film, but it established a sympathetic feeling between Jean and myself,
and I think it was because of this that Jean decided to go
with me for the part. In the film, I wore old, dirty work
clothes, and I had a small flute carved out of bark.

The picture was about tenant farmers who worked the
cotton fields of Texas, from a book called *Hold Autumn in
Your Hand*. We made most of the film outside of Madera,
California, which is cotton country, in the San Joaquin
Valley in central California. The area was populated by a
sect which had left Russia a long time before and had
found its way to Mexico, worked their way across the bor-
der and then up into central California. They did not
believe in allowing their reflections to appear in a mirror,
so their reactions to the making of a motion picture were
interesting. Renoir thought of bringing some of them
into the picture, but the idea of an image was against their
religion. If the camera pointed towards them, they
would run. We didn't use their house, for religious
reasons and also because it was in good shape; we needed
something more run down, and so Jean had to have one
built. Renoir gave me a lot of freedom in this part, and I
did much improvisation, including running over hills and
chasing animals. It was a marvelous part to play and
great to watch this man at work; in terms of interplay and
freedom for actors, he gave us a sense that we were creating right at that moment. There was a remarkable cast:
Betty Field and Zachary Scott, Percy Kilbride, Blanche

Yurka, Estelle Taylor, who had been the wife of Jack Dempsey, Charlie Kempner, a fine actor who was killed in a car accident soon after finishing the film, J. Carrol Naish, who played my character's uncle, and Beulah Bondi.

Renoir, the Frenchman, really understood the farmer of Texas. He articulated this well in his book and in a play he wrote which I later produced and directed for PBS called *Carola*, with Leslie Caron and Mel Ferrer. There was a line in the play: "The farmer of one country has more in common with the farmer of another than he has with the banker of his own country."

Jean was a sophisticate and an avant-garde artist, despite the naturalistic quality of most of his pictures. He understood painting on the highest level, having been raised in the household of his father with Cézanne, Pissarro, and Toulouse-Lautrec familiar callers at his home when he was a child. He knew French culture at its best. But he understood peasant life equally well; his sympathies were there. He liked their simplicity and their way of life. At breakfast, I saw him drink his coffee out of a bowl, as I had seen immigrants do when I was a child. His pictures like *Picnic on the Grass*, *A Day in the Country*, and *The River*, have to do with nature. He understood the working man also; in *La Bête Humaine* he made Jean Gabin learn to run the steam locomotive.

Again, I was working with a giant; Renoir was one of the major figures in the history of film. In all the years I knew him, whenever I was with him, he would say something that was an illumination — something I had never heard before.

His way was diametrically opposed to that of Hitchcock. They had a common ground in that they were storytellers; they were both writers. Hitchcock did not write the dialogue; he hired a writer, but the story was always told in his way. Renoir literally wrote, books and screenplays. At times, he collaborated with writers like Jacques Prevert and Charles Spaak, who were also poets.

With Renoir, you knew you were in the presence of someone special, and it rubbed off on you. One got a sense of what the business could be — what it was really about. With Renoir, one saw what it was like to be a great artist. In his person, he defined humanism.

Lewis Milestone

In 1944, having done three pictures in one year — *The Unseen, Spellbound,* and *The Southerner* — I decided to settle in Los Angeles and I sent for Peggy and Susanna; our son, Michael, had not yet been born.

Through the grapevine, I heard about a picture that was going to be made called *A Walk in the Sun,* to be directed by Lewis Milestone. George Chasin, later a major figure at MCA but then working for the Small Agency, was my agent at the time, and got an appointment for me with Milestone.

Milly was imposing to look at, like a Russian general. His face had a Tartar look about it. He was a formidable presence with an air of toughness, but underneath all that he was a beautiful man with great charm. He loved the good life—perhaps too much.

He was a superb storyteller, and had been one of the pioneers of Hollywood, having arrived just after World War I; a part of Hollywood history, he had been one of the founders of the Directors Guild. As a Russian immigrant, he had arrived from Europe at the age of fourteen, not knowing any English. He learned the language on the corner of 47th Street and Broadway in New York, standing in front of a cigar store. His speech was a delicious mixture of a European and strong New York accent.

Milestone's account of his arrival in Hollywood is a fine piece of local lore. He was in the army and was required to fill out forms concerning his civilian life. He saw that the man next to him had listed his income as five hundred dollars a week. Impressed, Milly introduced himself; where, he wondered, did the man manage to earn five hundred a week? The man, who was Richard Wallace, the well-known director, told him Hollywood, on the West Coast. So Milestone decided that was where he would go as soon as he got out of the army.

He arrived in Hollywood with a little money saved from his job as a door-to-door salesman of family portrait photographs, and found work in a small, independent cutting-room. The owner, in those days of silent films, picked up whatever work he could get. He took thirty dollars a week out for himself and fifteen for Milly. But Milly was a New York boy; he used to arrive at work in a derby and fancy clothes. Because he was a Broadway fellow, he took a taxi. The boss, struggling to keep the business going, couldn't tolerate Milly's arrival in a taxi; if he, the boss, couldn't afford one, then neither could Milly. Milly was ordered not to come to work in a taxi. But the boss had the wrong man; Milly quit. It was the first of many times he was to do so.

Milly later worked with Thomas Ince as a cutter. One day when he was driving onto the Culver City lot (later occupied by Selznick) the guard stopped him and said that he had to punch in. Mr. Ince felt his employees were taking advantage of him by coming in late — Milestone's habit was to arrive at about eleven — and wanted to know what hours they were spending on the job. So Milly was instructed to punch the clock.

"Oh," said Milly. "Where is it?" The guard pointed it out. Milly walked over and punched the clock by smashing his fist into it. "There, I've punched it. Tell Ince if he wants me, I'm in the bar across the street," he said. Ince, on being given this information, pronounced the son-of-a-bitch fired.

Now it so happened that in those days there was no system for coding films. The cutter would edit the scenes and after marking them with a grease pencil he would fold them over, put a rubber band around them, then throw them into a can. In this can were many pieces of film. The way the old timers worked was very interesting. I was amused to watch Milestone, who rose to be the foremost cutter in silent films. He would still use the old method of having the film around his neck. He would pick up the film in his hands; even with the moviola there he often ran it through his hands until he came to the frame he wanted, then he'd mark it. I remember going to see Chaplin in Switzerland and noticing that he had eczema on his hands. When I asked him how he got it, he said, "From cutting a lot of films." The emulsion caused it.

So Milly had left cans of unidentifiable, un-coded film. Ince went down and tried to put the picture together, even one reel together, but it was hopeless. He ordered Milly rehired. The recalcitrant was secure in the knowledge that he was the only one who knew how to make sense out of the film in the can.

He was tough, he was volatile, and very often he was not able to control his temper.

I read for him, and he liked the reading. He was also very sensitive to theatre people and liked stage actors. He knew a great deal about the Group Theatre; he had brought out Clifford Odets to write his first screenplay, *The General Died at Dawn*. He was interested in people who came from that kind of background. I was hired to play Archimbeau in *A Walk in the Sun*. Two of my lines in the picture were memorable. "We'll fight the next war in Tibet," and "You kill me." People still come up to me and quote them.

Milestone chose a very interesting approach in the direction of this film. He selected his favorite location in Agoura, where he had made *Of Mice and Men*. Today, it is a suburb and people drive into town from there every day, but before the freeway was built there was just a two-lane road and it was quite remote. Quarters were taken at the Malibou Lake Club, above Agoura in the mountains; people stayed there in the summer. The entire company was asked to live at the club, even though it was only forty miles from downtown Los Angeles. Milly was trying to develop a camaraderie, as he had in *All Quiet on the Western Front*. He wanted to establish a relationship between all the fellows who were in the squad which moved through *A Walk in the Sun*. Later, we shot *The Red Pony* on the same location.

We shot the film all around Agoura, and also in Hidden Valley; some scenes were done on the Goldwyn stages. We shot one night scene on a stage: it was on a landing barge, against a backing. As we stood on the barge with the rifles slung on our shoulders, pointing straight up, one rifle went off and put a hole through the backing. Two soldiers had been hired to take care of the equipment we had borrowed from the army, but we discovered they went hunting at night and had neglected to clean this particular rifle, leaving a bullet in it. Someone could easily have been killed.

The company lived at Malibou Lake for most of the shooting of the picture, which was about eight weeks. Milestone was right; most of the relationships that developed were the relationships in the story itself. At the end, most people began to go back into town and Milly permitted that; finally, in the last week or so, we gave up the Malibou Lake Club. But by then the relationships had been formed — friends in the movie were friends in fact, and similarly enemies in the script didn't like each other. He had cast the film well; it was a fortunate development. We scarcely knew each other when we started working, but that soon changed. Richard Conte, who played one of the leads, became a life-long friend. I spoke the eulogy at his funeral, as I did at Milestone's.

Dana Andrews and Richard Conte were the stars; it was John Ireland's first picture. George Tyne, Pepe Benedict, Huntz Hall and Sterling Holloway were also in the cast. Milestone had a strong sense of camaraderie with a male cast. It's reflected in the body of his work: *The Front Page, All Quiet on the Western Front, Two Arabian Nights, A Walk in the Sun, The Purple Heart, The Halls of Montezuma.* When he shot *All Quiet on the Western Front,* he actually built trenches and the actors lived in them. Rats began to inhabit them with the actors; it was close to the real thing. He maintained that the actors got something out of that, and in our movie, this was true; we did so by living together on location.

Milestone was a fine craftsman; a Hollywood director who learned the business in Hollywood and contributed to what came to be known as the Hollywood picture. If he got the right kind of story, he could do it well. If he got the wrong kind of story, he was in trouble. To a certain extent, this is true of most directors. But when he was given *Rain,* with Joan Crawford and Walter Huston, it was, as Milly said, "The only time the Lord's Prayer has ever gotten a laugh." It just wasn't his cup of tea. He wasn't a cerebral or intellectual director, though he was a man with a fine mind of its own kind. Like William Wyler, George Stevens, and John Ford, he was a special kind of director — a craftsman.

There was something in Milly that was remarkable, of real size which never fully emerged. *All Quiet* was a masterpiece and in this instance he fulfilled his talent, but his career seemed to be blocked. He never achieved what he appeared to be capable of when he first started. I have to say, dear friend that he was, that this was because of his personal complications: temper, temperament, inability to get on with the front offices at all and resistance to authority. Jim Tully once wrote a piece on Milly in which he thought that he had the possibilities of being Eisenstein, but never would realize them because of his personality. He meant that Milestone loved the good life, the cafe life. He married a beautiful lady, a Lee of Virginia, Kendall, who was one of the great hostesses of Hollywood. Her parties were legendary. Milestone loved that life — and it all closed in on him after a while.

The blacklist was the final blow; it drove him to Europe. He never quite got going there; he made a picture with Sam Spiegel, on Melba, which was a poor one and this ended his relationship with Spiegel. He made a war picture with Dirk Bogarde.

Milly always shot his pictures very well; he had a good eye. His pictures are well composed and look beautiful in a rather stylized way. He went by the Hollywood rules: he didn't pan unless the actor was moving. No tricks — although he did try to work out his dissolves, so they moved from one scene to the next in an interesting way, such as a billiard ball into a doorknob. He never lost his skill as a cutter. The overall story of Milestone ends sadly, but during the mid 1940s he was one of the top directors in Hollywood.

On *A Walk in the Sun,* he loved to stand around on location in the winter cold of the mountains and tell stories. There was always a dice game going on. I remember an assistant coming to tell him that a shot was ready, when Milly was twenty dollars down in the game. He refused to shoot the scene until he was even again and had recouped his twenty dollars.

Milestone got to do *A Walk in the Sun* in a unique way. There was a man in Hollywood by the name of Samuel Bronston, who wanted to be a major producer like David O. Selznick. He set about this by approaching directors who were prominent: Rene Clair, Julien Duvivier and Milestone. He asked each of them what stories they wanted to shoot. Rene Clair chose Agatha Christie's *Ten Little Indians,* which he made. Duvivier's choice was a Broadway play, *Decision,* which I do not believe was ever done. Burgess Meredith recommended *A Walk in the Sun* to Milly as fine material for a film. Bronston bought the book for Milestone and Milly hired Robert Rossen to write the screenplay. The screenplay was, to a great degree, the dialogue that was in the book by Harry Brown.

We started shooting. Two weeks into the picture, Bronston informed Milestone that he didn't have any money. Milestone went into his own pocket and met the first week's payroll from his personal finances. In the meantime, we were hit by terrific rains; all the equipment got stuck in the mud. A circus was wintering nearby in Agoura, with a couple of elephants; we had the elephants haul the equipment out for us. It was quite a sight.

Milestone finally came up with a man named Johnny Fisher, who owned a bar on Melrose Avenue called the Nineteenth Hole. Johnny Fisher had been raised on the Lower East Side of New York City and was a fierce fighter. He had the potential to become a professional pugilist, but his father wouldn't allow it because whenever Johnny fought, he wanted to kill. His father had also taught him that whatever he did in life, he should always have a cash register going for him; that was why Johnny kept the bar. He was also a bookie, and tied up with folks in Las Vegas, so he had access to money. There was a strong black market at the time, and as a consequence, laundering of money; one way to do this was to put the money into movies.

I don't know how Milly was introduced to Johnny Fisher, but Johnny came up with the money to continue the film. Early in life, Johnny had been sentenced to prison in the state of New Jersey in connection with a crime having to do with beer running. This was during prohibition. He was not a man to be trifled with, either in person or in the company of his Las Vegas friends. He admired Milly enormously and made a good partner for him; Milly knew how to handle a man like Fisher.

Johnny's only stipulation was that he wanted to protect his investment; he wanted it under surveillance.

The squad of *A Walk in the Sun* started out consisting of fair-haired, newly shaven boys of seventeen or eighteen, though some of them were war veterans who had seen combat and had been mustered out because of injuries. They were a nice, upstanding group. As Archimbeau, I played the point of the squad — the guy out front. One day shortly after Johnny Fisher had come into the picture, I was marching along and turned around. The fair-haired boys had disappeared; the squad now consisted of mostly dark men in need of a shave and pushing thirty. Johnny's friends were now the extras.

Thanks to them, the picture became known as the greatest traveling crap game in Hollywood. Every morning, it was the first thing they wanted to do, and it went on all day long. Milly approved; he thought it was good for the spirit of the production.

Milly finished shooting the picture, but because of Bronston's dropping out, the release through United Artists had been lost. Milestone went to Darryl Zanuck, with whom he had a longstanding friendship dating from Milly's giving Zanuck his first job as a writer of serious pictures. When Milly was given his opportunity to direct at Warner Brothers, Jack Warner asked him whom he wanted as a writer. Milly had said, "That guy who sits out on the fire escape and writes *Rin Tin Tin* pictures." It was Zanuck. Zanuck was now head of Twentieth Century-Fox and that too is a story: Milestone was to have formed a partnership with Joe Schenck. They had a falling out, so Schenck formed a company with Zanuck, which became Twentieth Century-Fox.

Zanuck agreed to release the film. They changed the title to *Salerno Beachhead*, and Fox took its thirty-five percent distribution fee. Fox made a little money out of it; Milestone got nothing, except the money he laid out and perhaps his salary. The picture never made a profit. When it was re-released, it again had its original title, *A Walk in the Sun*. It's a good picture and with it began my friendship with Milly. A year later, he offered me a job as his associate and gave me a piece of his company, The Milestone Corporation.

Before this happened, I did a play in Los Angeles — *Volpone* — for the Actors Lab. It was a great success. Morris Carnovsky directed it, and the cast included Hugo Haas, J. Edward Bromberg, Phoebe Brand, Ruth Nelson, Houseley Stevenson and Rhys Williams. As a result of my reception in this play, I was signed to a contract at MGM.

This was considered an honor; MGM was the foremost studio of the town at the time. In 1945, they had a large roster of stars — Gable, Tracy, Garland, Kelly, Rooney, Garson, Crawford, and many others, though Garbo was no longer there. To be signed as a player under contract to this studio was very encouraging. I made three pictures there: *The Green Years*, directed by Victor Saville; *A Letter to Evie*, which Jules Dassin directed; and *The Beginning or the End*, which was about the atomic bomb and directed by Norman Taurog. After *A Walk in the Sun*, I had also made a picture called *Young Widow*, with Louis Hayward, Jane Russell and Marie Wilson. It was produced by Hunt Stromberg Sr., but as a picture, it was not much.

While I was under contract to Metro, Milestone was given a deal by a new studio called Enterprise Productions. This was a most worthwhile and interesting company. David Loew, who with the Hakim brothers, had produced *The Southerner* and was the son of Marcus Loew, formed a partnership with Charlie Einfeld, Warner's top publicity man. They had the idea that a studio should be an attractive place to work with a supportive management, first class commissary and a general air of good will. Unfortunately, the studio had only one successful film, *Body and Soul*. Other films made there did not do well and Enterprise was forced to go out of business.

Milestone's first production with the new studio was *Arch of Triumph.* Irwin Shaw had written the script, which Milestone, having accepted the project, promptly rejected, saving only one line: "Anything you can settle for money is cheap." When Shaw severed himself from the project, Milestone asked me to come on board and work with him on the script. He had no intention of writing it, nor had I, although I think he respected my ideas about structure and scenes and the values of a script. For the actual writing he brought in Harry Brown, the author of the novel of *A Walk in the Sun.* He could write good dialogue.

Milestone proceeded to lay out the book, preparatory to writing a screenplay. We worked at Milly's home on San Ysidro Drive, exquisitely decorated by Mrs. Milestone. Milly had an office upstairs with an adjacent room where his secretary worked. He would have the secretary extract all the dialogue from the book. Then he selected the scenes he wanted from the novel and set the book's dialogue into them. This was a scissors and paste job which he would hand to the writer to put into playable form. He was slavish in his devotion to the material. He had worked this way on *All Quiet on the Western Front,* which had turned out to be a masterpiece; he believed that having bought a property, he felt he must stay with it.

Finally, we had a screenplay, but a major problem evolved as we started to shoot. Ingrid Bergman, a woman of great beauty and talent, was also a very strong-minded person. She was not a star who was just waiting to be told what to do. She was bright, worldly wise and quite definite. She had underlined all the areas in the book that she was determined would be retained in the screenplay. They did not necessarily coincide with what Milestone wanted to retain.

Another problem was that Charles Boyer was very close to the French government and to the French consul in Los Angeles. I admired him greatly; he was an intel-

lectual and brilliant. He was a very good actor who had
come out of the French theatre to become a major international star. When he sat in the projection room, Ingrid
would tell him as she watched the scene, "Oh, Charles, in
Sweden we call you 'bedroom eyes.'" Both of them had a
style. They were cosmopolitan, sophisticated, big league.
Their style and manner has led me to believe over the
years that there was a special kind of aristocracy in Hollywood, only to be found in the picture business. The
way Ingrid met her directors — including Milestone and
Rossellini — was to write to them; she wrote to tell them
she wanted to do a picture with them.

Milestone was in the middle of a sandwich: Ingrid
with her interests as an actress, demanding her underlined sections of the book; Charles Boyer, as a semi-offi-
cial figure, acting as a propagandist for France. In
consultation with the French government and on his own
behalf, he wanted to eliminate those areas of the book in
which the French government looked bad, because of the
way they treated certain refugees. So some very dramatic
material had to go.

Later, when we were already shooting, Charles
Laughton came into the picture, playing the character of
Haake, the heavy. He thought the character wasn't German enough, and should be rewritten. He was going to
do that himself. At the time, he was working with Brecht
on the English adaptation of Brecht's *Galileo*. They were
going to have to stop while Laughton did the picture, so
Charles thought it might be a good idea if Brecht worked
on this picture with him. For dialect, he wanted Hanns
Eisler to coach him. Eisler was working as a composer of
film scores, and had an impenetrable German accent.

PARKER: This seems like such a potpourri. Milestone
was a major director. How could this come about?

LLOYD: It came about because of the financing; the picture cost about four million dollars, which was an enormous sum in those days, and everything was riding on Bergman and Boyer.

Milestone was caught; he couldn't say no to Ingrid, she was dazzling to him. He wanted to keep her as a star, which is why he had Brecht write original scenes for her, to satisfy her objections. Boyer also had to be placated. At Enterprise, the situation was different from that at most major studios, where a director could go to the front office and ask the head of the studio to bring the stars into line. Einfeld was a publicity man, and Loew was a quiet, gentle personality, a talented painter and a collector of works of art. Milly became confused; he was trying to please Ingrid, trying to please Boyer, and when Laughton arrived, trying to please him.

I was no help. He'd consult with me; I would recommend we stick to the original script we had. The picture was going to be too long as it was, without adding extra scenes, which were good for what Ingrid wanted to play, but not good for the film as a whole. From her point-of-view, she was not wrong; it was just a question of whose point-of-view should prevail.

There was a scene in the picture about which I had always had my doubts. It was a scene where Boyer and Bergman, as refugees, were supposed to go to the south of France to get away from it all. A big set representing a large rock near the sea was built on a stage at Enterprise. At this point, we had hired Brecht to do an original treatment for a film we hoped we could have ready after *Arch of Triumph*.

During the shooting, Laughton came on to replace Michael Chekhov who had become ill. Laughton was very difficult, and as we were already shooting he had us over a barrel. I went out to his house with Milestone; he lived on the cliff at the edge of Pacific Palisades and it was fast crumbling under him. It was a beautiful home, exquisitely done, filled with paintings — Cézannes, Renoirs, Pissarros, and a collection of pre-Columbian art. Charles looked like a bag of potatoes; his shirt had martini stains all over it. In his study, he complained he had no clothes; he had nothing to wear. As he did so, he held a gold-plated stick, given to him by the Comédie Française when he played *Le Médecin Malgré Lui* there, in French. The stick had belonged to Coquelin. Laughton was an amazing man; a devil — he was unpredictable and had a kind of genius. It was wonderful for the business, to have someone like him. We got Frank Acuna to make him an entire wardrobe. Driving back from the meeting, Milestone told me, "I'm giving Charles to you. You're going to sit with him and rewrite all of the Haake scenes."

We were having great difficulty with one section of the script and it occurred to Milly to have Brecht work on it. It was about the plan to bring the Charles Boyer character from Europe to America. Brecht said he would like to see everything we had already shot before he wrote the scenes; in addition, he wanted to see some of Milestone's other films. After viewing all the film he had requested, he came up with a very interesting observation: the scene in which Bergman and Boyer go to the south of France, and recline on the beach, would make it difficult for the audience to accept them as refugees whose day-to-day existence was so precarious. He suggested the sequence be removed so that the impact of their predicament would not be reduced. He then outlined the additional scenes he had in mind.

But Ingrid would not consent to removing the south of France sequence. She wanted it kept in the picture because it gave the character another color. Brecht maintained that keeping the scene was a mistake, but he proceeded to write new material nonetheless. One scene was based on his escape from Denmark when the Nazis invaded that country; he had been number five on Hitler's list of people to be killed. Brecht's scenes were shot, but were never used in the picture; the south of France scene was retained.

For two weeks, Laughton and I met in the offices at Enterprise while Milly was shooting. Every morning at ten o'clock, Charles would begin work on the bottle of Scotch he had requested, meanwhile reading *Mein Kampf* and insisting that we incorporate some of its writings into the dialogue of the character. I got along well with him. Brecht came to visit us, bringing Paul Dessau, a composer he worked with in addition to Eisler. Brecht suggested an idea for a movie, which I flipped over: it was *The Tales of Hoffman*, with Dessau adapting the score.

On a Sunday, I went to Milestone with the idea; he liked it and told me to go to Charlie Einfeld's house, a quarter of a mile away, and tell it to him. I interrupted his Sunday afternoon nap. He turned the idea down; it didn't appeal to him. He had also vetoed the scenes in the movie which Brecht had written. I was totally depressed. A couple of years later, *The Tales of Hoffman* was made by Michael Powell, with Pressburger, but not in Brecht's version.

Laughton and I finally got the script the way he wanted it. Milestone agreed to shoot it. So we had Boyer's point-of-view, Ingrid's point-of-view and Charles's. It was a mess. We finished shooting after ninety-nine days; Milly was under a terrible strain.

In the last third of the picture, the script got uprooted again. We conferred with Boyer and Bergman during the day, and at night we would adjourn to the office of David Lewis, the producer. There would be drinks, after which we'd go across the street to Lucy's for dinner, then more drinks. With the booze and the food, by the time we talked about what had to be rewritten, Harry Brown, the writer, was stretched out fast asleep. Milly, David Lewis and I would decide what we were going to do with the script and next morning it was my job to tell Harry Brown what we had decided.

In addition, Brecht was angry with Milestone. He had agreed to write scenes, but he wanted to be paid for them; Milly wanted him to write the scenes as a package deal with the treatment he was doing — a quite separate project from *Arch of Triumph*. Brecht gave in, but felt badly about it; I think Milly was wrong not to give Brecht the money as he certainly needed it. The original treatment was to be for Bergman, so that after *Arch of Triumph*, Milestone could do another picture with her. An appeal could have been made to the Writers Guild, but Brecht was keeping a low profile; two years later, he would go in front of the Un-American Activities Committee.

We finished cutting the picture. Louis Gruenberg, who wrote the opera of *Emperor Jones*, did the score. We all piled into a chartered bus and went off to Santa Barbara where we ran the film. The preview was a disaster. We brought the film back and tried to fix it. The art director of the film was Bill Flannery, but Milly had an idea, and for this he brought in William Cameron Menzies, who was one of the great Hollywood names. Milly wanted to connect each sequence of the film with footage of Germans marching across Europe. He liked films with soldiers, and it was also his way of showing the period and the onward march of fascism.

Menzies designed this idea, in stylized fashion; it was shot and inserted into the completed picture. But it was the first thing to go, because it held up the action; it didn't work. It was a mistake which cost twenty-five thousand dollars — a lot of money then.

Next, it was thought that the music was at fault. Franz Waxman was asked to write an entirely new score, but of course it made no difference. The picture was re-cut and taken to Florida, without Menzies's material, shorter, and with the new score, but it died. Charlie Einfeld, who was one of the most brilliant publicity men in town, didn't know how to handle it, got cold feet and withdrew it.

At a party at Milestone's house, David Selznick told Milly in my hearing that when *Duel in the Sun* got bad notices, he flooded the country with the picture, and got his money back before the audiences could make up their minds. He advised Milly to do the same — to suggest to Einfeld that if he did this, with Bergman and Boyer he could get his money back. But Einfeld withheld the picture from release too long. Word got out that it wasn't good, and by the time it was released, it was doomed.

I worked very hard on the picture and made real contributions; it was the first experience I had had in this area, and I took a lot of personal abuse from Milly — and gave some. It was a really violent experience. I didn't get any credit on the film. Today, for what I did, I'd probably be made vice-president of the studio.

After *Arch of Triumph*, Charlie Einfeld gave Milly a title, *No Minor Vices*, and suggested he come up with a picture to go with it. Harry Brown and Milly started with the title and wrote a script; later, the heirs of George Bernard Shaw sued them, as they felt it bore a close resemblance to *Candida*. The leads were Louis Jourdan, Lilli Palmer, Dana Andrews, Jane Wyatt and myself. Jane Wyatt played the girl I was in love with; Louis Jourdan played the interloper into the marriage of Dana Andrews and Lilli Palmer; Dana was a dentist. *No Minor Vices* kept Enterprise going as a company, though they had to scrounge for money. Based on the credit of David Loew, they had had an eighty percent bank loan, but after *Arch of Triumph*, things got tougher. *Body and Soul* did well; it was a plus for the studio, but it couldn't make up for what *Arch of Triumph* had lost. Enterprise made another picture called *Streets of New York*, which was Stanley Kramer's first movie, but it made no money. Some Joel McCrea westerns were shot at the studio, but it was just exchanging dollars: the money that was spent came back, which paid for studio overhead.

While we were shooting *No Minor Vices*, we were waiting for Brecht to save us. Milestone had the hope that Brecht would provide us with a treatment that Ingrid would be keen about, and that she would agree to do, which would put us all back in business.

For six months Brecht had been paid two hundred and fifty dollars a week; his secretary/mistress, Ruth Berlau, was paid seventy-five dollars a week. Brecht said he wrote in German and needed someone to translate as he went along. He always traveled with a retinue of women — his wife and one or two mistresses. He escaped from Germany to Denmark; from there he went to Finland and then to Russia. From Vladivostok, he came to the United States. In Russia, he had no money to live on, but he had a letter from Feuchtwanger, authorizing him to collect royalties which Feuchtwanger's popular books had earned, but which couldn't be taken out of Russia; Brecht lived on this money while there.

When he came to America, he settled down on 26th Street in Santa Monica with his wife and children.

We understood that his hiring Ruth Berlau was a way of supporting her, and we were amused by it. We also knew what the treatment was going to be about: Brecht said that one of the tragedies he had witnessed in this country was that of the middle-aged ladies who sat in bars alone. He was motivated by one remarkable photo in *Life* magazine, of a woman leaping to her death from the upper story of a hotel on fire in Atlanta. In her hand she was holding a pair of shoes; Brecht was intrigued to know why. The opening shot of the treatment was the curb of a sidewalk and a pair of shoes. The camera dollied, the shot loosened, and there was the woman's body, laid out with the others.

Milly wanted to know what was happening with the treatment, so I called Brecht and told him the time had come. I waited a couple of days for it to be typed — and perhaps finished. When I got it, it was twelve pages long. I took it to Milestone.

To put this in context, it is necessary to recall the scenes Brecht had written for *Arch of Triumph* — which were not ultimately used. In one scene, the character played by Boyer has been given a boat ticket, from Europe to America, by a wealthy American woman modelled after Barbara Hutton. He has no intention of using it; he wants to take a hotel room next to Haake, the Nazi played by Laughton and the head of the concentration camp where Boyer's wife died. He means to make Haake's acquaintance and then kill him. So he sells his boat ticket to a Jewish family, who are lacking one ticket for the son; they escape, and he has the money for the hotel room.

Brecht and I went to Milestone's house after dinner one night to discuss the scene. Brecht was not being paid, except for having been hired to do the treatment; Milly was clearly upset, as one could feel that the picture was in trouble and a lot of money was at stake. Even at his best, Milly had a life long problem with his temper; it was always too quick to come to the surface.

As we discussed the scene back and forth, over and over, it was evident that I agreed with Brecht on the way it should go. Milestone was working on it with a pencil in his hand, which was fatal; while he had a good sense of story and character, he could not write — but he insisted on writing. He was also a very naturalistic director, and almost literal in his way of going from step one to step two to step three. He could never go from one to three to five.

The more Brecht and I became separated from him on the ideas of the scene, the angrier he got. He started screaming at us. In spite of Brecht's great standing as a playwright, Milly turned on him. "You're an idiot!" screamed Milly. "You're an idiot!"

Norman Lloyd at age twelve.

Peggy Craven (Mrs.
Norman Lloyd) in 1930.

The Apprentice Theatre Company at Dublin, NH, in 1933. Left to right: Bill Phillips, Norman Lloyd, Kappo Phelan, May Sarton, Theodora Pleadwell, Norma Chambers; Alexander Scourby in foreground.

Norman Lloyd as the clown, in *Injunction Granted*, 1936.

Julius Caesar, with the Mercury Theatre players, 1937. Left to right: Richard Wilson, Bill Ash, William Alland, William Mowry, Joseph Cotten and Norman Lloyd.

Norman Lloyd and Alfred Hitchcock at Grand Central Station, shortly after shooting *Saboteur*, 1941.

Norman Lloyd as Fry in *Saboteur*, 1941.

On location in Madera, CA, for *The Southerner*, 1945. Left to right: cameraman Lucien Androit, Jean Renoir, J. Carroll Naish, Norman Lloyd, unidentified.

Norman Lloyd as Fuiley in *The Southerner*, 1945.

Norman Lloyd as Archimbeau in *A Walk in the Sun*, 1944.

Left to right: Lewis Milestone, David Lewis, Louis Gruenberg, and Norman Lloyd, 1948.

Norman Lloyd as Mosca in *Volpone*, 1946.

Left to right: Norman Lloyd, Claire Bloom, Nigel Bruce on the set of *Limelight*, 1952. Charles Chaplin at right background.

Norman Lloyd (l)
and Louis Calhern
(r) in *King Lear*,
1951.

Norman Lloyd (l) and Nina Foch (r) in *Measure for Measure*, 1956.

Sondra Locke (l),
Bo Hopkins (c),
and Norman
Lloyd (r) in
Gondola, 1971.

Norman Lloyd as
Dr. Daniel
Auschlander in *St.
Elsewhere*, 1987.

Director Norman Lloyd in rehearsal for *The Cocktail Party*, 1951. Left to right: Lloyd, Vincent Price, William Schallert, Patricia Neal, Harry Ellerbe, and Reginald Denny.

Norman Lloyd (r) rehearsing Royal Dano (l) and Joanna Roos (c) in *Mr. Lincoln*, 1952.

Norman Lloyd (c) directing "The Lifework of Juan Diaz" for the *Alfred Hitchcock Hour*, 1964. Cameraman John Russell stands next to Lloyd as he talks to Alejandro Rey.

Norman Lloyd with John Houseman during the production of *The Taming of the Shrew*, 1956.

Left to right: Leslie Caron, Jean Renoir, and Norman Lloyd during the production of *Carola*, 1972.

Norman Lloyd with his children, Susannah and Michael.

Left to right: Arthur Laurents, Norman Lloyd and Charles Chaplin on the tennis court at Chaplin's home.

Norman Lloyd with James Agee during the production of *Mr. Lincoln*, 1952.

Norman Lloyd and Joan Harrison.

Norman and Peggy Lloyd lunching with Alfred Hitchcock at his home in Santa Cruz, 1960.

I took this personally, first because of Milly's temerity to scream at a man like Brecht, and secondly because I had brought Brecht into the project. I began to scream back at Milly. "How can you dare talk to this man like that? How dare you talk to this writer that way?"

Milly whirled on me. "And you're an idiot, too!" he yelled. Brecht and I left, and I drove him home in my '48 Ford coupe. "That man," said Brecht thoughtfully, "is not an artist. That man is a heavyweight prizefighter."

But Brecht needed the weekly salary and Milly needed the treatment so the relationship continued. Milly was not a bad man; he was a "mensch." He was always irascible when working, and I suspected he really didn't like to work — it made him unhappy. But he wanted the money, and he loved pictures; he was deeply insecure. He had a great sense of whether an actor was honest in a scene; he could spot phonies, which is why his war pictures are so good and so truthful.

When Brecht handed me his slim treatment and I took it to Milestone, Milly saw it as absolute crookedness and thievery on Brecht's part: six months salary of two hundred and fifty dollars a week, to produce twelve pages! He kept on repeating it — twelve pages — until I pointed out to him that he hadn't read it; after all, it was the quality, not the quantity which mattered.

He read it, and hit the ceiling. As always, he started screaming and yelling. He refused to accept it, he didn't consider it a treatment. If this was all Brecht could deliver after six months, Milly had been robbed. Reaching for the one thing he thought would hurt, he ordered the girl — Ruth Berlau — fired.

For myself, I found the treatment fascinating. Brecht called it *The Grey Goose*. The woman, who ended her life by jumping out of the hotel window with her shoes in her hand, had, when she was young, fallen in love. But life with her true love would have been poverty stricken; when she finds the opportunity to marry someone who can give her money, a position and a chance to go into business, she takes it. Her life consists of episodes in which she leaves a series of romantic involvements, each time for a better financial situation, always putting security first. When she has accumulated a fortune, she seeks out her first love again, but in a critical situation to do with money, she leaves him. Brecht's point was that there are women who can never give themselves totally in a relationship because they need the security of money more.

Milly never submitted the piece to Ingrid. I filed it among Milestone's papers; it is probably still there.

I met Brecht at Lucy's restaurant, opposite Paramount, to communicate, as gently as possible, Milly's reaction. He did not care that much about it; Brecht's interest was in getting some money. He was willing to write another treatment, and asked me if I had any ideas. I suggested to him that inasmuch as he had taken historical figures, (St. Joan, Galileo) and given them modern treatments, he might be interested in doing the same for Joseph and his brothers. "One of my favorite fairy tales," said Brecht, and agreed to give it a try.

He took the idea, current at the time, of grain for art; the United States would trade its grain for Italian paintings to help rehabilitate that country after the war. Joseph, a young man from a poor family, was an Italian banker who acted as broker for the deal. An Italian patron with many paintings was Potiphar, married to a beautiful woman. The story took place in modern banking circles.

Again, I found it fascinating, and Milestone rejected it. Like *The Grey Goose*, it is probably still in Milestone's papers. Brecht was never able to move the deal onto the next monetary plane. But he sold his house in Santa Monica and was able to move back to Germany with a small stake.

These were the failing days of Enterprise; *No Minor Vices* was not successful. With the failure of Kramer's first film, Enterprise, too, came to an end.

The lot was subleased by David Loew and Charlie Einfeld from Harry Sherman, an old-time producer of Westerns. As Enterprise began to move off the lot, Sherman was informed by his aides that things were beginning to disappear. He issued an edict that no one was to drive off the lot without having his car inspected by the guards at the gate. On the last day, one of the Enterprise executives was stopped by the guard, and as he protested vigorously and indignantly, his car was searched. In the trunk, the guard found large quantities of paper towels, soap and other supplies of that kind.

It was around 1948. I went into a picture produced by Walter Wanger and directed by Anthony Mann, called *The Black Book*. It was Arlene Dahl's first movie, and also starred Dick Basehart and Robert Cummings. It was made at the suggestion of William Cameron Menzies. He had designed *Joan of Arc* for Wanger and realized that after this movie, a great deal of scenery was left over; he proposed another film should be made to utilize these sets.

I also made a picture called *Scene of the Crime* for MGM with Arlene Dahl and Van Johnson. It was one of the first films in a documentary style and it was a good movie; I played a stool pigeon, and in one memorable scene was hung by my collar from a lamppost, with a pigeon in my pocket.

More important during this period was my work on *The Red Pony* with Milestone. It was a Steinbeck story from his book, *The Long Valley*; Milestone had bought the rights from Steinbeck after he made *Of Mice and Men*.

Milestone succeeded in making a deal with Charlie Feldman, one of the major agents in town. Charlie was very stylish, always immaculately dressed; he had an outstanding list of clients including Marlene Dietrich, John

Wayne and Myrna Loy. Among the people working for
him were Ray Stark and Ben Benjamin. Charlie Feldman
had the clout to pick up the phone and call a studio head
on a first-name basis. He lived a cosmopolitan life. I
had known of him in Brooklyn, where he was brought up;
he had been an orphan who was adopted by friends of
my relatives.

Milly and I went to New York, where Feldman was, to
work on the script and Steinbeck joined us during the
afternoons in the hotel, where we talked about the film,
though not too much work was done. In an effort to
make it more commercial, Feldman insisted on our casting Myrna Loy as the mother. Much as I admired her
work in light, sophisticated comedies, I could see she was
miscast. She was not a ranch mother in a family that had
to do a hard day's work to keep the ranch going; she
didn't look the part. Lou Calhern was also in the film,
and Bob Mitchum played Billy Budd.

We made the picture in Agoura, Milestone's favorite
location, but luck was not riding with him this time. The
film did not turn out well. The only distinguished element was the Aaron Copland score, still one of the best
ever written for a movie. It has become a staple of the
symphonic repertoire in this country. The film also combined live action with animation, for which Milly hired a
group who had seceded from Disney, known as UPA; this
was their first job. The genius of the company was John
Hubley, one of the most talented of all animators. Later,
UPA had great success with Gerald McBoing Boing, but in
this first feature they were paid by the accepted foot, and
had to work over and over to make everyone happy —
they lost their shirts to get their start. Hubley later did
some brilliant sketches for *Galileo*; they were not used in
the show, but Brecht thought they were works of genius
and used them to give the actors the spirit of the show.
We exhibited them in front of the theatre.

PARKER: Milestone seemed to wield an unusual amount of power and independence in the studio-dominated production days, somewhat like directors do today.

LLOYD: Back in the days when I first came to Hollywood, the sets were like feudal courts; the director was the king and he ruled by fear. Fear was the order of the day, from the top on down. Fear was the way production departments were run. I don't think that exists today. Of course, there's always the insecurity, the fear of losing your job, since so much of it is whim. You might lose your job just because you look at someone the wrong way.

PARKER: Absolutely. They can pick a director just because they like the way he parts his hair. This is particularly true in episodic television where a director is looked down on and is considered a technician. There's no creative sense.

LLOYD: A real director is a Director with a capital "D." Milestone was a man who had great charm and compassion which often moved him to tears. But he did rule by fear and temper, as many did. When his will was being contested, Milestone's physician, Dr. Parker, was on the stand and was asked about Milestone in his last days in the hospital. "Well, he was like he always was," said the doctor. "What do you mean?" asked the lawyer. Dr. Parker replied, "He was a director — he directed. He directed me on how to treat him. You couldn't tell him anything. He had to direct you on how to do it."
Even if you disagreed with him, as I often did, he would not give you the benefit of being right. He would say, "You're right — but for the wrong reasons." I'm sure this was the code of the times in which he was raised. You could never be right and your superior wrong.

New elements have entered directing pictures today. I was asked at a seminar if a director should learn how to make his own deals. I said, yes, of course; it's no different from what it's always been. You have to be rather shrewd about getting jobs. But today you have little chance to be signed on for a year. In the days of the great studios, they'd give a director a picture and he'd shoot it, then they'd give him another, and he'd shoot that. Some were under contract to Metro for years.

It seems to me that apprenticeships, learning by working with the master filmmakers, is less in operation nowadays than in the past. People like Bobby Wise and Mark Robson started as cutters working with Orson Welles. Orson was their age, but he was so advanced at that time that it served as an apprenticeship — in addition to their working with other knowledgeable craftsmen.

The technical side of film, the state of the art, has advanced over the years. The equipment is so much better, and many new directors have become fascinated with that. At the end of his life Renoir said, "The most important thing in the film is the actor." He meant the actor is the story. Hitchcock once said, "What really matters is what happens in front of the camera." What has happened is a preoccupation with the technology of the camera and all that goes with it.

PARKER: Milestone seems to belong in an elite group of directors, those that made their mark, within the studio system. Others I can think of include: Frank Capra, George Cukor, William Wellman, Billy Wilder, Vincente Minnelli, and William Wyler.

LLOYD: That makes me think of a story.

I was at the Milestone house a few days after Mrs. Milestone died and William Wyler came in with his wife, Tali.

I was moved to see these old fellows together; they had been through a great deal. They started to talk, and Wyler was prompted to tell the story of first coming out to Hollywood as a young man.

Uncle Carl Laemmle brought him out. He went to work at Universal as a gofer on a set with a director named Bob Hall. Watching Hall shoot, he gradually got a strong sense of what was required to shoot a film. Wyler possessed a sensitivity and sensibility and he began to be offended by Hall's directing. One day he was watching Hall set the camera at a certain angle. Willie, who was nineteen, thought that this angle would not tell the story properly and he could no longer contain himself.

"Excuse me, Mr. Hall," he said, "But I think that you would be better off if the camera were over there," and pointed in another direction. Hall told him to get lost and Willie backed off. He didn't want to get fired.

Five years passed. Wyler was now directing at Universal — the beginnings of his career. He already had a couple of films under his belt. About to shoot a scene needing ten extras, he ordered his assistant director to gather a group of extras from which he could select the ten he needed.

When the assistant told him they were ready, Wyler looked at the men who were lined up against the stage wall. Standing among them was the former director, Bob Hall. He was an extra, looking for a job. Willie was absolutely startled to see him and felt very badly about it, and Bob Hall was among the ten he picked.

Wyler went on shooting the picture and after a time he became aware that every time he made a set up, someone was staring at him. It went on for a couple of days — at that time, these pictures were done in a week — and then Willie couldn't take Hall's staring any longer. He told his assistant that it made him nervous to have Bob Hall on the set. Willie had the assistant pay Hall off for the entire week and give him an adjustment for overtime and whatever else he could tack on to make certain Hall was given more than he ordinarily would get. And so Hall departed.

Several years later Wyler was making a picture of *The Children's Hour* called *These Three*. He was one of the top Hollywood directors by this time. For some reason, in this version, there was a scene which took place in Germany; it was not in the play, which they changed considerably. In those days, they didn't go to Germany to shoot the scene; they built a set, of a café exterior and a cobbled street, on the Goldwyn lot.

Wyler was an Alsatian and spoke German fluently. When he walked on the set and looked at it, it offended him. The signs were all wrong, they were misspelled and the set dressing was not to be believed. It didn't look like a café in Germany to Wyler, and he said he wouldn't shoot it, none of it was right. The assistant asked him what he was going to do.

"I'm not going to worry about that," said Wyler. "You have to find somebody who knows Germany and can dress this properly and get the signs right."

A young fellow stepped up. He said, "Excuse me, sir, but I am Austrian, and I certainly agree that everything is incorrect. I would be very happy to correct all of it for you."

Wyler asked him what he did; he said he was in the production office. Wyler instructed the young man to get the set right and in the meantime he found something else to shoot.

He came back the next day and the set was perfect. The signs were correct and the dressing looked legitimate. Wyler thanked the young man from Austria, then instructed the cameraman where to put the camera. The young Austrian stepped forward and said, "Excuse me, sir. I think perhaps if you were to put it here —."

Wyler had a trigger response. "Get —," but he stopped short of repeating Bob Hall, and said, "You're right."

"And that," he recalled, "is how I met Fred Zinnemann."

A New Theatre

During the time I was working on *The Red Pony*, a new theatre, the Coronet, was being built on La Cienega Boulevard by a couple named Berkoff. They had a dance studio and their ambition was to own a theatre. I was approached by a theatrical attorney, Paul Schreibman, to go and see the two-hundred-and-sixty-seat house with a view to getting involved in it with him. Although it was unfinished, I found it had great charm; I told him I was interested and asked him what his ideas were. He said he could get half the money necessary to start a theatre, if I could raise the other half.

At that time I was unhappy with the Actors Lab; I had played Mosca in *Volpone* there with great success but nothing had happened for me after that. I had taken them an unproduced script about which I had been very enthusiastic, but the board of directors had found it simply depressing. "It makes you want to cut your throat," was the comment of one board member when they returned it to me. The play was *Mother Courage*, by Brecht. I told Schreibman I would see what I could do.

I took the proposal to John Houseman. Jack and I were suffering, in 1948, from the same malaise: we still felt close to the theatre, but cut off from it. Jack has always been stage-struck; as a major film producer, he constantly has had the need to run a theatre, and there have been seven theatre companies to prove it.

I showed him the theatre and like me, he was charmed. He agreed we should get together with Schreibman to form a company.

We formed Pelican Productions. Anyone who wanted to be on the board contributed twelve hundred dollars. Those who contributed, in addition to Jack and myself, included Joe Mankiewicz, George Coulouris (who, typically, sent his letter of resignation before we held our first board meeting), Nicholas Ray, Irene Selznick and others.

We decided to open with *The Skin of Our Teeth,* which had been done in New York but had not been seen on the West Coast. At the same time, it was Houseman's idea to form a film society. There were then no cinemas showing classic films in Hollywood; these were available through the archives of the Museum of Modern Art in New York, and we showed them during the day and on Sundays. The projectionist was Curtis Harrington. We also borrowed paintings from people in town who were interested in the theatre, including Stravinsky; we had paintings by Max Ernst and Morris Graves, who was a discovery of Laughton's; he was not then well-known. We had a very distinguished looking lobby, for which Ray and Charles Eames gave us chairs. The theatre was constantly active, with plays and films.

The Skin of Our Teeth was a success. It was directed by Paul Guilfoyle; Carol Stone played Sabina, Keenan Wynn and Jane Wyatt were Mr. and Mrs. Antrobus, and Blanche Yurka played the fortune teller.

For our second production, we did *Galileo.* Brecht had already written the play when he arrived in this country and had given it to Laughton, whom he wanted to play Galileo. Laughton sensed that it was a magnificent part, and he spent two years with Brecht adapting it into English. When they tried to get a production, they took the play to Clurman, to Kazan, to Welles and Mike Todd, with no success; they were unable to find a producer. As I got to know Brecht and Laughton, conversations led to my knowledge of the existence of the play, and when I read it I knew it was a major piece, an event in the theatre.

Joe Losey had come to me with a story for a film he wanted to show to Milestone, with the idea of having Milly produce it; Joe would direct it. It was called *The Sabine Women*, which later became the musical film *Seven Brides for Seven Brothers*. I read it and turned it down, but I suggested that Losey contact Laughton and Brecht with a view to directing *Galileo*. Losey already knew Laughton, having stage-managed *The Fatal Alibi*, a play Laughton had done for Jed Harris in New York in 1932. Losey also knew Brecht, and was hired to direct *Galileo*.

Hanns Eisler did the music, and Robert Davidson designed the show. Anna Sokolow started doing the choreography, but Brecht fired her, saying that he could not abide her Broadway commercialism; this was the most awful thing he could have said to her. She had come out of the Martha Graham company and was a serious artist of enormous integrity.

The show was really Charles Laughton's, but Hugo Haas was also very good as the Cardinal, and there were other fine actors in it; Frances Heflin, Van's sister, played the daughter. In our two-hundred-and-sixty-seat theatre, for the limited run, there were no empty seats; tickets were unobtainable. I tried to get Houseman to extend the run, but this was not possible; the next show was already booked.

Galileo went on to New York, where it was killed by Brooks Atkinson — who, many years later, changed his mind and gave it a good review when it was revived there.

We next did *No Exit*, again a play seen for the first time on the West Coast. Our production featured John Emery, Tamara Geva and Nancy Coleman. The set was designed by Howard Warshaw; he was an eminent painter, and this was the only set he ever designed.

As we were the first company in the new theatre, the finishing touches were still being done on the building when we got there. The question arose as to what type of house curtain would be appropriate; Laughton suggested it should be a painting of a Thrifty Drug Store, because that was the most indigenous California artifact. We ended up with a Jacques Carot reproduction of street players.

We also had our own wardrobe department; for *Galileo*, it was headed by Mrs. Brecht — Helene Weigel, one of the greatest actresses in the world, who because of the language difficulty, could not act here. Later, in Germany, she played Mother Courage and took it to Paris and London.

One evening, after an exhausting day on location with *The Red Pony*, where the temperature in Agoura had been over one hundred degrees, I was having dinner at home before going to the Coronet for rehearsal, when the telephone rang. I answered it.

"Hello, Norman."

"Yes."

"Brecht, here."

"Yes, Brecht."

"I wish to speak to you about Charles playing with himself."

Laughton, out of extreme nervousness, would, in the first scene of the play, thrust his hand deep into his left trousers pocket and play with his genitals. Lest the reader misunderstand, this was not part of his characterization but rather a totally unconscious activity. It was evident to all of us at dress rehearsals and only ceased to catch the eye when Laughton would put on the Leonardo robe which he wore through the remainder of the play.

Brecht continued. "You must speak to him and get him to stop." I replied, "No, Brecht."

"But it's your theatre. You are one of the managers."

I came up with a solution. "Joe Losey is directing the play. Get him to speak to Charles."

"He will not do it."

"But Brecht, you have been working closely with Charles for two years. You should tell him."

"I will not do it."

"Neither will I."

Brecht reached for the law. "The Sheriff will close your theatre." I remained adamant. "I will not speak to him." There was a pause. A bass voice came on the line. "Norman, this is Helly speaking" (Helene Weigel, Brecht's wife). "Do as Brecht says."

"Helly, I'm not the person to do it."

"Very well," she said in that great voice that came from the center of the earth. End of conversation.

The following evening the young female assistant to Helly in the costume room was seen running across the stage, Laughton galumphing after her shouting, "Who sewed up the pockets of my trousers? Who sewed up the pockets of my trousers?"

While there has never been a confirmation of the fact, to this day it is assumed that it was Helly who committed the deed even though the young costume assistant, collared by Laughton, was the one who was made to obtain a razor blade and undo every stitch.

After *No Exit*, we did *Dark of the Moon*, again the first production outside of New York. The cast featured Hurd Hatfield and Carol Stone. Earl Robinson did the music, and Pete Seeger sang the songs.

Next, we did the first production in English of *The House of Bernarda Alba*. It was directed by Vladimir Sokoloff and it had an original score by Darius Milhaud, for four instrumentalists. By this time, however, we were running downhill financially. With such a small theatre, unless we sold out every performance we would drop behind. The first sacrifice we had to make on this production, which had a beautiful, all-velour set designed by

Eugene Lourie, was to eliminate the score to save our-selves the cost of the four musicians; there we were, with an original Darius Milhaud score that couldn't be used because we couldn't pay for it.

We did one more production which we thought would be more commercial as it was half magic show and half revue; then we folded.

Our productions had been very heavy; they were al-most all very large shows. *Dark of the Moon* had thirty or forty people in it, with an orchestra and dancers; *Galileo, The Skin of Our Teeth,* and *Bernarda Alba* all had large casts and were big shows. We needed to sell every seat at every performance, which was just not possible.

Houseman and I put in a little more money, but when we closed we had a debt of sixteen thousand dollars, which Jack personally paid off.

Charlie Chaplin

At the time of the Coronet Theatre, I began seeing Charlie Chaplin often. In the most calculated and specific sense of the word, he was one of the artistic geniuses of the industry. Chaplin was a nineteenth-century romantic. He was the greatest combination of artist and business man that the motion picture industry has ever known.

Jean Renoir once observed that without Charlie Chaplin there would not have been a Hollywood. There is much truth in this: in the days of nickelodeons and little storefront theatres, Charlie made a group of one- or two-reelers which would be distributed around the country — indeed, around the world — and these would play to great business. The owners of the nickelodeons kept playing them until Charlie made another picture six months later, or even longer. It was Chaplin who, more than any other figure, created a great mass audience for the medium.

Milestone, whom many thought the ranking cutter of silent days, pointed out to me that Chaplin, in one of his pictures, established in three cuts a classic way of telling a story. Cut number one: The first shot is of a lake. A man who has been swimming comes out of the lake, walks up on shore and looks in horror at where his clothes were to have been; they are obviously not there, but in their place are prison clothes of the twenties with black and white stripes. He holds these up in dismay.

125

Cut number two: the exterior of a prison. Steam comes out of a whistle as it goes off; out comes a truck, filled with prison guards with rifles, hell bent for leather. Someone has escaped and they are tearing down the road.

Cut number three: as the truck is speeding down the road, coming toward the camera in the opposite direction, with the familiar walk, is Charlie dressed as a minister.

In three cuts, he has given the exposition: 1. A prisoner has escaped; 2. the chase; 3. Charlie is the escaped prisoner and the man on the shore of the lake was a minister. To Milestone, these three cuts were the most perfect example of how to cut and tell a story, combining exposition and action, with the greatest economy.

Chaplin, like other silent filmmakers, adhered to the theory of a tree is a tree, a rock is a rock, (from the story of the time, "We're making a picture about the African jungle — meet you in Griffith Park by the zoo. A tree is a tree, a rock is a rock —"). They filmed a great deal in Griffith Park. Charlie told me they would go to the park and see a bench. He would direct the actor or actors to sit on it and to trip him as he came by — and they would go from there. With that, he would start a one-reel film. Once when we were sailing across Catalina Channel on his boat, Chaplin pointed out where they came to the channel to shoot their own stunts. They jumped off one side of a boat right in the middle of the channel while being photographed and then came up on the other side of the boat. It was very tough; the actors really earned their keep. Amongst other things, Charlie was a great roller skater; in the film *The Rink* he did fabulous things on skates.

While he was making *The Cure*, he told me, Nijinsky and Diaghilev visited the set. As Charlie performed, Nijinsky watched, until suddenly he burst into tears, thrusting his head into his hands. Charlie stopped, cut the scene and went over to Nijinsky. Had Nijinsky been offended in some way? "No, Charlie," replied Nijinsky in his strong Russian accent. "You have not offended me. You're so funny, so funny." Then he burst into tears again.

The Russians loved him. Feodor Chaliapin, who was about six feet seven to Charlie's five feet six, met him one night in Paris, at a white tie affair. As Charlie described it, each of them was elegant in evening clothes. When they were introduced, Chaliapin exclaimed, "Charlot! Ah, Charlot!" and embraced him, pulling him close with such fervor and love that when he broke away, Charlie felt a pain in his nose. He discovered that printed on the end of it was an indentation from Chaliapin's diamond stud. Charlie saw the way to make marvelous humor out of the damnedest situations.

He formed United Artist, of course, with D.W. Griffith, Douglas Fairbanks — who was his closest friend — and Mary Pickford. I was often with Chaplin when he was selling United Artists to Krim and Benjamin. By that time, Charlie had developed a great enmity for Mary Pickford, who was his equal from a business point of view. It was tough to make a deal with this lady. Charlie was trying to unload the company and wanted to get out of it but she was making it difficult to finalize the sale. This was sad, as Charlie had been close to Douglas Fairbanks — so much so that they had even built houses near one another. Eventually the company was sold, but Charlie knew he had a formidable opponent in Mary Pickford.

Charlie realized the value of his work, financially; there is a story which captures his attitude towards art and money. He used to say, "As long as I have a million dollars, everything will be all right."

In 1918 or '19, there was a company called Essanay Films. By then Charlie was such an extraordinary figure in the world of entertainment that they wanted to make eight two-reelers with him. They called a meeting at the Plaza Hotel in New York, and Charlie took the train from

Los Angeles. He was a figure of enormous, worldwide fame; wherever the train stopped, people lined up at the stations to see him, running from one end of the train to the other, calling his name. It was like a triumphal procession across the country. One of my earliest memories is of sitting in a high chair as a baby, with a wind-up Charlie Chaplin doll walking across the tray; it was a source of wonder to me later, when I got to know him, to remember this.

In order to protect himself to some degree, Chaplin registered at the hotel as Charles Spencer, his middle name. With him was his half-brother Sydney, two years Charlie's senior, who was, according to Charlie, never impressed by anything. Sydney Chaplin had himself been a star — and the best Charley's Aunt I ever saw; he made a great hit in a picture called *The Better 'Ole* and in the 1920s, when there were no taxes, he was offered nine thousand a week by Famous Players to be their leading comic. In 1927, he decided he had enough money, and he retired to do what he loved more than anything — ballroom dancing. He and his wife, Gypsy, went around the world, looking for orchestras and ballrooms. He could never understand Charlie; he thought it was silly to work so hard.

At times, Sydney functioned as Charlie's business manager and negotiator, at which he was absolutely first class. When Charlie made *The Great Dictator*, Sydney had Charlie buy the land they used for the location; after shooting the picture, they sold it at a profit.

At the Plaza, Charlie and Syd had a suite at the other end of the corridor from the Essanay people. Before the negotiations started, Charlie and Syd decided they wanted a million dollars for the films — a fantastic sum for those times.

Charlie had brought his violin along to soothe his nerves. He loved to play the violin, which he had strung so he could play it left-handed — the opposite way from the usual stringing. He recited with delight how he had handed the instrument to Jascha Heifetz and invited him to play a tune. When Heifetz tried, the most awful sounds came out. Charlie then took the instrument and holding it in his right hand and bowing with his left, played a tune, to Heifetz's chagrin. Sydney, still treating Charlie as his younger brother, ordered him to play the instrument in the bathroom because he couldn't abide the sound. So Charlie stood in the empty tub and played away on his violin while Sydney went down the hall to negotiate. He came back in an hour with an offer of $500,000; Charlie, still standing in the tub and not interrupting his playing, said that it was a good sum, but not nearly enough; they had decided they wanted a million dollars. Sydney should go back and keep negotiating.

Syd went back and returned with a $600,000 offer, but Charlie protested it wasn't enough. Syd returned to the negotiating table and got an offer for $750,000. Charlie turned it down. In about half an hour, Sydney returned again; the offer was up to $800,000, take it or leave it.

Charlie continued to play his violin. He replied, "Tell them I'm an artist. I know nothing about money. All I know is that I want a million dollars."

Sydney left, and in a short time came back. "Charlie," he said, "throw away your violin and get yourself a bull fiddle. You've got a million dollars."

Charlie's argument for being paid well is the best I've ever heard.

Charlie took his first million and literally buried it in the ground somewhere, so that he knew no matter what went on in this world, success or setback, he would have a million dollars socked away in cash. It lay in the ground and was never touched. When, years later, he was prevented from returning to the United States by the authorities, there was a mysterious, very quick visit by Oona Chaplin to the United States from Europe. I am of the opinion that the trip was to get that million dollars — that he told her where to go to dig it up.

That's what he meant by, "As long as I have a million dollars, I know everything's all right."

I worked with him in two capacities; as an actor in *Limelight*, and as a co-owner of the property, *They Shoot Horses, Don't They?*

In *Limelight*, it was fascinating to watch him; as a director, he was basically an actor. He instructed the cameraman, "Get me in the cross-hairs and stay with me." He knew he was the star, the money, the primary interest. Every take in which he appeared was printed; he permitted himself this luxury, he said, because he had no one standing behind the camera for him, the only way he could get a perspective on it was to look at it the next morning in the projection room. Not a frame was cut until Charlie came into the cutting room. He might watch five takes of a given scene and throw them all out, going back to re-shoot them. Often he would take a look from one take, a gesture from another and a walk from a third take to complete a scene. He needed that freedom, so no sequence was cut without his being there.

I played Bodalink, the choreographer, in *Limelight*. My big scene was in the theatre, reciting the narrative line of the choreography in one long speech. When Charlie looked at it, he felt it was too much like *Hamlet*; he admired it on its own terms, but he wanted a lighter reading for the picture, and we did it again the next day. He was equally objective and kind with Nigel Bruce, and with Buster Keaton. He had enormous respect for Keaton, as did Buster for him, and one was moved at seeing the two together. It was overwhelming to contemplate what each had done in films.

With Claire Bloom, whose first picture this was, and with Sydney, his son, matters were different; I began to see a Charlie that I had heard about, as a director. Insofar as the camera was concerned, he was not too interested;

he set up his shots simply. His films had their own look; he had his own world, and all his pictures reflected that. But to Claire Bloom and Sydney, he was hell on wheels. The only way he could direct was to act, so he would get up and act their parts. He played the leading man straightforwardly, but he acted the woman fantastically; his body expressed everything about the meaning of the scene and its emotional level, more strongly than what he said. He could translate it more specifically with movement than with words.

At the same time, he was terribly impatient with these two young actors. Charlie would not sit in a chair; he squatted right under the lens and acted the scene, back and forth, back and forth with increasing anger as he felt he wasn't getting what he wanted. It was totally disconcerting for the actors, as he was only a couple of feet away — not in the orchestra, ten rows back in the dark, knocking himself out, as he would have been in the theatre. They were constantly aware of all this movement, which would ruin their concentration; then he would sail into them, shout at them and show his impatience. It was an unhappy time for Claire and Sydney.

It was all complicated by the fact that every time Charlie did a picture, he knew the world was looking at him. He was like a major painter, or a major composer who had a new work; the world awaited a Chaplin film. It was not just an average director making a picture for a studio. He was conscious of his place in the world, on a list with Nehru, Gandhi, Einstein and Shaw as the great men of the century. As an actor, therefore, if you weren't carrying out the intentions of his scene, you were personally affronting him — personally limiting his approach to the world. You were going to affect how he stood in the eyes of the world. This contributed to, and ignited, his naturally combustible temperament which was a mixture of darkness and melancholy, great lightness, brilliant humor and savagery.

Charlie had the gift of going all the way. I believe that if he had wanted to, Charlie could have killed a man — but not a butterfly. Once when we went to play tennis, he saw an injured butterfly trying to get along on the ground. He watched it from the balcony of the tennis house and said, "Oh, the poor thing. I can't go down on the court. I might hurt it. Do you think you could take it and put it in the grass?" I did so. Yet, in the lobby of the Alexandria Hotel in downtown Los Angeles, he hauled off and hit Louis B. Mayer on the jaw. One weekend at Catalina, Peggy and I were with Charlie and Oona on their yacht, and Oona, who was a superb swimmer, was in the water when a motorboat came dangerously close to her. The boat kept going and Charlie was not able to start his own boat quickly enough to chase it, but if he could have, he would have killed the man. His anger was monumental.

It was this extreme temperament which made him consider it a personal affront if a scene wasn't played as he envisioned it.

He started *Limelight* with his old cameraman, Rollie Totheroh, but after looking at the footage he took Rollie off the picture. Rollie, who had been on Chaplin's payroll for many years, was kept on the set, with salary, as adviser. Charlie hired Karl Struss, who had done *All Quiet on the Western Front* and other major pictures; he wanted an updated look, but he would not go with any of the new, young cameramen.

Chaplin's lot was at La Brea and Sunset; it now belongs to Herb Alpert and his record company. It still looks like a row of little English houses. It used to go all the way to the corner of Sunset, where he had built a tennis court and a large frame house. He may have intended to live there, but I don't think he ever did; his mother, whom he brought over here, or a half-brother named Wheeler Dryden may have lived there for a while.

He had a cottage dressing room which was a wood-frame bungalow, characteristic of the Hollywood bungalows in all the silent movies. In it were a sitting room, dining room, kitchen and a room for Charlie to change where his costumes were kept in the closets. I saw the great shoes and the canes there; the secret of the shoes was that he had another pair inside them. One night when I went down to the studio with him to look at a film, I tried to make off with one of the canes — I suppose the only word is steal it. As we were talking, I had it in my hand; he just kept on talking, about something else, and as he did so he lightly took it out of my hand and put it back in the closet. He'd read my mind.

While he was working on *City Lights*, he told me, he used to sit in that bungalow. From nine in the morning, which was his call for the first shot, until six at night he confronted a blank piece of paper — trying to create ideas to shoot while he kept the entire company waiting for him to come out and be funny. But he could think of nothing to come out and be funny about. He said, "I'd sit there looking at the clock, waiting for six to arrive." He felt he couldn't leave any earlier, as it would be bad for company morale.

With *City Lights*, which turned out to be a masterpiece, he told me he had other problems. He spent six weeks rehearsing and shooting the prize fight, but when he looked at it, he thought it wasn't funny. So he threw it all out, and within a week he redid the scene completely; the successful version which is in the movie was done very quickly.

His writing, like his directing, was controlled by his temperament. He wrote whatever scene he felt like writing, not necessarily in chronological order; sometimes it could be two-thirds of the way through a script, sometimes at the beginning. If he didn't feel like writing at all, he would go to the piano and improvise. He wrote beautiful music for his pictures this way — including

"Smile" for *Modern Times* and "Terry's Song" for *Limelight*.
He didn't know how to write down the music he composed; someone would record it, transcribe the music into
written notes and then orchestrate it, subject to Charlie's
approval.

By the time I worked with him, he dictated his scripts
to a secretary as he paced back and forth. He found that
the most convenient way to work; he seldom sat down
and wrote longhand. Sometimes he scribbled notes but
more often he performed at the same time as he talked,
acting it out. He wrote his lyrics in longhand.

Bob Aldrich was the first assistant director on
Limelight. I got him the job; I had known him on *The
Southerner*, when he was Renoir's first assistant. He had
been the top first at Enterprise and had worked on *Arch of
Triumph* and *Body and Soul* in this capacity. He had told
me he felt *Limelight* would be Chaplin's last picture, and
so he was eager to do it; I promised that if an opening
presented itself, I would talk to Chaplin about him.

It did; Charlie told me that he was worried about the
cost of the picture. "I need someone who will drive this
thing through and realize the value of a dollar." It was
all his own money, and even though there was a unit
production manager, he wanted someone on the set who
would be like a cop. Bob was the toughest and the best.

As he was very ambitious to be a director but had not
yet found the opportunity, Bob formed the habit of standing behind directors. He stood behind Charlie, snapping
his fingers and pounding his palms impatiently as Charlie
was trying to figure his shots and set up scenes. Charlie
said nothing. Meanwhile, Bob was very critical of the
way Charlie was directing. "It's his money, but we're
wasting time. He can't direct. He's the greatest actor in
the world, but he can't direct." The direction was not the
way Bob or any other Hollywood director would see it; it
had to do with setting up Charlie as an actor.

One day — and I'm sure Charlie plotted this as carefully as he plotted the script — we were doing a scene which took place in a theatre. We were on the set at the old Pathé studio in Culver City. Shooting was to start at nine, but it was nine when Charlie arrived. It was a chilly, damp December day, and he was wearing an old threadbare topcoat which he must have brought when he arrived from England. He had on a hat, tilted over his eyes, and the thick glasses he wore in his later years. He looked desolate and forlorn.

"What are we waiting for?" he asked Bob. "Well, sir, excuse me, you, sir — you're in the first shot," Bob replied.

"I am?"

"Yes, sir."

Charlie asked, "What is the first shot?" Bob told him, scene twenty-three. Twenty-three didn't mean anything. What was the scene about?

It was the one where he walked down the corridor on his way to the dressing-room, Bob told him.

"Well," said Charlie, "I don't feel like doing that scene. What else have you got?"

Aldrich's eyes would have fallen out of his head, except that he wore glasses; you just didn't do that in Bob Aldrich's world. He was a member of the Rockefeller family; he was a man of scrupulous discipline. On a set, you made a schedule and you stuck to it. Now he was confronted with a man saying, "I don't feel like it."

But Charlie had asked what else was scheduled. Scene twenty-four, Bob told him. Numbers didn't mean anything to him, Charlie insisted; what was scene twenty-four? "It's where Buster Keaton comes into the dressing-room with you," said Bob.

"And the next scene?" asked Charlie.

Bob knew about numbers by this time. "You and Keaton in the dressing-room." Again, Charlie didn't feel like doing it. Bob went through the entire morning schedule with him; he came to the end of it, and Charlie had thrown out the entire thing. "Find me something that I can direct," he told Bob. "I don't feel like acting."

Bob came to me and said, "He's crazy. It's his money, but he's crazy." But Charlie was doing this deliberately. Bob found him a couple of scenes to direct.

We broke for lunch. Charlie had already written much of the score; though we were far from having finished shooting the picture, he had recorded the music on acetate with an orchestra. He had a machine on the set to play it. After lunch, the Royal Ballet arrived. They were appearing in town, and the big event for their day was a visit to the Chaplin set. Charlie was ecstatic; he had a new audience, a company of dancers.

He put the music he had written for the movie's ballet on the machine. With the entire Royal Ballet standing around and watching, Charlie danced a solo to his music. Melissa Hayden, the leading American ballerina who danced for Claire Bloom in the movie, was also watching. (After she completed her work on the film, Chaplin gave her a hundred pairs of ballet shoes in gratitude.)

Charlie horsed around until about five, when the Royal Ballet left. Then he suddenly turned to Bob and said, "Let's get a day's work done here — we need to shoot some scenes." It was time to go home — but Chaplin felt like working. Bob was bewildered, convinced Charlie was crazy; he did not realize at the time that Chaplin was doing this deliberately.

The beauty of the film is that it is the deepest story of Charlie and Oona, told in theatrical terms. It was Charlie at that point in his life where he felt he could no longer make people laugh.

PARKER: Didn't you start work on a production of *They Shoot Horses, Don't They?* with Chaplin?

LLOYD: Horace McCoy's book first came to my attention in 1948, though it had been published in 1934. When
I read it I thought it might make a film; I inquired about
the rights and found they were available.
  I played tennis with Chaplin about four times a week.
We played in the late afternoon, five o'clock in summer
after the heat had lessened, earlier in winter. After the
game, we sat in the tennis house for a while to chat, and
Charlie would often invite me to the house for a drink —
scotch old-fashioned, his favorite. In winter his butler,
Watson, made a coal fire in the living room; this gave
Charlie a feeling of England. It was a lovely room, with
many beautiful things in it. Sometimes he'd have me call
Peggy to come over for dinner and with Oona, just the
four of us would dine. Over the years, it developed into
a warm friendship.
  Sunday afternoons were special at the Chaplins.
They were centered around the tennis court. Charlie and
Oona would invite friends and their children to come by
at about three in the afternoon. Peggy and I would go
with Susie and Mike and arrive to find not only friends
but visiting celebrities. While the serious minded played
tennis, the children gathered on the lawn near the pool
area; non-players watched or chatted in the tennis house.
At four o'clock, the butler, Watson, would appear in his
supercilious way, followed by his retinue bearing tea and
pastries whereupon there was a move by all but the tennis
players to the refreshments. These were beautiful days,
much loved in the remembrance.
  On one of these occasions, Charlie asked me what I
was doing. The Milestone job was over; the Coronet had
closed, and I was acting again. I told him I was thinking
of taking an option on a book in which I was interested.
His response was immediate; he offered to share any venture I wanted to do, fifty-fifty.
  I was astounded; the greatest figure in the motion picture business was making this marvelous offer. I told

him what the property was. He handled the situation as he always did, with a spin on it; he reacted as if he had never heard of *They Shoot Horses, Don't They?* He thought a bit and then said he did remember something about the book. It turned out that he knew the property very well — but his business instinct took over and his guard had gone up. I sensed he was planning something.

He agreed to produce it, and I would direct. "Is there a part for Sydney?" he asked. He knew damn well there was a part for his son, Sydney. I ventured that Sydney could play the young lead; Charlie instructed me to find out the price of the property without using his name; he would give me the money.

George Wilner, one of the top literary agents in Los Angeles, handled Horace McCoy. I asked George if I could buy the property outright, with no options; Charlie had told me to do this. I said I wanted to direct it and I was confident I could get a production.

On Charlie's instructions, I made an offer of three thousand dollars for all the picture and theatre rights. I would never have had the courage to offer such a low price on my own; I would have thought twenty-five thousand more appropriate. As it turned out, Horace McCoy was broke at the time, and he was willing to take three thousand. Also on Charlie's advice I went to a good lawyer, Martin Gang, to draw up the contract. He included all film, theatre and filmed television rights to the book; he omitted live television. Charlie gave me the three thousand dollars, which I deposited in my account, and I paid for the property with a personal check.

Charlie was preparing *Limelight*, and when I talked to him about the screenplay of *They Shoot Horses*, he seemed reluctant. His mind and heart were on *Limelight*. We did manage a couple of sessions; he realized that the book had no story and he started to invent one; the scenes he conjured up were stunning. I think it's a major loss that this picture was not made with Charlie.

He revealed that he had been to dance marathons; they fascinated him. He had known about the book, and had ideas about it long before I read it. In our sessions we began to develop a story and relationships between the characters. What Charlie had in mind was so moving, so Chaplinesque.

The leading character took on the flavor of Chaplin.

He was planning it for his son, Sydney, and at one time we thought of his playing it with Marilyn Monroe. Sydney and Charlie Jr. had known Marilyn when she was first trying to get a job in the picture business. Now she was moving along, and was a real possibility; she would have been quintessential in the role.

I kept notes, but they have been lost. I remember fragments; during the dance marathon, which was held in the ballroom on the Santa Monica pier, there were breaks every hour for participants to eat. The leading character would go out onto the pier and have a sandwich. He looked at the gulls and gave them crumbs. He built up a friendship with one gull who would wait for him — or he would scan the skies for the bird at the meal break.

In the early '50s Charlie embarked for Europe. While at sea he was informed by the U.S. State Department that he could not come back to America unless he passed a moral turpitude test; he had not become a citizen and therefore he was vulnerable. He went on to London with his family and made it plain what he thought of the whole thing. In bitterness and anger at what he felt was the injustice done him, he absolutely would not answer any correspondence about *They Shoot Horses, Don't They?*; he just dropped it. He vowed never to make another film in the United States. I wrote and informed him that people were inquiring about the book. Raoul Levy was interested in it. I went to see Levy at the Sherry-Netherlands and he talked about a four-picture deal he had with Columbia.

He asked if I would permit him to say that *Horses* was one of his four pictures. He showed me stills of an unknown actress who had recently made a picture for him in France; he thought she might be right for the girl. It was Brigitte Bardot.

There were several other people who, over the years, wanted to buy the property from me. I was in partnership with Charlie; even though he was not answering my communications about the book, I felt I could not morally make any move without his approval.

When I was playing The Fool to Louis Calhern's Lear in New York at the National Theatre, Horace McCoy came to my dressing room. He had the money to buy it back; he asked me to sell it to him because Cocteau wanted to make the picture with him. When the book was published in 1934 in the United States, it was not popular domestically but was successful in France; the French found it an interesting picture of certain aspects of life in the United States. Later, when the word came into use, it was considered one of the first existential novels. McCoy, therefore, had important literary standing in France — and Cocteau was a unique picture-maker.

There were various Hollywood people who wanted to buy it: Jerry Wald called me to his office one morning at eight o'clock, to talk about it. None of the offers involved me; people just wanted the property.

In 1962 I went to Europe and stayed with Charlie in his house in Switzerland. He would not bring up the subject of *They Shoot Horses*; he talked about his autobiography, about everything else. He was in such a fury about how he had been treated by this country that he didn't want to consider coming back or making a picture here. I waited for him to talk about *Horses*; I didn't want to press him. That was a mistake on my part; perhaps I should have.

I had not reckoned with the copyright renewal; it was about to come up. We had owned the property for fifteen years but it had existed since 1934, and its copyright was due to expire.

Martin Ritt had a company with Paul Newman and was interested in producing it, with me directing. Paul would play the lead and Joanne Woodward, whom I had directed in the James Agee Lincoln films, would be the girl. I was working at Universal, on the Alfred Hitchcock television show. Lew Wasserman came into my office in the Hitchcock bungalow; Paul Newman and Marty had sent him, he said, to discuss a deal for *They Shoot Horses*. The first thing I knew was that I wasn't going to get into any deal discussion with Lew Wasserman; he was the master of them all in this area. In those days, he was very close to Hitchcock and I would see much of him; his bungalow was opposite ours and he was very friendly. I told him the copyright would expire in eight months. When this happened, if the author were alive, he simply paid a dollar and the property was copyrighted for another twenty-seven years. In this case, McCoy had died, so the property reverted to the estate. I had to go to Mrs. McCoy for a renewal. Lew said we would talk again when I got the copyright sorted out.

I went to Mrs. McCoy; she told me I should talk to her son. I met with Peter McCoy (who became chief of protocol for President Reagan) but he wasn't interested in renewing with me; I had not made the picture in sixteen years and he wanted it made; he had other offers.

We lost the copyright, and the property was bought by United Artists, who paid the McCoy estate forty thousand for it. They did not get the European rights; these still belonged to Charlie and me, as the European copyright is based on the Berne Convention, with the copyright running fifty years from the death of the author. To clear all rights, United Artists came to me to buy the European ones. As I still could get no answers from Charlie, I acted on my own and sold them the rights for fifteen thousand dollars. I sent half the money to Charlie.

When I saw him in Italy later, he didn't mention it. We never discussed the property again, once he was barred from coming back into this country. Eventually, he did come back, for the Academy Awards ceremony where he was given an honorary Oscar. By that time he had mellowed a bit. But in the days when we owned *Horses,* he was terribly bitter and angry about his treatment at the hands of the government.

The picture was eventually made. It was sad that I never made it with Charlie; it would have been a memorable experience.

Omnibus
and Early Television

In 1951 I went east to play The Fool in *King Lear*, directed by John Houseman with Louis Calhern as Lear. I loved the role. It sometimes happens that you get a part with which you are so sympathetic and so in focus that everything flows. The relationship of Lear to the Fool reminded me of my situation with Milestone — in that the Fool is trying to open Lear's eyes to what is happening around him so that he can deal with it accordingly. The Fool's inability to do this and Lear's inability to deal with the situation made it very moving for me — it seemed I was living my life with Milly and his intransigence again. Lou Calhern was an old friend of mine, and of Milly's; we had worked together on both *The Red Pony* and *Arch of Triumph*, and I had acted with Lou in radio on the *Arthur Hopkins Hour*, so it was easy to relate to him. It was a joy for both of us. Usually, The Fool is played in stylized fashion, in the tradition of a court jester. For me, it was natural to make the character fully human, Lear's closest friend. It wasn't even acting; it was directly from my life experience, and I think the audience felt that.

For me, Lou was a superb Lear — kingly. He was an oak. His presence filled the theatre and he played the part without sentimentality. In truth, one felt at the curtain that Lear had learned nothing from the experience and would have made the same mistake over again.

I returned to Hollywood to do a picture at Metro, *The Light Touch*. At the same time, there was a new television program called *Omnibus*.

James Agee had become a permanent part of American literature. He may have had genius; at any rate, he made you think he was a genius. He was striking to look at, and he had a beautiful, tortured personality. He was given to drink and excessive smoking — a man driven to extremes. He felt he wasn't writing as he should be, that he compromised by working for Time-Life as the foremost film critic in America — when he should have written more novels and poetry. He loved films; I got to know him through Chaplin.

Jim was going to write five episodes about Abraham Lincoln for a new TV program. It was for CBS, but the Ford Foundation was providing the money. This program was to be an attempt to bring to the country television that was devoted to things of a cultural nature. *Omnibus* was to be its name. Robert Saudek represented The Ford Foundation and Bill Spier was the director of the overall show. In addition to the Agee episodes, they hired Leonard Bernstein, then a young conductor, to do his performance-lectures, talking about the orchestra and the music. Alistair Cooke did the introductions.

Robert Saudek had been a roommate of Agee's at Harvard and asked Jim to write for the show. The scripts were about Lincoln in Kentucky, Indiana, and New Salem, Illinois — from his birth to the point where, as a young man, he left New Salem for the first time to go into the Illinois state legislature.

I got a call, in Hollywood, to come East to direct these shows in New York. The line producer, on a sublease agreement, was Richard de Rochemont; he and his brother, Louis, had worked on *The March of Time*. Dick left that organization and then formed a company to make documentary pictures. He was a producer of rare taste and knowledge, and I look back on my work with him with great warmth. The offer of the job could only have come through Jim Agee. I did not know de Rochemont before this time.

I arrived to find that Royal Dano had already been cast as young Lincoln, which was a fine start; he had worked on *The Red Badge of Courage,* for which Jim had done the script and Jim cast him in the leading role. The cameraman was Marcel Rebière—a highly gifted French cameraman who specialized in documentaries. De Rochemont hired him to make the series look like a documentary, which I thought was a fine idea. After the first episode, which we did on the old Fox stage at Fifty-fourth street and Tenth Avenue, we shot most of the rest on location in New Salem, Illinois, where Lincoln had lived.

The town of New Salem had been reconstructed through a grant from Hearst, using all the original foundations, and it looked just as it had when Lincoln lived there. Reading the scripts, which were beautifully written, it occurred to me that Jim, as a person, had much in common with Lincoln. He came from the East Tennessee mountains; there was something of a country boy about him. Not only did he have a great admiration for Lincoln but he also shared a kind of melancholy with him, in the sense that Lincoln was preoccupied with death — and they were both poets. I began to realize that while Jim was using historical events and the facts of Lincoln's childhood, youth and young manhood for the construction of the series, he was really writing about himself. He used Lincoln to say a lot of the things he wanted to say. I was fortunate — again — to be working with this rich talent.

The scripts had a definite style; Jim was a documentarian. He had written, with Walker Evans, *Let Us Now*

Praise Famous Men, and he knew most of the documentary group in New York.

We cast Joanne Woodward as Ann Rutledge; it was her first film. Jack Warden played Jack Armstrong. Among the bit players were Pat Hingle and Joe Campanella.

These actors were brought to my attention by Eleanor Kilgallen and Monique James, whom I met for the first time when I went to New York to cast the Lincoln films.

Eleanor was beautiful, with alabaster skin, proper with her white gloves, surprising with her Broadway lingo, sharp and committed. Monique, standing in her stocking feet as high as her desk, her shoes beside her, was the indestructible force that overcame the immovable object. Monique is best described by the story of her trying to sell a client. In approximately her words: "The producer said, 'No.' I went to the director. He said, 'No.' The writer said, 'No.' The executive producer said, 'No.' I went back to the producer, the director, the writer, the executive producer. They all said, 'No.' I was beginning to get discouraged. (Note the use of the word beginning.) So I started over again. The producer said ..." etc. The end? The client got the part. It is to her everlasting credit that Lew Wasserman, while she was in his employ, barred her from the lot. He needed to obtain a moment of peace, no doubt. Together, Eleanor and Monique were very special. Loyal to their clients, fierce in representing them, constantly amusing and colorful, they are cherished by those of us who had the great good fortune to be their charges.

Jim chose to structure the films by opening with Lincoln's second Inaugural Address, "With malice towards none and charity towards all." We had a still of the Inaugural Address, and Jim's narration pointed out that the gentlemen in the still were already putting on their hats ready to leave, before Lincoln had finished his speech. We next used the great photograph of Lincoln by

Alexander Gardner — a portrait printed on a glass plate which, symbolically, is cracked. Over the photograph, we used a moving speech by Lincoln about his sense of the country and the future — in which he seemed to know he had not long to live. Nor did he; he was shot three days later. Then we staged the catafalque scene, which Griffith had also included in his movie with Walter Huston and Una Merkel. In it, Lincoln wakes in the middle of the night, and when his wife, Mary Todd, discovers him wandering through the White House, with a blanket around his shoulders, he describes a dream of lying on a catafalque with a procession filing by. Both Jim and Griffith saw it as a premonition; they may have taken it from Sandburg's book, as Jim used that extensively.

We next did the assassination, in a stylized way — very quickly, with cuts. Two cards had been put in the box before the Lincolns arrived; one said "Reserved," the other "Taken." Jim ended the sequence on the two cards, the "Taken" one splattered with blood.

From there we went to the house across the street where Lincoln was laid on a bed. He was too tall for it, and had to be placed diagonally. Blood soaked the pillows, which were constantly changed. Lincoln must have had great strength; he lived all through the night with the bullet right behind his ear. The sequence was done according to the report of a young doctor who was there, so it was historically accurate. He described feeling the carotid artery and the pulse, and how the landlord came in to clean and worried about the blood on the bed, showing no sympathy at all. After Lincoln died, pennies were put on his eyes. He was wrapped, nude, in a sheet and his clothes were folded on a chair. He was put in a plain pine box and taken out of the room. Our last shot was of a soldier taking the clothes and following the procession.

The sequence of the funeral train followed, going through the country at eight miles an hour during the day as people stood beside the tracks and watched. Before I arrived, the documentarians from *March of Time* had shot about five thousand feet of film of the train, which was of the period and owned by the Baltimore and Ohio railroad. We went down to the tracks at Flemington, New Jersey, where Richard de Rochemont lived and where there was a train only every other day. On the day the track wasn't used, I got a flat car and shot people watching alongside it. In the weeds I found an old iron sign reading "Look out for the railroad," which we put up at a crossing. We had horses and carriages. We had to be careful not to show the telephone poles which did not exist in the period we were shooting. I had a small boy run after the train, waving to it as if it were a circus train leaving him behind.

On the Fox stage in New York, I shot a scene of people filing past the coffin. There was a last shot of a flower being put on the casket. We had sent for a number of extras, among whom were blacks; one of them was an old black woman, in her eighties and so arthritic that her hands were like claws. She, I decided, should put the flower on the casket; when I went to tell her this, Jim was already there; he had also decided she was the one for the job. With her crippled black hand, she placed the white flower on the casket.

Instead of using music, underneath all this was Walt Whitman's poem "When Lilacs Last in the Door Yard Bloomed." I read it myself. When the old lady put the flower on the casket and the Whitman poem ended, the narrator said, "That was the end — and now the beginning. Only the stars remember the beginning." From a shot of the night, we went back to Hodgkinsville, Kentucky, where Lincoln was born, and from then on took the story in continuity. We had started with Lincoln at the end of his life and then went back to his birth.

In that scene Nancy Hanks, played by Marian Seldes, was having a difficult time delivering the child. There was a superstition that if you thrust a plow under the bed and lifted the bed, it would bring on the birth. Crahan Denton, playing Tom Lincoln, did this. I think the superstition arose because the woman's fright was so great when the plow lifted the bed that it brought on the birth. There was an episode of all the trials Lincoln went through as a little boy. There were scenes which showed the death of his mother which resulted in a desperate life for him and his sister, Sarah. We showed how they were left alone in a cabin in the wilderness while his father went back to get a wife, Sally Ann Johnson.

When I finished shooting in New York I went out to New Salem, Illinois. But footage was also needed from Hodgkinsville, Kentucky, mostly silent material of the cabin and its interior, the little boy learning to draw water from the well, riding in the wagon as black slaves went by, and the family sitting outside the cabin at night. As I couldn't be in two places, de Rochemont said that I had better go to New Salem and get started on the remaining episodes. He knew a still photographer who had a very good eye and who could do the second unit footage in Hodgkinsville, if I approved. He showed me a film the young man had made; if I liked it, de Rochemont would hire him.

I didn't much care for the film, but the camera work was interesting. The young man had operated the camera as well as directed the film. I told de Rochemont it would be fine to hire him — and that's how Stanley Kubrick came on board. I went off to New Salem to continue directing the film while a couple of the actors went to Kentucky with Stanley to do the second unit. Marian Seldes sent me, from Hodgkinsville, some interviews Stanley had given about his directing the Lincoln film. When I read them, I knew he was going to be an enormous success; when you have an ego like that, at twenty-one, nothing will ever stop you.

After their first showing, the films were used extensively in educational programs. When John F. Kennedy was shot, the films were played, particularly the funeral train sequence, day and night, over and over again.

PARKER: You seemed to branch off into television work during the early 1950's. Much of the talent from stage and film seemed to follow suit.

LLOYD: In 1951 MCA was the leading talent agency in the business and had enormous clout. An extraordinary list of agents made up this organization under the leadership of Jules Stein and Lew Wasserman, and they had an outstanding list of clients. Being an enterprising and innovative organization, MCA looked at the new medium of television and decided to get involved.

Carl Kramer, who had started the company in Chicago with Jules Stein and Taft Schrieber and was one of the top executives, was given charge of the project. His primary concern was handling the money for the operation, but deep down inside him, apparently from the days when he went to college, he had had a desire to get into the creative end. When I first met him, Carl would never reveal that. Some time later, when the relationship between us had changed, he went to his desk, on top of which were the trade papers, *Wall Street Journal* and so forth. Surreptitiously opening a drawer, he brought out a volume of Schnitzler.

When the television project began, he was tough and pragmatic. He had the kind of mind that drove — that made MCA what it was. The company had put up one hundred thousand dollars, which they could well afford, to rent facilities at a studio called Eagle-Lion. It butted up against the Goldwyn Studios on Santa Monica Boulevard. Their intention was to do half-hour films for television. Tape was not yet available; television was either live or on film.

Carl Kramer hired Richard Irving, a young director and actor who had done theatre work, and Axel Gruen-

berg, one of the top radio directors. I thought this was
shrewd. He also hired a carpenter, an IA man, named Joe
Manecci, to do the sets. He would build whatever he was
asked. The sets were, in fact, all the same but they were
dressed differently.

At the beginning, the half-hour shows were shot in a
day-and-a-half. There was *The Gruen Theatre* for the
watch company and *Chevron Show Time* for Chevron gas.
Bill Williams starred in a series for Coca-Cola called *Kit
Carson*.

After a number of these day-and-a-half pictures had
been made, Kramer decided to upgrade them and make
them in two days. At this point Jay Kanter, one of the
younger agents at MCA but a prominent member of the
company who personally represented Marilyn Monroe
and Marlon Brando, recommended to Carl that I be hired
for this television project. The operation was now called
Revue Productions. Jay felt I might be interested as I
wasn't doing much, and I had just come back from New
York. I went to work directing the two-day shows.

It was tough, because not only was it necessary to
work very fast, with material which was not the greatest,
but the equipment was much less efficient than it is today.
The crab dolly did not exist, and that is the one piece of
equipment that made modern television possible. Before
it, there was the Fearless dolly — for which it was necessary to lay an actual track. This was hammered down
with nails every time a dolly shot was needed. When this
had been done and you looked at the shot and found it a
bit off, it was not possible on our schedule to pull up the
track and move it over; you had to restage or take your
beating like a man. With the advent of the crab dolly,
which can be moved everywhere like a crab — to and fro,
sideways, — it became easy to adjust a shot.

Nor were there the lenses that exist now; there was no
zoom lens with its amazing ratios. When you have the
crab and the zoom lens, you have great mobility without

having to lay tracks and lock yourself in. Nor was the
film as fast as it is today. Sometimes we would go overtime on the schedule and Carl Kramer would say, "If you
fellows keep this up, you're going back to a day-and-a-
half." We tried to avoid that.

In those beginning days we went out and scrounged
for scripts. I'd call up friends and ask them if they had a
script, or I'd find a story and ask someone to dramatize it
— if the story could be bought for very little money. At
that time, residuals were unknown and writers were paid
a very small sum. It was necessary to be a member of the
Directors Guild to direct, however.

When we had gathered eight scripts, we gave them to
Joe Manecci who, as head carpenter, would budget them.
They were all shot on stages. We made our own dead-
line; when we had eight scripts, we would get to work.
We had some good actors: Buddy Ebsen did two of the
shows, Vincent Price and Alan Mowbray one each. We
also used Francis Ford, John's older brother; he was very
old then. When John first came into the business, he was
a propman and Francis was the star.

I worked for about a year. MCA-Revue Productions
moved from Eagle-Lion to what is now CBS/MTM Studio
Center in the Valley, and was called at that time Republic
Studios. The lot had been built by Mack Sennett and was
owned by Herb Yates when Revue took over a section of
it.

At Republic, MCA built up Revue Productions to be
the biggest organization of its kind in television. They
were the producers, both creatively and financially — as
well as the distributors, salespeople and also the agents,
although as agents they took no commission. As both
producers and agents, they became so big that they
bought Universal and moved over to that lot. At about
that time, MCA gave up the agency under government
pressure. Now MCA owned a studio.

Many of the personnel went into other agencies; some

formed their own. Freddy Fields and David Begelman formed an agency, and George Chasin, Arthur Park and Herman Citron formed another. Wasserman wanted some of the people to stay with the company, and Jennings Lang, Eleanor Kilgallen, Monique James, Pat Kelly, Jay Kanter and Jerry Gershwin were some who did stay.

Working at Eagle-Lion was not satisfying to me; you had to work at extreme speed. My experience directing stock served me well; it allowed me to give a little more to the actor and to the story than someone who had been a first assistant director in films.

As the operation grew, MCA brought in some production people from Columbia pictures. Columbia had a very tough production head who used to brutalize his assistants and production people. Three of them joined Revue Productions as it began to expand. From the MCA point of view, they were just what the doctor ordered, as the MCA men knew nothing about making pictures. With these men from Columbia, MCA could be confident of getting its dollar's worth every day. Revue was oriented towards the production department and if you worked there you always felt great pressure.

Six years later, after I had been to New York and done some theatre work, I was brought back to MCA by Hitchcock, for the program *Alfred Hitchcock Presents*. But then, when the production department got after you, there was Hitch and his operation to keep you separate and apart; I was protected by Hitch.

Back to the Theatre

PARKER: Though you were constantly at work in either films or television during this period, you always seemed to find time for the theatre. Your first venture was with the La Jolla Playhouse.

LLOYD: The playhouse came about at a time when there was no television. There were actors in Los Angeles who had worked in the Broadway theatre and missed it; some of them had no opportunity to go back to New York to do a play, and some could not, as they were under contract to a studio. The theatre in those days seemed very remote when you were a Broadway actor in Los Angeles making movies. Actors felt a kind of guilt and had a feeling that they had deserted their true calling. Today, there is a kind of off-Broadway equivalent in Los Angeles, a flourishing theatre activity in many small theatres, that did not exist then.

Several actors under contract to David O. Selznick loved the theatre and wanted to have one. They were Gregory Peck, Dorothy McGuire, Joe Cotten, Jennifer Jones and Mel Ferrer.

Greg Peck came up with the idea of using his old high school in La Jolla. There was an auditorium with a stage that was usable, at best. The actors went to Selznick, who shrewdly saw the value of it; it would allow them to let off steam. He loaned them fifteen thousand dollars, and

155

Greg went to the La Jolla authorities and got permission to use their stage.

I first went to The La Jolla Playhouse in 1948 to direct *The Road to Rome* by Robert Sherwood. Eve Arden and Wendell Corey were in this production. I was invited there by Mel Ferrer, who did a fine job of managing the theatre in its early years. However, he soon got tied up in other projects and John Swope took over in 1953. John (a popular photographer) was a man of impeccable taste, great warmth and charm who had much compassion for people. It was a loss to the theatre that he did not pursue his producing career after La Jolla.

In 1951, I returned to direct *The Cocktail Party*. The stars were Patricia Neal and Vincent Price; also in the company were Estelle Winwood, William Schallert, Harry Ellerbee and Rose Hobart. This company, with Marsha Hunt replacing Pat Neal, went on to become the national company. As it travelled, I put different actors into it: Vincent Price became ill when the show was in San Francisco and Dennis King replaced him; Julie Haydon, of *The Glass Menagerie* fame, replaced Marsha Hunt.

Also with Vincent Price and Marsha Hunt, I did *The Lady's Not for Burning* in 1952; the production went up to San Francisco. In 1953, I directed Dorothy McGuire, Don Taylor and Lamont Johnson in *I Am a Camera*; Jean Parker, Don Taylor and Tommy Gomez in *The Postman Always Rings Twice* and Allyn Ann McLerie and J. M. Kerrigan in Shaw's *You Never Can Tell*. Then I did *Dial M for Murder* with Brian Keith and Douglas Montgomery.

PARKER: These people were no longer connected with Selznick. Did the theatre just continue?

LLOYD: It continued in the summer for several years. They paid back the money that had been borrowed from Selznick.

In 1954, I directed *The Winslow Boy* with Vincent Price and Dorothy McGuire; then there was Howard Duff in *Anniversary Waltz*, Joe Cotten in *Sabrina Fair*, *The Seven Year Itch* with Don Taylor and a new play called *The Vacant Lot*, which did not go well.

During 1955 I directed *The Rainmaker* with Teresa Wright, Lee Marvin and Jimmy Whitmore and another new play, *The Native Uprising*, with Howard Duff. We did *Billy Budd* with Vincent Price and then one of my favorite shows, *The Time of the Cuckoo*, with Claire Trevor.

All these actors were a joy to work with. Dorothy McGuire, eternally youthful, whose love of theatre is infinite, brings that love into her performances and endows them with her special beauty. Vincent Price, committed to the theatre, is forever stage-struck. Name the play, name the street-corner — Vincent will be there. What a delight to work with! La Jolla tapped resources in him that surprised us all. There were Claire Trevor, consummate actress of great depth, and a loss to our profession when she retired too early; Pat Neal, exciting with the gifts of a great leading lady; Lee Marvin, a major actor, his talents scarcely tapped in films; Teresa Wright, who quietly went her way playing role after role in American dramas with unforgettable performances; Jimmy Whitmore, an actor who embodies our best traditions; and Howard Duff, whom the audiences loved because they believed him — not a dishonest bone in his acting body. Through it all was John Swope with his notes and criticism always right on the nose but delivered in his enormously attractive indirect way.

This was in the 1950's, but the community was tuned into the 1920's. It was an audience that, in my view, saw the theatre as something lightly amusing, a good filler between drinks, dinner and 11:00 p.m. — when you started to drink again. I know that the people of La Jolla would be up in arms at this indictment — but this was thirty-five years ago.

The pay was minuscule, but we loved anything to do with the theatre. There was no television to absorb the energy. We couldn't make what might be called a "serious theatre" in La Jolla at that time. Our big hits were *Sabrina Fair* and *Anniversary Waltz*. You couldn't do better than that.

PARKER: How did they take *The Cocktail Party*?

LLOYD: Rather medium boiled. *Lady's Not for Burning* did well, but that's sugar-coated culture. They did not like *Billy Budd* at all, nor *The Winslow Boy*. We speculated whether it was worthwhile continuing the theatre there. People would come down from Los Angeles to see the shows, but without the community we couldn't stay in business.

The most characteristic story about this situation concerns *You Never Can Tell*. We had not done well at the box office with it — this wise play, which Shaw had written as a mainstream play — for his Broadway, so to speak. It was light and it was meant to be commercial — but Shaw could not write anything that did not have a great deal of wisdom. It's a play about the relationships within the family, particularly in respect to the father who has been away for some time, and returns. What are his rights — if indeed he has any? What can he demand of his children? It didn't do well at the box office.

A little later, we were preparing *Don Juan in Hell*. I think it very amusing that the publicity man requested of John Swope that Bernard Shaw's name be in the smallest letters possible outside the theatre. If it were put in its proper, larger type, he believed, it would drive away the audience.

This was a problem for anyone who had even a modicum of seriousness about theatre. But from a directorial point of view it was great fun, because I had a play to do almost every week. I had very good actors coming down from Los Angeles. It was stock, though we thought it was a little better because of the caliber of the actors.

It was an Equity company. Jimmy Nielsen ran the backstage area and directed many of the plays before I arrived on the scene. He was a superb production manager and a solid director; he had been Katharine Cornell's stage manager and he was precise and first-rate at his job. It was very valuable to have a director who could direct traffic. If a director starts to break up the play in this kind of situation and fragment it in what he thinks is a more profound way, he is going to find himself in trouble, fast. You need to get on with it, to stage it.

I have always enjoyed the challenge of having to direct under pressure, both in television and in the theatre, and having to meet those stock requirements through a kind of shorthand. Through an immediate rapport with the actors, you can quickly get in some ideas. I think we were successful with *The Cocktail Party*, and with Shaw.

If you have a play that has great quality, you have a chance to raise the level to more than just a stock production. It's when you get into bad material that a fascinating result occurs.

There are some directors who are much better with bad material than with good. The latter makes a demand of them, and perhaps they can't get to that level. Good material often constrains them, or intimidates them, or they don't know how to be faithful to good material. There are directors who, with bad material, can improvise on it, be relaxed with it and have a certain freedom of invention — because they feel no sense of responsibility. It may appeal to a director's real taste, which frees his gifts. Bad material, and I think this is a truism, very often makes a good film — particularly if it tends toward melodrama, because the natural style of film is melodrama; certainly it is the style of television. In selecting material to direct, one is often seduced by something very well written and literate without realizing it doesn't really lend itself to being a film. There are times when melodramatic pulp makes a good film. Truffaut's *Shoot the Piano Player* came from a pulp story. He made something special out of it, a picture which had a social point of view.

There are directors who are craftsmen; they complete the job on time and on budget. But for a director to give a piece its overtone, that extra something, he must find an identification; a responsive chord has to be struck within him. I am talking about material one hasn't written — not about those who write their own scripts.

One is fortunate to fall in love with whatever one is directing even if one knows it's of minor value. It gets difficult in this business; as time goes on, you think, "I'm not going to fall in love with it. I've done too much of that kind of material." You have a hard time revving yourself up for the job; you "phone it in." For my own part, now, I find it very difficult to get really interested in anything in the way of fictional material — even in watching it.

Chaplin said to me, toward the end of his life, "It's all artificial." He had begun to lose the zest for the artifact. He said, "The very word 'art' is in the word 'artificial.'" It was getting laborious. Fortunately, when he was a young man he didn't feel that way and we have all that marvelous work.

There is a statement of Ionesco's which I think is important to all directors. It's from an interview in 1982 in Los Angeles. He said: "In the 1950's we rebelled against the realistic theatre because we understood that realism is not realistic. It is a document, a system of theatrical, literary or other conventions. Documents are the work of political partisans. We cheat with documents, but poets cannot lie because they deal in imagination and imagination is revelatory. The politician can lie, but the poet doesn't lie. He invents, which is entirely different."

I came out of the La Jolla experience brimming with a mad desire to direct. I had had great luck with the actors and with the production people and it had been very exciting. Sometimes I couldn't get the actors up to pitch. When Pat Neal was in *The Cocktail Party*, she was very good as Celia, but in some ways, I could not get her up to speed. Someone sent Vincent Price, who was playing the psychiatrist, a telegram which said, "We will be coming to the opening with the author." This referred to another play Vincent was considering. Vinnie said he was confused by the telegram. He showed it to me saying he couldn't make heads or tails of it. I asked Vincent if I could borrow the telegram. He consented.

I called the company together. I said, "I have here a telegram sent to Vinnie and I'm going to read it to you. You can act accordingly." I read the wire.

"You mean T. S. Eliot?" asked Pat Neal. "What else could it mean?" I replied. She said, "Oh, I'm going to throw up." She ran off-stage and did so, but she was fantastic that night.

After the opening, I confessed that the telegram had been about a play someone wanted Vinnie to do. She laughed; I must say she took it very well.

It's a difficult play, and Pat had only had a week's rehearsal. I wasn't faulting her; I was looking, as a director should look, for something that would get her up in the air. She was remarkable in the part. Pat could have been the Katharine Cornell of her time.

But we have never taken good care of our talents. We lost Broadway and we lost our talents. In Brando's career, there is nothing to discuss in regard to theatre; he can't be considered in comparable terms to Richardson, Gielgud or Olivier as a leading actor. The nearest one to approach this was Henry Fonda — but although he had a rich career, the best in our country in our time, it had no classical aspect to it. The actor who could have had it all, on the highest level, was John Barrymore, but something in his character rejected it. *Counsellor at Law*, his film with William Wyler, was made from an indigenous Broadway play, in which Paul Muni created the role. It was real Broadway, New York theatre. It was not avant-garde theatre, not original theatre — but that's what Broadway was, that kind of play. It had a vague social statement and it was Yiddish. Broadway was Yiddish. Now it's British Yiddish.

In those days, it was professional theatre; professional Broadway theatre. You just don't see it — it was something. It didn't have this genius attitude all over it. With regard to films, it carried over when many actors emigrated out to Hollywood. There was a terrific group; Eddie Robinson, Lee Tracy, Spencer Tracy, James Cagney and Humphrey Bogart.

These were all professional Broadway people; they were not geniuses. They went out and did a job. We don't have anything like that now.

There were a lot of good actresses in those days also. Barbara Stanwyck is typical of that kind of actress; she's had a superb career. Claire Trevor is another, as was Maggie Sullavan. They had a tough, good-hearted Jane quality, but they were brilliant at their craft and they had emotion and humor.

PARKER: What about the Phoenix Theatre?

LLOYD: The Phoenix Theatre was founded by T. Edward Hambleton and Norris Houghton. Houghton had been a scene designer and was rather well-known for a book that he wrote in the early forties, *Moscow Rehearsals*. Norrie had been one of the first people to go to see Russian theatre and he wrote very well about it. T. Edward Hambleton was an interesting and attractive fellow. He came from a well-to-do Baltimore family and had been producing in the theatre with little economic reward, but with great resiliency; he was known for his smile. All his productions had some aspiration — one could always see what attracted him to the play, even though it might not work. He was quiet and reserved, a real manager.

T. and Norrie had discovered the old Yiddish Art Theatre at Second Avenue and 12th Street which was built in 1927, the last legitimate theatre to have been built in New York City at that time. It had been the theatre of Maurice Schwartz; since then, it has had many histories — most flagrantly, as a burlesque house. It was a lovely theatre of about nine hundred seats.

I was brought into the company chiefly by Hume Cronyn, who was going to do *Madam, Will You Walk*, a posthumous play of Sidney Howard's. Hume felt that to direct and to play in it would be too much of a chore; he asked me to co-direct and also to act in the piece. The play was to be the first production of the Phoenix Theatre, and Hume, Jessica Tandy and I were to play the leads. When Hume was on stage, I could be out front directing — and when I was on stage he was not, and could direct.

It worked out well; it's not a situation I would recommend under most circumstances, but the show had many technical tricks and effects, and this arrangement made it easier. When it came down to a difference of opinion, I acceded to Hume — so that we could get on with it, not because I agreed all the time. The show was pleasant enough, but it never had the imaginative execution that it might have had; it was a polite evening in the theatre.

When Sidney Howard wrote the play, he wanted George M. Cohan for the lead. The Playwrights' Company produced it, with Cohan and Arthur Kennedy, but it closed in Washington before coming to New York. The Playwrights' Company was formed by Howard, Robert Sherwood, S.N. Behrman, Elmer Rice and Maxwell Anderson — who had become disenchanted with Broadway's producing organizations.

The play was flawed and unrealized, but it had great charm — the same charm, people said, as Sidney Howard himself. The play dealt with the devil in its subject matter. There was a rumor that Cardinal Spellman indicated to Cohan his displeasure with it, and this contributed to its closing in Washington. It had needed a rewrite, which Sidney Howard, who was killed in a tragic accident at his farm, did not live to do. A rewrite was done by Robert Sherwood, but the play remained on the shelf after its first unsuccessful production.

Howard's agent — and the agent of virtually every major Broadway playwright until Audrey Wood came along — was Harold Freedman. He felt strongly about the play, and when T. asked him for a good American play to start the Phoenix season, he took *Madam, Will You Walk* from the shelf and gave it to him. Freedman stayed close to the production. He stipulated, as did Howard's widow, that the original be done, not Sherwood's rewrite, and he protected the text so that it was never a point of discussion. Freedman addressed T., Norrie, Hume, and myself in the Phoenix office after the first dress rehearsal; I remember him saying, "Now, I want everyone to be quiet because I'm going to talk." And so he did, making good sense. He was an admirable representative for the play.

After the second dress rehearsal, the same group met with Robert Sherwood, who agreed that the original was a better play than his rewrite. He was an imposing figure, standing six foot seven — a theatre eminence.

The play was pleasantly received. The New York critics and audiences wanted the Phoenix to succeed; T. Edward Hambleton was so attractive and well-liked that everyone wished him success.

Coriolanus, directed by John Houseman, was the second production. Houseman was in California before the show went into rehearsal. He was producing at Metro; we were living in his house in Rockland County.

He asked my help in casting the three clowns in *Coriolanus*. I found him three actors that he was happy to accept. They were Jack Klugman, Gene Saks, and Jerry Stiller.

The Phoenix then embarked on a big musical enterprise, *The Golden Apple*. I knew John LaTouche, the lyricist, and they asked me to direct it.

LaTouche, whom I had known since the thirties, was a talented, strange man who had started with great flair, enthusiastically received as a lyricist. He did *Ballad for Americans* and, after several other shows, *A Cabin in the Sky* with Ethel Waters, which has some beautiful songs including "Taking a Chance on Love." He then had a long dry spell; he was still writing, but nothing was catching on. Shortly before *The Golden Apple*, he had done an evening with Jerry Moross, who did the *Golden Apple* score. It was a show called *Ballet Ballads* — four ballets to which there were words — which was well received off-Broadway. *The Ballad of Baby Doe*, in which Beverly Sills starred, was to come later. LaTouche was looking for the recognition he had had as a young man.

Jerome Moross was long recognized as a fine musician and composer, but special; he, too, had not had Broadway acceptance.

The designers were William and Jean Eckhart who, not long after, decided they had had enough of the Broadway experience and went back to the University of Texas where they taught scenic design. They were enormously gifted and I thought them brilliant designers; their sets for *The Golden Apple* were absolutely extraordinary.

The choreographer was Hanya Holm; *The Golden Apple* was the show she did just before *My Fair Lady*. Hugh Ross, the conductor of Schola Cantorum in New York, was the musical conductor. In the cast were Stephen Douglass, who had been the lead singer in *Damn Yankees*, Kaye Ballard, Portia Nelson, Priscilla Gillette, Jack Whiting, Jonathan Lucas, and Bibi Osterwald.

I had never directed a musical. When I began re-hearsals, I found I had an enormous problem: there wasn't one word of dialogue. Everything was set to music, so that what I was directing was a kind of compli-cated opera. Moross saw it staged to definite notes — entrances, exits and moves.

Directing one entrance, I waited through eight bars of music before the actor appeared. When he did come on, we waited again for his cue to sing. Without consulting Moross, which I should have done, I turned to the pianist and told him to cut it down to four bars, so we could get on with the show. "You can't do that!" protested Moross indignantly. "It's in sonatina form!"

I pointed out to him that the audience didn't know it was in sonatina form; they would simply be waiting for something to happen. Moross had his way, and the audience waited.

The Golden Apple is the story of Ulysses brought up to date. In the first act, the piece is in story form, with the parable rather obvious. The second act is a series of revue numbers — still supposedly involving Ulysses, but the story doesn't develop. One of the revue numbers is the hit song of the show, "Lazy Afternoon," sung by Kaye Ballard as Helen of Troy. It has become a standard.

I kept insisting something should be done to join the two elements together to avoid a dichotomy in the show. The authors rewrote parts of the first act, but did nothing to the second, and the problem was not resolved. They had a proprietary feel for the show, which had taken them two years to write. This was understandable. And I, with my story sense, was coming from pictures, where if one scene doesn't work, you substitute another. But in this case, the entire fabric was music and lyrics; if any part was disturbed, it all unraveled. It was too late for a major rewrite, which should have been done before we went into production.

I had fought for this, and before the production started rehearsals, I had quit. I had found the protective attitudes of LaTouche and Moross very unpromising, and I told T. I didn't think the show would work. LaTouche was a friend of many years standing; Peg and I would visit the old apartment building he lived in, where Paul and Jane Bowles also lived. A fire occurred there. Paul and Jane, who were mysterious and had other apartments in other places, went to Brooklyn Heights to live; La-Touche had nowhere to go, so he lived with us for some weeks. We had great admiration for each other, but when we began work on *The Golden Apple*, I encountered his mad, almost violent protection of his work for the first time.

T. gently and diplomatically mended the rift, and I went back, still with misgivings. The show was a hit, but actually it never worked and, at the end, no one was speaking to anybody else.

The glue that held it together was the choreography. Hanya was a surprise to me; it seemed that her assistant was doing all the work, but Hanya went on to the biggest hit of its time, *My Fair Lady*. Whenever I worked with a choreographer, the relationship between the choreographer and the assistant has been a mystery to me. At times, the assistant's contribution seemed to be larger than the choreographer's.

The Golden Apple won the Critics' Award; I left the Phoenix Theatre. They moved the show uptown to the Alvin, where it didn't do well at all; it had been right for the smaller house.

I came out of it with the sense that I should never direct a musical, which I had found to be a very special field. Musicals were changing at that time; when I saw, shortly afterwards, the production of *West Side Story*, I was sure that musicals should only be directed by choreographers. The old days, when George Abbott came in to pull it all together — after the book had been rehearsed in one place, the dancers in another, and the singers somewhere else, were gone.

I did not return to the Phoenix until 1956, when *The Taming of the Shrew*, which I directed at Stratford, Connecticut, transferred there.

In 1954 I worked for an industrial film company, directing three short films. Coming from show business, I found myself in a different world; the language was different and so were the attitudes and the responsibilities. It didn't sit well with me. But at the same time I stayed in the theatre by going to La Jolla.

PARKER: You returned to the Phoenix Theatre a few years later.

LLOYD: I was asked to go to Stratford to appear as Lucio in *Measure for Measure* in the theatre's second season — summer, 1956. During the first season, the theatre had many problems and as a consequence the regime had changed. The artistic directorship was given to John Houseman and he gathered some of the people who had worked with him in previous years, one of whom was myself. He also brought in Hiram Sherman and Whitford Kane from the Mercury and in addition there were Morris Carnovsky, Pernell Roberts, Nina Foch, Mildred Dunnock, John Emery and Fritz Weaver. It was a good company.

After I had performed in *Measure for Measure,* Houseman asked me to direct *The Taming of the Shrew.* The costumes for the show, designed by Dorothy Jeakins, were traditional but a pleasure to the eye in their rightness. The look of the show was unusual because of the louver pieces that gave visual interest to the raked stage. These pieces were set in different patterns for each production, thus giving the stage a new look for each play. They hung from the grid. This concept was the work of Rouben Ter-Arutunian. The show was lit by Jean Rosenthal.

My thought with the piece was to give it a vaudeville style. It seemed to me that Shakespeare had not intended it to be profound — although anything Shakespeare touched had meaning, so that while there was vaudeville in the show, you still had scenes that had importance and content. It is one thing to say you will direct a play as vaudeville; it is quite another thing to do it. Not long before, *Taming of the Shrew* had been a great hit as a musical, *Kiss Me Kate*, with a book adapted from Shakespeare by Sam and Bella Spewack. The New York *Herald Tribune*, which was still in business then, thought it would be amusing to send Sam and Bella Spewack as critics to review the production. They ended their review by saying, "It will make a better musical." They had their little joke.

There is nothing more irritating in the theatre for me than obvious romps in which the actors think they are funny showing irreverence to the great master, Shakespeare. It's a question of finding the tone — how to do it so that it is real and still make it vaudeville. How can you be inventive enough, in the staging, in stage business, in character concept — inventive enough to give it a vaudeville facade yet still give it meaning and still make it real — with a tone? That wasn't easy. I think we achieved it at Stratford.

For the induction scene, where all the actors arrive and prepare to do a play, the actors came on carrying various poles and pennants and set up the stage. This was done with a nice choreographed sense, because living nearby in Stratford was Balanchine. There were forty-five actors in this entrance and I suggested to Houseman that we ask Balanchine to choreograph it; we would do it to music and have a pretty, dance-like effect — though it was less dance than mime. So Balanchine came and staged the scene; it was a pleasure working with him. We had Christopher Sly and the Page on the balcony above, in the Globe tradition — the Page played by my daughter, Susanna, and Christopher Sly by Mike Kellin, who gave a rich performance.

The one costume where Dorothy Jeakins went wrong, in my view, was the one she designed for Christopher Sly. The problem was that Dorothy was on the West Coast and I was in Connecticut; we exchanged conversations by phone. She designed the show, then brought the designs east. In the design she showed me for Sly he was a rather elegant, princely fellow who got drunk. I saw him as more like a tinker, wrapped in burlap, with lots of pots and pans banging around as he came through town. It appeared to me that she had misread the play in this regard. She is a dear friend and one of the foremost designers of our time — but she refused to understand what this ought to be.

During our phone conversations, we had never really discussed how Sly should look; we just thought of him as a drunk. Sometimes when you talk to a designer, he or she will sketch as you are talking — it's a form of communication. But Dorothy was three thousand miles away. I took it for granted that she would capture the particular look I wanted for Sly.

There was a great to-do over this, and it was interesting to me that one person connected with the show saw Sly with a princely elegance and I saw him in burlap. Dorothy fought for her way. We were in the basement of the theatre arguing at a great rate when Houseman came by and got into it. This was something he loved because in the years gone by he would have to find a place to lose his temper once a day. So did Orson.

They had to scream. This argument with Jeakins was one he could really grab onto. He said to me, "Let me take care of this," and then he shouted and screamed at poor Dorothy — though they were good friends. Finally she caved in. It was quite a battle; it has always fascinated me to see directors fighting for their concept in a departmentalized situation and how the departments fight because each thinks it is directing the show. In any case, after all the fury, we got a lot of burlap and wound it around Sly and gave him pots and pans to bang away on; he was really a great slob.

Three years later, just after we had moved into our present home in Los Angeles, Jeakins came to visit us. She brought a house gift — the original plate of Christopher Sly; the rejected one. We said, "Thank you, Dorothy," and put it on a wall which it graced for many years. In 1982, we had a call from Dorothy. She was giving a show of her costume plates at a gallery and asked if she could come and borrow Christopher Sly. She took the plate — to show what Christopher Sly looked like in her view, and people were going to think that's how he looked in the production. She said, "Oh, I'll see that you get it back, Norman. I wouldn't want you to be without it."

Pernell Roberts, as Petruchio, was superb. He was a fine Shakespearean actor; he had made a hit off-Broadway as Macbeth, and in *Measure for Measure* he was an impressive Barnardine. As a young actor, he had it all. Nina Foch played Katherina and was beautiful, witty and strong; Petruchio's servant, Grumio, is an old complaining fellow, and Morris Carnovsky played him to the hilt. He spoke Shakespeare's dialogue, but in addition he built up an entire ad lib of his complaints in Italian gibberish.

The show was successful. It moved to New York and played the Phoenix. We rehearsed again after a short layoff. Morris turned against the Italian gibberish. "All that stuff I did at Stratford, it's awful. Why did you let me do it?" I said I found it funny. He said, "It's terrible. I'm taking it out."

"Shakespeare will be relieved," I told him. "Go ahead, take it out." He rehearsed without it for about a week. A couple of days before we opened in New York he said, "It needs that Italian gibberish. We've got to put it back in. I've got to put it back in." I protested I wasn't arguing with him — but he was prepared to fight for it.

That's a real actor's story. Carnovsky found something so funny and so right which gave his performance a rhythm. When he had time to think about it during the layoff, he decided he wanted something else. But Carnovsky sensed after rehearsals started again that it wasn't the same quality he had had previously — so he put back the gibberish.

A director should know when not to play the card as well as when to play it. In this case, I had to let Morris find that he was wrong.

Morris is a creative man, and a fine teacher; he is astute, and an intellectual about acting. When he directed *Volpone,* every night there were notes, and such notes; they were like little books. Hugo Haas, who shared a dressing room with me, couldn't take them and fended Morris off by telling him the notes confused him. English, he said, was not his native language; he spoke Czech in his mind. But I liked talking to Morris every night and I didn't mind the notes. He knew acting on its best level and he knew how to get it from an actor from the point of view of The Method. As a director, he could speak the actor's language. This was something all the Group Theatre directors could do — when I worked with Kazan, he was the same. They were teachers by nature.

Fritz Weaver played Gremio, the old suitor, in a marvelous performance; he is a superb character actor. He played him as a staggering, lanky old man with a tall hat. In his hat he kept a live moth — and he had a special light which Jean Rosenthal arranged. One of the best pieces of business in the production was when Gremio met Katherina. Off came his top hat, the moth flew out, saw the light and went right up into it. Every night before the performance, the apprentices went out in the field and gathered moths. There are many aspects of directing that people don't think about — I did stop short of casting the moths, who were a delight to behold and well behaved. The business worked every night.

Among Petruchio's eight servants were Peter Bog-danovich, Rene Auberjonois, Michael Lindsay Hogg and David Scott Milton. The servants were played as slobs, as unruly boys. That may have been the most unfortunate piece of direction that I gave, because the servants got dirtier as the show went on. They resorted to getting dust from the floor to put on their faces. Finally, I told them they were carrying things too far and asked that the makeup be held to a minimum, but every time I went back to see the show the makeup was worse than before. When the show was in New York, I asked them, "Don't you guys ever run out of make-up?" They poured on everything they could possibly find. They were just starting in the theatre and one of the joys in theatre is to make-up. They were amusing and fun.

I tried to keep the play very bright with brilliant colors, to which Jeakins contributed, as did Jean Rosenthal's lighting. Irving Bazalon did the music, which I asked to be in the style of Prokofiev's "Lieutenant Kije Suite." The show had great speed and nicely invented business. It had a large sweep and a good sense of movement. We used every part of the big new Stratford theatre and its enormous stage.

It was the first real hit at Stratford; *Measure for Measure* was well-received, but it was a little time before it caught on because the first show, *King John*, had not done well and audiences were cautious in responding to this new venture. But *Measure for Measure* was received with respect and gradually, through word of mouth, people started to come. *Taming of the Shrew* was an outright hit. It had a gaiety that found an audience immediately; it was good summer fare and it was what the audience wanted.

When it moved, with *Measure for Measure*, to the Phoenix, neither play went as well as it had at Stratford. Once we left the spaciousness of Stratford for the much smaller Phoenix, the plays became compacted, pressed in. As a consequence, the shows lost their bounce and gaiety. It is not unusual for a show to move from one theatre to another and in moving, to lose something. If I had redirected *Shrew* for the Phoenix, there would have been no reason for it not to work, but we transferred the shows as they had been in Stratford; particularly in the performances, the loss was evident.

At the conclusion of the Phoenix engagement, I received an offer from Alfred Hitchcock to be associate producer of the television shows *Suspicion* and *Alfred Hitchcock Presents*. The Hitchcock show, which lasted a total of ten years, was at the start of its third year, and Hitchcock was making certain changes. He had been the producer, with Joan Harrison as his associate; now he elevated her to producer. They were also taking on another series of hour shows called *Suspicion*, ten of which would be made by Hitchcock's company and the other twenty-two by various other companies. Some would be done live in New York, and some shot on film.

Alfred Hitchcock Presents

I think it is fair to say that *Alfred Hitchcock Presents* remains one of the outstanding successes in television history. Twenty-three years after the last episode was made and thirty-three years after the first, the original series still plays. Before the show, Hitch was known throughout the world as a director, but the television show gave him even greater fame and fortune.

Hitch was a superb executive producer; I learned how to be a producer from both Hitch and Joan Harrison — who had also learned from him. He had the ability to delegate, while at the same time being very clear as to what was demanded.

The shows were produced by a company called Shamley, Inc. — the name of the English village where Hitchcock and his wife, Alma, had had a cottage before they came to America. Hitchcock was sole owner of the company, so we had to be very careful about the money because it was his. He was proud of the fact that he never directed any really big budget films. Once, at Metro, he went over budget; he made *North by Northwest* for four million dollars, and he and the studio were virtually not speaking by the end of the shooting because of the money spent. The picture was an enormous hit.

The television show had to reflect Hitch. This was something we sensed; no one sat down and said this, but it was taken for granted by Hitch when he hired Joan

Harrison and myself. We understood his storytelling style so well that we easily fell into it.

Joan Harrison, who was the producer of *Alfred Hitchcock Presents* when I was brought out from New York to work on the show as associate producer, was most sympathetic to my being hired. A classic English beauty, Alice of Wonderland grown up, she had been Hitch's secretary and had accompanied him to America when he came to do *Rebecca*, on which she received one of the writing credits. Joan eventually produced feature films, *Phantom Lady, Ride the Pink Horse*, and *Uncle Harry*, among others. At a time when women producers were a rarity, she may have been the sole female producer of feature films in Hollywood.

She is now married to Eric Ambler. In her producing days, her charm and diplomatic skill, encased in a will of iron, enabled her to work effectively with writers and directors.

Members of the crew held her in great esteem. She would appear on the set dressed in immaculate taste, beautifully coiffed. The crew was proud to be working with her.

Her sense of the Hitchcock story was strong and Hitch trusted her choices. I learned much from watching her work and shall always be grateful for her encouragement. She is a dear friend.

In the early days of the show we stayed pretty much with material that had already been published; there was then a rich body of good short story material. The genre was suspense, with a twist, and with an overlay of humor. We got the cream of it; television was still a new medium and nobody knew how to do these stories as well as Hitch.

We also favored published material because you knew what you were buying. In the ten years that the show ran, there was only one story that we did not shoot after having purchased it — a story by Roald Dahl that we bought in the last year. In contrast, when I was doing *The Name of the Game* we had two hundred and fifty thousand dollars worth of stories on the shelf that we were never going to use. But if a story was approved by Mr. Hitchcock, you had to make it work. Joan Harrison and I looked for material and read it, though we soon hired a reader — Gordon Hessler, now a director — who sifted through the material and brought us what he thought was plausible. If we liked a story, we had it synopsized in two or three pages and the synopses were sent to Hitch's office.

When he read them, he decided, "Yes, let's buy it," or "No," or "Put it on the reserve list in the event we run into a jam. But it has problems and I don't really see it." He was understanding about the reserve list because as the years went on it got more difficult to find stories.

Once the story was approved, we hired the writer; Hitch was not consulted on this. We developed the script, cast it, hired the director and did the show. After it was shot, we took the rough cut to Hitchcock and looked at it with him. He was tolerant and generous; never, to my knowledge, did he ever ask for anything to be re-shot. This was partly dictated by the fact that it was his money; he had a very practical point of view about television. Very, very rarely he would suggest: "If you have a close-up there, you might want to use it."

I remember only one aesthetic that he offered: "Remember, it's a close medium." In television, you get an establishing shot and then you get in close, as fast as you can. I believe he was right. No matter what else is tried, there remains nothing more remarkable than the big head in close-up on a television screen. In your living room, you're seeing into the depths of the eyes of the individual. We made some interesting shows that were imaginatively staged, but we always came back to this basic premise of the close shot.

On the half-hour shows, we built to a commercial after the first eleven minutes, which was the FCC ruling; there was a commercial at the beginning, one at midpoint and one at the end, making the show essentially two acts. When we got to the hour show, it then became three acts.

Every one of Hitch's famous lead-ins, for ten years, were written by Jimmy Allardice. They were brilliant. Jimmy has never been given his due. Most people think that Hitch wrote them. The relationship was remarkable in that Jimmy Allardice found his perfect voice in Hitchcock; he said all of those wild things about the world through Hitch, who was willing to do any outlandish lead-in that Jimmy wrote. In a sense, Jimmy was a part of Hitch's television persona. He wrote material based on Hitch's personality and pushed it onto another level. Hitch would go to that level and make it even more outlandish — so that he would appear as his brother, Albert Hitchcock, as well as himself, or Jimmy would put Hitch inside a bottle, or have him wear golf knickers, or put him with a lion.

PARKER: Were they shot for each show separately?

LLOYD: In the half-hour days, we did thirty-nine shows. We waited until we had a dozen scripts and then we gave them to Jimmy. He told us he didn't want any until he could have a dozen. But nothing happened; Jimmy would just sit and ignore them. We'd call on a Wednesday, and say, "Jimmy, we're shooting the lead-ins Monday — it's the only time we can get the stage." He'd say, "Monday? My God, oh dear, Monday!" He hadn't written anything, but by Monday he would have all twelve. He would never write unless he was under the pressure of having to shoot; if he had the shows a month before, nothing would appear. His work was always a delight; he did one of the great writing jobs in the history of television.

PARKER: How did they get together?

LLOYD: Jimmy was from Yale; he had co-authored a play called *At War with the Army* which, as a film, was the first hit of Dean Martin and Jerry Lewis. After another, less successful play, he was brought to Hollywood to write for the first year of *The George Gobel Show*. It was the show's most successful season. MCA took Jimmy from the Gobel show and gave him to Hitchcock, and Hitch adored him. Jimmy would have him talk about his belly this way, his jowls that way, talk about his speech this way — and Hitch never blinked an eye; he did everything Jimmy wrote. It made him very lovable to an audience; it made Hitch a major star of show business. It took Hitch about two days to shoot each series of twelve or so lead-ins and we did them three times each season.

When we brought Hitchcock the rough cuts of the filmed stories, he watched them and would have little to say; if he didn't like one, he simply nodded and said, "Thank you." If one was particularly good, he would let you know.

The directors had to have a feeling for the material; it required a sense of suspense and irony. We did not do a mystery show; nor a detective show. We did a suspense show. In directing them, one had to know how to deliver the twists visually. Hitch said, about sound pictures, "What we do now is photograph dialogue; we've lost the ability to really shoot pictures." He meant the ability to tell a story with a camera — "to write with the camera" was the expression used in silent pictures.

PARKER: What, in your evaluation, are some of the best shows?

LLOYD: One can only say the shows that are remembered over the years were the most successful. Hitch directed about a dozen; I directed about twenty-five of

them. Robert Stevens was a very important director to us
— and to the early years of television — and directed
about thirty of them. Herschel Daugherty directed many
shows; Arthur Hiller virtually began his career with us. I
started Bill Friedkin on this show, and Lewis Teague also
started with us.

One evening Peggy and I attended a play in which
Joan Houseman was appearing at the Beverly Hills
Playhouse. It was called *Days of the Dancing* and, while it
was not successful, the writing revealed a considerable
talent. I soon asked the author of the play to do an adaptation of a Nicholas Blake novel for the hour show.
Robert Redford and Zohra Lampert played the leads. It
was Jim Bridges's first writing for the screen, large or
small. Jim is a natural. There was never any question
but that he would be successful, for in addition to his
talent he knew how to work with people, an inestimable
gift not given to all. He did some eighteen scripts in the
time he wrote for the show. "The Jar," from a Ray Bradbury story, and "The Unlocked Window" remain the best
known, but all his scripts had a human, modest quality
which was particularly effective in a suspense piece. In
"The Jar" he added a regional flavor that was rich in its
authenticity.

Henry Slesar wrote more scripts for the Hitchcock
show than any other writer. He wrote fifty-five, most
from his own stories. We first came upon Henry in the
Hitchcock magazine. He had a story in that publication
every month, with three other writers who were also published every month. We decided to bring all of them out
to California and give them assignments. Imagine our
surprise when we learned that all four writers were
Henry Slesar. To say he is prolific scarcely does justice to
the man who became a typist of dazzling speed in order
to keep up with the stories pouring out of his head. He
possesses the outstanding gift of being able to create
original stories, a gift denied most writers. These stories

had a unique structure for our time; a beginning, middle, and an end. In his quiet, gentle way, Henry was indispensable to the show.

"The Life Work of Juan Diaz", written by Ray Bradbury from his own story, which I produced and directed, was a particular favorite of mine. Ray Bradbury was always exciting to work with for the flow of ideas were original and dramatic. "Juan Diaz" was, in my view, the best screenplay he wrote for the Hitchcock show and in the performances of Frank Silvera, Pina Pellicer and Alejandro Rey, his intentions were realized. This story of a man who earned more for his family as a mummy than he could as a live human being contained a compassion that was deeply moving combined with the most intriguing dramatic ideas. I've always enjoyed doing a Bradbury story because it's never without inherent drama. To be around Ray with his wild-eyed charm makes working with him a delight.

Three of the most famous shows were "Lamb to the Slaughter", a Roald Dahl story directed by Hitch and starring Barbara Bel Geddes; "Specialty of the House", a Stanley Ellin story starring Robert Morley and directed by Robert Stevens; and "The Man from the South", written by Roald Dahl, in which I directed Steve McQueen and Peter Lorre.

"Lamb to the Slaughter" was about a woman who killed her husband with a frozen leg of lamb. She put it in the oven to roast, and when the police arrived she served it to them as they talked about the lack of any evidence. In those days on television, you had to have retribution; murderers were not allowed to get away with it. This gave us an interesting challenge, and Allardice's lead-out was a triumph of invention. To meet the Broadcast Standards and Practices requirements, Hitch said in the lead-out that she remarried and became displeased with her second husband, reached into the freezer for a leg of lamb and hit him over the head with it. However, the freezer wasn't working properly, the lamb was soft and so she didn't put him away and was caught in the act. That was Jimmy's way of working it out. Audiences didn't take it seriously. They enjoyed the humor of it.

"Specialty of the House" was Stanley Ellin's first story; later he became a successful mystery and suspense writer of both short stories and novels. Robert Morley played a man who belonged to an eating club. He went there on Thursdays, when a particular dish, lamb armistan, was served; he relished this dish and ate a great deal of it. Lamb armistan was human flesh; the reason the chefs permitted him extra large portions was that they were fattening him up to serve to the other members. That was a very special show.

"The Man from the South" was a story about a young fellow, Steve McQueen, who had lost all his money gambling in Las Vegas. He was approached by a man, Peter Lorre, who offered to play a game with him and give Steve a chance to win some money. He had seen him light a cigarette with a Zippo lighter; the bet was that Steve could not light the Zippo ten times in a row without missing at least once. Steve said he could; the stakes were that Peter Lorre put up a Cadillac against Steve's little finger. They took a room in the hotel. Peter Lorre ordered a hammer, nails, twine, and a bottle of scotch. He tied Steve's hand to the table and separated his little finger. He had the bellboy bring a meat cleaver. They had picked up a man in the bar to referee. As he counted "One," Peter raised the meat cleaver and Steve lit the Zippo.

Lionel Lindon, known as Curly Lindon, was the cameraman; he subsequently won an Academy Award for *Around the World in Eighty Days*. He had lit the cleaver so that every time it went up, a light hit it — we were shooting in black and white. The light reflected and glistened, and Peter would have a lovely smile of anticipation.

It was a suspenseful story with a tremendous twist, and it was very popular with our audience. We learned that children were playing a game called "Zippo" in the schools. Fortunately, they were not using cleavers — but they were using Zippo lighters, trying to light them ten times in a row in bets with one another.

In the tag to the show, Lorre's wife burst into the room to break up the proceedings. "He does this everywhere he goes," she said. She showed the car keys to Steve, saying, "It's cost us four Cadillacs and three fingers." As she handed the keys to Steve, the audience could see she had only two fingers left. Katherine Squire played the wife. We made a special glove for her with two fingers.

There were many shows that were memorable. We maintained that unless one out of every six shows brought hate mail, because it shocked the viewers, we were not reaching our audience. "The Man from the South" brought such mail. There were some stations that informed the network they were not going to play it — and indeed did not.

We tried to inspire this hate mail, which we felt represented audience interest. One show, which brought a good deal of it, featured Arthur Hill. He was a school teacher from the South who had a disagreement with his wife, and in a huff, he left her. He took three hundred dollars, virtually all their savings, and went to Las Vegas. The story picked him up just as he had lost all his money at the tables. He walked out of the casino and into the parking lot. As he crossed the dark lot, his foot hit something — a money clip with a wad of bills in it. He picked it up and saw initials on the clip. He hurried back to the motel where he was staying and counted out ninety thousand dollars.

Very nervous about the whole thing, he put the money under the mattress and tried to give the matter some thought. Tossing about, he decided that the honorable thing to do was to return the money to the person who lost it. But how?

He decided to put the money in a safe deposit box and run an ad in the local newspaper saying a sum of money had been found; if the person who lost the money could identify the money clip by specifying the initials, he would meet him and give him the money. The newspaper man looked at him strangely; next, the police summoned him, wanting to know where the money was. He refused to tell them.

Finally, someone requested a meeting. At the newspaper office a man (Rod Cameron) stated the initials on the clip and described it. He accompanied the school teacher to the safe deposit box where he was given the clip and ninety thousand dollars.

Rod Cameron told Arthur Hill, "I like what you've done. Why don't you come to the casino with me? We'll have some dinner. Feel free to play the tables. Why don't you invite your wife here and have a little vacation on me?"

Arthur Hill thought that was a great idea. He went back to the casino with Cameron, who gave instructions that he should be given anything he wanted in the way of chips, on the house. Leaving Arthur Hill at the tables, Cameron headed for his office.

A few minutes later, one of the lackeys came out and said, "He'd like to see you in the office." There, Rod Cameron was on the phone. "It's your wife," he said. He had gotten the number from a friend in the teacher's hometown so he could call and invite her to Las Vegas.

On the phone, the wife was hysterical. She revealed that strange men came to the house and were holding her prisoner; they said her husband had something they wanted. Arthur Hill said, "I don't know what they are talking about." He looked over to Rod Cameron.

"Where's the other ten thousand?" asked Rod.

This proved to be one of the six shows. People wrote in that Arthur Hill, by returning the money, had done the most stupid thing they had ever witnessed. In their eyes he deserved what he got and hoped the lesson would be observed by everyone. This man was castigated for his honesty.

At about the same time there occurred in real life an incident in which a porter found a bag of money that had fallen off a Brink's truck. He returned it to Brink's and got a great deal of publicity. He had to move out of his neighborhood because of the abuse; his boy in school couldn't take the vituperation that was heaped on him for having a father who was so stupid as to return the money. It's a great lesson about audiences — these are the audiences you're playing to and trying to get ratings from.

The shows were shot in two or three days. Hitch never rehearsed; he shot "Lamb to the Slaughter" in two days. I shot "Man from the South" in two days with one day's rehearsal. Other shows would take a little more time.

Good actors wanted to do the show because of Hitchcock. We also specialized in bringing out New York actors. There was not then a community of New York actors in Los Angeles. Thus, we had a constant flow on the airlines.

There were two reasons we used so many New York actors when there was a large pool of Hollywood performers. One was a kind of snobbism. When the program started, Robert Stevens was one of the directors and, indeed, did most of the shows. He was from New York and commuted to Los Angeles. He felt very strongly about New York actors, having used them in his work on live TV. I suppose it's faintly humorous to say there was snobbism, but there was an element of that.

Secondly, these were very special pieces of material, more like little plays than they were films. The New York actor, particularly of the fifties, fresh from live television, had a special kind of vitality — and was virtually a new face. Later on, they all became fairly old faces — but at this time there was an advantage in using good actors unknown to television audiences, although they were known on Broadway.

On occasion we would bring people from England; Wendy Hiller, Robert Fleming, and George Cole — who had just scored a hit in Somerset Maugham's *Duo*. Of course, there were established English actors in Hollywood, such as Cedric Hardwicke, Edmund Gwenn, Margaret Leighton, and John Williams, who would appear on the show.

PARKER: They make finer portraits, like a pen-and-ink detailed characterization.

LLOYD: Yes. But we paid no more for these people; they'd get whatever the top dollar was for the show. We were careful with the money. At the end of its ten year run, Hitch sold the company, Shamley, to MCA for stock and the deal was so good that he became the fourth largest shareholder of MCA at that time. This gives you an idea of how much stock he had. He was always very careful with money on his feature films as well. He was proud that he made pictures at a comparatively modest price, and he expected the same of us with the television show. When he directed one of them, he would take great pride in bringing it in on the nose, on the minute, as if to say, "Well, if I can do it, so can you."

PARKER: Did Ida Lupino ever direct for him?

LLOYD: Yes. One in particular was with Claire Trevor. In connection with this show, I asked Claire how she liked working with Ida. Claire said, "I enjoyed it. But you know, it was the only picture I ever made where the director spent more time with the hairdresser than I did." Between setups, Ida would wander over to the hair and makeup departments and have them work on her. I guess she was still looking back on her days as an actress. Ida was highly thought of as a director in Hollywood at that time. She did small, interesting pictures. It's a pity she stopped working when she did.

When I first came on the show, we were also doing a series called *Suspicion*. It was an hour show, and it was originally the reason I was brought in — with the demands of thirty-nine half-hour programs in a season, it was impossible for Hitchcock and Joan Harrison to do it themselves and still take on an hour commitment. *Suspicion* was again a Hitchcock show, with a twist; Eric Ambler was one of our writers. He and Joan Harrison had met socially years before, but when she selected him to write one of our stories, they became romantically involved and married.

Suspicion lasted only one season. Hitchcock directed one show called "Four O'Clock", from a Cornell Woolrich story about a bomb attached to an alarm clock. To get the point-of-view of Hitchcock about stories — he once said of another story which had a bomb in it, "You know, Norm, a bomb is always a good thing."

It was in the second season of *Alfred Hitchcock Presents* that I started directing. Hitchcock liked what I did as a director. Later on, when he was feeling ill, he made plans to hand over to me one of the films he was making — *Marnie*, but it never came to that. At the end of his life, he was preparing *Short Night*. His hope had been that I'd direct and that he would produce it from his desk. But he told me the front office wouldn't permit it, because then they couldn't call the film a Hitchcock picture. We had worked it out so that I would direct the principals in Finland, as Hitchcock wasn't well enough to go over there. In our relationship he felt confident in me as a director, as did Joan Harrison.

The course in which I was eased, and I offered no resistance to it because I was intrigued by the possibilities, was that of a film executive. The studio wanted a producer, someone who would put pictures together. MCA was still trying to operate the studio as it had been in the old days, which meant they needed executives to whom they could entrust a project, who could animate projects, or find ideas. I went along with that for a while, and in the course of it I drifted away from directing. Occasionally, I would drop back into it; I directed *Companions in Nightmare*, a World Premiere film for NBC.

PARKER: Was this in the course of the Hitchcock half-hour?

LLOYD: *Companions in Nightmare* was later. In the course of the Hitchcock half-hour and hour shows I directed about twenty-five episodes.

PARKER: Are these available?

LLOYD: Yes, in syndication. The show started in 1955, finished in 1965, and still plays every day somewhere. I have people tell me they saw a show that I made thirty years ago. We shot in 35mm because the studio had that equipment. They picked it up when they bought the studio from Universal; in those days, everything was 35mm.

Television in the Sixties and Seventies

When the Hitchcock show was over, Lew Wasserman set me up in a beautiful bungalow on the lot and suggested that I go into the theatrical feature area: buy properties and make movies. My own desire was to direct, but the management wanted me to produce.

For them, producers were the ones who went out and found the material. There were exceptions, of course; Hitchcock was their star and he was essentially a director, though he was his own producer. They could always make exceptions in the case of directors who were already successful. But in the main, when Wasserman took those people whom he had his eye on in television, and put them in the theatrical area, they were put into producing situations.

When you worked in a studio, there was a front office which had a story department. The story department was supposed to help you in finding stories, but this was not quite the case. The traditional studio system was that the story department distributed to the producers on the lot, over the course of the year, hundreds of synopses. Mainly, they were synopses of books but occasionally they were plays.

If you were interested in any of these, you would discuss it with the story department and then, should they care to pursue the property, with top management. It's safe to say that ninety-eight percent of the material was unusable and the synopses were not done well. If you expressed an interest in a particular piece of material, you might find that someone else had been there before you, so you missed out on it; you were in a competitive situation that was a bit puzzling. The idea seemed to be to make pictures — but what you really found was that the idea was to get into a position where it was possible to make a picture, and there were numerous people in the studio who had the same idea.

You waited to find a story in synopsis, or a writer would come in and tell you a story, or you tried to stir up the agents locally and in New York. After a while you got very itchy because time was passing; you were being paid and you knew that every day you came to work, working simultaneously for and against you was the computer. The computer was saying how much you were being paid and how much you were producing — more specifically, how much you were generating in the way of income for the studio. For eight years on the Hitchcock show, I was a darling boy, because the Hitchcock show did very well and I was part of the team bringing in gross income. At the end of the year when it came time to pick up your option, you were considered in terms of how much product or income you had generated for the studio. After six months, if you were on a yearly option and nothing was happening, you got rather nervous if you wanted to keep the job.

In my own experience, I found it very difficult to contact Ed Muhl and Mel Tucker, the two men who had been retained by Wasserman to run Universal. They had been managing the studio for Nate Blumberg, and when MCA bought Universal they continued doing so. Unless you got yourself close to the seat of power, you could not get off the ground. Ed Henry became a sort of hatchet man, operating out of the Tower to each of the producers, between them and Wasserman; although he was not responsible for any shows himself, he was in a position of importance. Jay Kanter couldn't get anything off the ground and he went to England, where he did some interesting pictures. George Chasin gave up and returned to the agency business.

I couldn't get Muhl or Tucker to approve of anything; in some instances they may have been right. In others, I wonder. For example, John Hubley called me from New York with an idea. He was one of the most brilliant men in animation that our industry has ever known; he had established a company in New York, working with his wife Faith, and they had won a couple of Academy Awards for their animated shorts. I told him I would be interested in doing anything he wanted to do, and we proceeded to lay out a picture in live action and animation.

It might be seen in the perspective of *Star Wars*. John Hubley, with a writing partner, took an unfinished story by Mark Twain, *Captain Stormfield Goes to Heaven*. The captain ran a steamboat on the Mississippi River when the new-fangled freight train arrived. Stormfield maintained his boat was faster, and a race was arranged. The boat beat the train to a bridge, but had to create so much steam that it exploded, and Captain Stormfield found himself gliding through the firmament in his boat. At a sort of entrance, he explained who he was, but they had never heard of him — nor of Earth, either. But, they said, perhaps he was looking for a place called Heaven.

Given directions, Stormfield went off through the stars and arrived at Heaven. There, a celebration was going on with all the great figures of history present — all except Moses, who was bored with everybody. There the unfinished Mark Twain story ended.

Hubley and his writer had taken that and continued the story as live action and animation. In Heaven, they had Stormfield, an old curmudgeon, meet an Indian girl. Through a series of scenes with historical figures, Stormfield mellowed and fell in love. After this, he is sent back to earth — given another chance because he has learned to love.

The idea was skeletal, I realized, and there was much to be done. Knowing John's brilliant visual skills, I thought the whole idea of going through the heavens in a steamboat was delicious; I went to Tucker with it, and he looked at me askance.

PARKER: They would have done that with *Star Wars*, too.

LLOYD: Yes — *Star Wars* was turned down by Universal. Jules Stein tried to find out who had said "no" to it.

On the Mark Twain story, Muhl told me, "I can't visualize it," which I thought was honest: he was not an unintelligent man. He had come from the accounting department, but he was a well-read man and had a practical mind, and Universal made down-to-earth, practical films; he was in the business to make money. I respected his opinion. A further deterrent, he pointed out, was that an entire system would have to be created in the studio to make the film, which he thought the studio wasn't prepared to do.

PARKER: What year was this?

LLOYD: This was 1965. During this period, the front runners like Jay Kanter and myself, who were in line to become major producers and/or directors on the lot, were not getting anywhere; those who remained in television and came to do theatrical features later managed to avoid that. Matters had cleared up a bit; Muhl and Tucker were out by that time. One day, shortly after Wasserman put me in the feature area, I walked into the commissary and Frank Price was sitting there. He was producing a television show, *The Virginian*. He looked at me and said, "You are a lucky son-of-a-bitch. He's put you into pictures." Frank eventually had his wish, then went to Columbia, where he did very well. Jennings Lang wasn't in pictures then; he was still a major force in the television area.

Finally, I bought a book which I thought I'd have a chance to make. I wasn't enthusiastic about it — but that doesn't mean much because I've found that I'm not enthusiastic about most things. There are projects I've loved — the Galileo play and the Lincoln films — but not many commercial things. I did like the Hitchcock show, which was commercial, and I had a lot of fun doing it; I was enthusiastic about the *Hollywood Television Theatre,* which was not commercial. I did love *St. Elsewhere,* which I took part in as an actor. But it was always difficult for me to settle on a property and say, "This I've got to do." Perhaps the bottom line reason I never made *They Shoot Horses, Don't They?* was that, while I saw its possibilities, I was never really enthusiastic about it. In this business, I think you have to sell yourself on a project.

At Universal I came across a book by Paul Bowles, whom I had known in New York years before; he had been rather successful as a cult novelist. In the thirties he had composed the music for a couple of shows I had done. At that time, the New York *Herald Tribune* had the best musical page in America, with Virgil Thomson as music critic and Edward Denby, the finest dance critic we've ever had in this country; Paul Bowles was the second music critic. I was in a production of *Twelfth Night* with Helen Hayes and Maurice Evans, before I got fired, and Paul did the music for that.

PARKER: What did you play in that?

LLOYD: I was Andrew Aguecheek. This was long before — thirty years before — I was at Universal. Margaret Webster directed; Maurice Evans was Malvolio and

Helen Hayes was Viola. At first they wanted me to play
Feste, but I have never understood that character. When
we opened in New Haven I got a telegram from the
Theatre Guild complimenting me on my performance —
they were the producers, with Gilbert Miller. The next
day, I was fired. I could never understand why. My understudy went in and played it for the rest of the run.
Some years later he got a nice check, because for eight
months on the road the Guild had kept paying him at the
understudy figure, but the Equity rule is that you receive
the salary of the actor who was fired — so eventually he
got the difference.

That was in 1941. Twenty-five years later, I was sitting in the commissary at Universal when I saw Helen
Hayes two booths away; I had always believed she had
had me fired. Maybe she hadn't liked my performance; I
was very cocky and brash, and I did many things I
probably shouldn't have done with a star on stage. She
saw me, and I saw her — but I didn't indicate recognition.
I finished my lunch and went to speak to someone in the
opposite direction.

A waitress tapped me on the shoulder and informed
me that Miss Hayes would like to talk with me before I
left the commissary. I went over to her table. "There's
something I've wanted to say to you for twenty-five
years," she said. "It occurred to me that I might never
see you again after you left the commissary. You were
brilliant as Aguecheek in *Twelfth Night*." For twenty-five
years, she had waited to make amends.

Paul Bowles's book, *Up Above the World*, was about a
middle-class couple — Laurence Olivier and Deborah
Kerr would have been good casting. They visit Central
America as tourists, and there they inadvertently witness
a murder — though they are not aware of it; they don't
know it's a murder. The murderer (a very elegant man
for whom Peter O'Toole would have been perfect), who
has a follower always dressed as a cowboy, sets out to get

control of the minds of the couple. He dopes them, and the story is about what happens to the couple after they've been doped — where they are taken and what's done to them. It's filled with visual effects of what happens on LSD. This was in 1965. This entire subject would have been new for pictures.

The studio bought it on my recommendation. It was very little money, around twenty-five thousand dollars, and I think Wasserman very much wanted to see me get started on the picture. My experience with him was first-rate, and I think he was sorely disappointed when I left the lot not having really done anything in features. Wasserman had not read the book when they bought it; later on I heard he disliked the story.

I went over to England and met with Pauline Mc-Cauley, a writer who had had a success with a suspense play that Eric Portman had done, and I brought her to America. She did a treatment, which the studio didn't like, and that was the end of the project. They still own the property. Early in his career Brian de Palma was under contract to Universal and came across it; he wanted to do it, but the studio would not approve it.

This was the closest I came to a production. At one point I was an early discoverer of *Rosemary's Baby*, but I couldn't get any response to it. Then I came across *Cotton Comes to Harlem*, but there was no response to that. These two properties were eventually made elsewhere.

The year elapsed and I was taken out of the theatrical feature area and put back into long-form television, where I did a World Premiere called *Companions in Nightmare*, written by Robert Joseph. Melvyn Douglas, Gig Young, Anne Baxter, Billy Redfield, Dana Wynter, Patrick O'Neal, and Louis Gossett were in it.

Its premise was that in a group in therapy there was a killer; the first part was a group therapy session. Directing it, I realized it was impractical to do with only one camera. It should have been done on tape, but the studio didn't have the facilities; with multiple cameras, one could keep the action going properly, more like a theatre piece. I tried to get two or three film cameras, but there was enormous resistance. First, I wanted to go to NABET, because they had cameramen who knew how to operate with multiple cameras. The cameramen at Universal used one camera, unless it was for an action shot. We needed one camera for a three-shot, with another camera, for example, getting a close shot. This drove the cameraman to distraction because it affected his lighting. I could not swing it. I started out with two cameras, but I noticed they were both on virtually the same angle. I ended up shooting with one.

The show proved to be successful, one of the best of the World Premieres. It was a flawed show, with no real ending, and I found it unsatisfactory, but it was well acted. After the World Premiere, I left Universal and went to England, for Fox, to produce a series called *Journey to the Unknown*. It was a suspense series, but with a mystic element to the stories. It was made at Boreham Wood Studios, and the experience of working there was exciting. The physical facilities — the sets, the wardrobe that was available to you, the locations — the looks of those places — were outstandingly good, particularly for the period pieces; we had stories which ranged from a modern setting back to the eighteenth century, and that could be done in fine style in England.

PARKER: What year was this?

LLOYD: This was 1968. For these shows we brought over an American star, and then filled the remaining roles with English actors.

PARKER: What was the reason for doing it in England?

LLOYD: The costs. We brought over Barbara Bel Geddes, Chad Everett, Patty Duke, and Roddy McDowall. We had fine writers, like Julian Bond, Jeremy Lamb, and Tony Skene.

It was my first experience of working in England, and one of the amusing aspects of it was the tea — morning tea and afternoon tea. I was horrified when the enormous ham and cheese sandwiches, on rolls, were brought around with the tea. My face must have given away my thought; someone said, "Oh, it's not true, sir, that tea holds up the work." But it did take a good half-hour every morning, and another each afternoon. For lunch in the commissary, they could order liquor, too; that was unknown here, though now you can get wine with lunch at the studios. I had a cameraman in England whose lunch was gin; well, it's cold in England.

After producing *Journey to the Unknown*, I came back to take over the segments of *Name of the Game*, which starred Tony Franciosa, for Universal.

PARKER: Had it already been in operation?

LLOYD: It had already been on the air for at least two years and was an enormous success; it was a seminal show. The executive producer was Richard Irving; the man behind it was Jennings Lang, who was head of the television department.

Name of the Game was a ninety-minute show; its pilot had starred Gene Barry in the role of the reporter. The show caught on, and it was one that set a style; I regret that I do not know who the writers of the early shows were.

PARKER: It was always about something. They also evolved this unique format of having three stars play the lead on alternate weeks. That is, Gene Barry one week, Robert Stack another week, and Tony Franciosa the third week. It wasn't an anthology, it had the three leading people rotate.

LLOYD: Exactly so. Susan St. James played the secretary; I believe she was the secretary to all three leading men. The format was built around a magazine which Gene Barry published, with the other two as reporters.

This show affected many shows. *Columbo* was a ninety-minute format, and there were others, like *The Bold Ones*. The show had a great sense of being of its day; its overall style was very much of the time. The musical theme, which Dave Grusin wrote, was jazzy and current, and the titles and graphics were brilliant. It was well produced; they put a lot of money into it.

PARKER: What was the cost per segment?

LLOYD: It was close to two hundred thousand; we had a week to ten days to shoot. Everyone connected with it moved along well, and it was a great feather in Lang's cap; he became known as the father of the long form, whatever that means.

Name of the Game was a hit television show at a time when Universal was the leading producer of television in Hollywood; they had eleven hours on the air. The making of the Gene Barry and the Robert Stack episodes went well, and audiences liked them. The Franciosa episodes, which were very good and also popular, were another matter.

Franciosa has an electric quality and he's a talented actor. He came to Hollywood with one of the best deals any actor ever had — a five-picture deal, three at Metro, two with Warner's. He made *A Hatful of Rain* and a couple of other pictures.

When I was asked to come in and take over the Franciosa episodes, there had been other producers before me; one was Leslie Stevens, another was E. Jack Newman.

They had done good work, but the core of the situation was that Tony Franciosa was impossible to handle. With E. Jack Newman, he had actually come close to fisticuffs in an office. Dick Irving asked me to meet with him. He said he thought I was the guy to handle Franciosa. "I think he'll respect your background in the theatre, and the fact you're an actor."

I told him I admired Franciosa as an actor. "But," I added, "I must tell you, Dick, that we saw *Hatful of Rain* in New York, with Franciosa and Shelley Winters." The night we saw it the stage manager came out between acts one and two and announced that Mr. Franciosa was ill and could not continue; his part would be played by Mr. Harry Guardino. I had understood this was not too unusual. The only thing I remembered, I told Dick, was that Franciosa never finished the performance. But I told him I would like to try; I thought the show was good and that it had some meaning.

I went to Franciosa's home for the meeting. After being admitted, I waited in the living room for about twenty-five minutes until he finally appeared. I felt we were getting off on the wrong foot — this had no style.

When Tony appeared, he was very leery; he was almost skittish. He wanted to be friendly but at the same time he was on guard. After the meeting he called Dick Irving and told him he thought it would be fun; he wanted to work with me. Clearly, I had been auditioned. I wasn't appointed by the studio, I was approved by Mr. Franciosa, and this is something to bear in mind in view of what eventually happened.

The first show we did was superb and Franciosa was outstandingly good in it. It was about a type of training for American soldiers, a simulation of a Vietnamese camp where American prisoners were held; we had Orientals to act as Vietcong, creating hell for the Americans. They were ordinary soldiers who were captured in a mock exercise — instead of being at boot camp learning to be

Marines, they were learning to be prisoners. The picture set out to show the terrible treatment our boys suffered in those camps. Oscar Rudolph, who directed the show, did a first-rate job.

Franciosa, as the reporter, suspects that excessive brutality is being used in the camp: there have been reports of boys dying in training, and he is seeking to expose the military. To do this, he poses as one of the soldiers in the camp. Tony was enthusiastic about the story, because he always wanted his stories to have a social meaning. Steve Forrest played the General, and was very good; all in all, it was a perfect *Name of the Game*.

Tony was happy, although in one fight sequence he went berserk and knocked down a tin wall. He was carried away by his own violence, and he could have been ripped to pieces. There had been a slight difference between Tony and me about his wardrobe. I was not trying to select his clothes; as an actor, I wouldn't want any director or producer to do that. But I had been warned that Tony was peculiar about clothes — it was hard to get him to make a decision, which made it tough to have his clothes ready in time to shoot. All I wanted was for Tony and the tailor to get together, agree, and make the clothes. It finally worked out; this is all part of picture-making.

We went on to do other shows. One very good one was about Victor Reisel, the labor reporter who was blinded by acid thrown in his face. Jack Klugman played that character, and it was an effective show; Klugman and Franciosa respected each other and worked well together.

PARKER: Would the same crew that shot a Gene Barry segment shoot a Tony Franciosa segment? In other words, was there any simultaneous shooting?

LLOYD: Not that I recall. Not while I was working there. It became evident that Tony had trouble learning lines. This difficulty lead to the use of the teleprompter, and a director had to accommodate his shots for Tony to be able to read it. But once a director did that, Tony wouldn't look at the teleprompter; he improvised the dialogue, creating difficulties for some of the other actors. Jimmy Nielsen, who directed the Victor Reisel story, confessed he was bewildered; Franciosa didn't know his lines, did not read the teleprompter, rewrote the dialogue. When the dialogue was changed on the teleprompter, he wouldn't look at it. Jimmy Nielsen was a super mechanic as a director, with great precision, a sense of perfection and pride in being on schedule and under budget. Franciosa was killing him — but with all the problems, we made a good picture.

I was experiencing difficulty in finding material for *The Name of the Game,* and the next show we did was based on a story from the reserve material of the Hitchcock show; the script for this episode was vulnerable. I had Harvey Hart direct it because Tony liked him, and I had already worked with him on the Hitchcock show successfully.

Next, I bought a story with a novel idea: a professor, living in Virginia and an authority on Shakespeare, claims to have found a first folio of *Hamlet* and to have it in his possession. Tony, as the reporter, goes to interview the professor who, it develops, is mad, and thinks he has the folio stashed away on the premises. I wanted John Gielgud to play the professor and I told casting to make him an offer; we had to do casting of this nature in concert with the network — which had not been the case on the Hitchcock show. There we were an autonomous unit and could do as we pleased.

When I told the network representative, Stan Robertson, that we were planning to cast Gielgud, he was dismayed. "Oh, you can't," he told me. "He's not a star."

I informed him that we had already made Gielgud an offer, and if he turned it down I had told the agent to make an offer to Ralph Richardson. "He isn't a star either," said Robertson. "You can't work with either one of them. We need star value."

I started laughing — then I saw a way out. My dear friend, Joe Cotten, was available, and they would accept Joe Cotten. He played the part, and very well.

Living with the professor in Virginia is his mad sister, played by Margaret Leighton, one of my favorite ladies and actresses. She didn't want to play the part because it was Southern, and she said she couldn't speak the accent. I told her that whatever she did would enhance the show. The character was one of those ladies who spends all her time in the attic. In addition to the *Hamlet* folio, the professor claims to have Shakespearean memorabilia from *The Merchant of Venice*.

Tony read the script and liked it. "It's good," he told me. "I want to do a speech from *Henry V*."

"In what context?" I asked him. "Just one of the speeches," he said. I protested that it made no sense; there was no reason for him to suddenly do a speech from *Henry V*.

"There's every reason. I want to show that I can play Shakespeare," he replied. "It won't be right, Tony," I said, "I don't want you to do it."

"I want to do it," he said.

He read the excerpt from *Henry V* to me and the reading was not good; the quality of his speech was all wrong. Leo Penn was the director, and I told him Tony wasn't to do any Shakespeare. I also told Tony it would be terribly unfair to spring it on an actor like Joe Cotten, who would feel he had to handle it in some way, and there would be nothing he could do.

I was in my office when Leo Penn came in from the stage. Tony, he said, was determined to do the *Henry V* speech. I told him to set it up in such a way that we could cut it out of the picture — which he did. Tony ad libbed something to get into the speech and then recited it.

Leo called me from the stage. "What shall I do?" he said. "First this guy wants to do *Henry V*, now he wants to break up the scene and do close ups and tight twos."

I went down to the stage. First I went to Joe Cotten and apologized; he was most philosophical about it. "There's no substitute for arrogance and ignorance," he said. "Mixed together, there's no way to stop him." I told Leo I was sorry, but he, too, could see that Tony was determined to have his way.

In Tony's dressing room, I told him I had heard about his *Henry V*, and that we weren't going to use it. "I want it in," he said, "And that's all there is to it. Furthermore, I've written some other stuff that I want to do in this scene, where I'm going to add some Ben Jonson."

It was the last straw. I said, "You're not going to put in any Ben Jonson. I happen to know something about playing Jonson; I did *Volpone* in this town and had a great hit in it. What you're putting in makes no sense. Your additional dialogue is illiterate. You cannot write a simple declarative sentence."

His voice rose. "I don't give a good goddam what you say. I say I'm writing this — and it goes in the picture."

I replied in a voice as loud as his, "I say it's not going in the picture because it's illiterate and my name is on the screen. I am not going to have my name up there with those words coming off the screen. I have something of a reputation for being fairly intelligent, and it could only mean that I was not around, or that I've lost my mind."

Back in my office I called Dick Irving. I told him we had an intolerable situation, with Franciosa rewriting on the set and insisting on his text being used. The original script, written by Anthony Skene, was quite stylish — and as Skene was living in England he would know nothing of any changes until he saw the show.

Dick Irving tried to reconcile the two of us, but Franciosa told him he was going to say his dialogue and would not stand for any interference. So Dick Irving came back to me, the same day, and asked if I couldn't work it out with Tony; we hadn't finished shooting.

I said that I was responsible for a text that had been approved by everyone, including Franciosa, and furthermore Franciosa's Shakespeare was an embarrassment I would not permit. I would quit, I told Dick, before I would allow Franciosa's dialogue and Franciosa's Shakespeare in a show with my name on it.

At the end of the day Joe Cotten and I drove together to the house of a mutual friend for dinner. I told Joe about my threat to quit and how sorry I was about Franciosa's treatment of him. By then Joe had done his major work in films — *Citizen Kane, The Third Man,* and *Shadow of a Doubt.* He had starred with Katharine Hepburn on stage in *The Philadelphia Story.*

He was still serious about his work, but he was not looking for great parts any more; he was relaxed and easy going, and he thought I should be, too. He advised me not to quit; he thought that would be silly. I was two months into my renewed contract with Universal; I had ten months to go. I had not talked to my agent; I was too angry, and I wasn't thinking straight.

The next morning Dick asked me if I still intended to quit — and I could tell from the way he asked the question that he hoped I would. Franciosa was working on the text and there was nothing Dick could do about it.

So I said goodbye — but before I left, I asked him one question. As the producer, I pointed out, I had represented the studio — so where did the studio stand on this; where did Dick Irving stand?

He told me, as an old friend, that he thought I was absolutely right. "But," he went on, "We — the studio — did tell the network we had a problem with Franciosa.

However, we are the middle men. The network said, 'We're not interested in your problem. Deliver him.'"

It was the beginning of what now exists on a wide scale, on television and more particularly in major films, where the actor or actress is the power. There is no studio that dictates.

No longer did the studios have the power they once wielded. As long as the actor could get the rating, that was all that concerned the network. Producers were easy to find.

I quit, with the studio owing me money. They didn't have to pay me; I broke the contract, I walked. It was 1969 or 1970, and they owed me well over sixty thousand dollars. I said, "The hell with it." My anger overcame me. When I look back, I can see that my anger and disgust with the situation had resolved itself in such a way that I just couldn't conceive of being a part of it any longer. Obviously I handled it badly; my agent at that time, Phil Gersh, was beside himself. He couldn't understand what had happened — that I had already kicked over the apple cart and there was no way back.

PARKER: Why do you think you handled it wrong?

LLOYD: The way you handle this is to go to the front office and tell them you will produce something else for them — that you just want to be taken off the show. But I was angry that the studio hadn't backed me up. I thought they might put me on *The Virginian* with Frank Price, and I didn't want to do that. Frank Price was making a name for himself as the producer of *The Virginian,* and he was doing a good job — but I didn't want to do that; I couldn't see myself on *The Virginian.* That kind of snobbism, or elitism, has plagued me.

They found another producer, Boris Sagal, who completed the series. About a year later the studio called me to come in and give a deposition on my experiences with

Franciosa; they were about to sue him for a large sum of money because of his behavior on the set. They wanted me to refresh my memory as to his actions — only in so far as they cost the operation money.

Meanwhile, Franciosa was suing them for defamation of character. I believe the suits were finally settled.

Not long after *Name of the Game*, Dick Irving called me back to the studio; he acknowledged they were in debt to me, and asked that I produce a two-hour film, *The Bravos*, with George Peppard. It was a pilot, but it didn't come to anything. They also had a series called *Movie of the Weekend*. I produced a script by Howard Fast, *What's a Nice Girl Like You...*, starring Brenda Vaccaro, Vincent Price, Edmond O'Brien, Roddy McDowall, and Jack Warden. It was faintly amusing, but it was just a job. I also directed one of the first episodes of *Columbo* with Peter Falk.

When I was producing the hour Hitchcock show, a play called *Prescription Murder* had been submitted to me. It was written by Link and Levinson and it had been out on the road, starring Joe Cotten, his wife Patricia Medina, Agnes Moorehead, and Thomas Mitchell, who played a character named Columbo, a detective. The play toured for six months and did good business, but it was felt not to be strong enough to bring into New York, even with that cast.

The play kept resurfacing. It was offered as television material. On the Hitchcock hour, I had read it and discussed it with Joe Cotten. He felt there was no third act. This may have influenced my thinking about the piece and I turned it down. Later on, it was submitted to me by the studio to do as a ninety-minute show. Again, I turned it down. "Oh, no, fellows, it's no good," I said. "I really don't want to do it." I suppose it was a kind of snobbism; I wasn't going to fool around with a show that couldn't get to Broadway — which was bad thinking on my part.

Don Siegel, whose offices were adjoining mine, was in the same spot; we were trying to find our way back. He was in television and had come over from Fox, where he had had a series. He was looking for a project. We each felt that if we found one, we could get moving again. A week or so after I turned down *Prescription Murder*, he pointed out to me that I had made a mistake. He had agreed to work on it. "I don't think it's any good either, but I'm on it, as executive producer — and on the computer, I'm working on something. They've got you as working on nothing — you're in trouble."

Of course, I see all these things clearly now; it's the way you jockey in the studio. Don stalled around until he got a western that he wanted to do with Henry Fonda. It was a good story, and he did it well, and it was a hit as a Movie-of-the-Week; that's how he got *Madigan*.

Prescription Murder circulated, and Dick Irving finally did it, with Gene Barry — and Peter Falk as Columbo. The management at Universal was enthusiastic about the idea of a series built around Falk in the character of Columbo because the show, contrary to my judgment, was an enormous hit. It did very well chiefly because of the character played by Falk. Another pilot for *Columbo* was done with Lee Grant as a lawyer/killer. Out of that came one of the most successful series on television.

Later I was asked to direct one; it was fun to do. The guest star was Susan Clark. Peter went on strike during the shooting. He apologized to me. "Nothing against you personally, Norman. It's just that I want more money." He sat out two days while we shot around him. He came to the studio every day and lunched in the commissary with the people he was striking against; he got the money. He knew how to handle his talent.

Around this time I had a most satisfying experience, playing Undershaft in *Major Barbara* at the Mark Taper Forum. Richard Dreyfuss played Bill Walker to great effect and Blythe Danner was an exquisite Major Barbara.

The show was well received. We did cut some of the play, but not very much. When *Heartbreak House* was produced at the Mercury, Bernard Shaw was still alive and wouldn't allow one line to be cut.

The most intriguing aspect of playing Undershaft is that one is playing a man who is a genius. To give genius on stage credibility it must be written by a genius. Therefore, I had my work cut out for me: it wasn't just a question of playing a munitions manufacturer, it was a question of playing a genius — written by a genius. It was one of my most heady experiences — on the nights you're in the groove, you're on a kind of thermal with Shaw and Undershaft and you could sense it out front. There was something in the air. The play is a masterpiece and one is fortunate to have had the opportunity to play it.

Shortly before *Major Barbara*, I played in *The Scarecrow* by Percy MacKaye for KCET's *Hollywood Television Theatre* on PBS. The play was written in 1905 and is set in New England, in the time of the witch hunts; Nina Foch played the witch whose former lover is the Devil, played by myself. Boris Sagal directed a fine production.

The producer of *Hollywood Television Theatre* was Lewis Freedman, who had founded it with a Ford Foundation grant. His first show had been *The Andersonville Trial*, directed by George Scott, which won an Emmy. During *The Scarecrow* I established a rapport with Freedman, and he asked me to produce and direct *Awake and Sing* when I finished *Major Barbara*.

Alex Segal, who had been the director, had quit; the starting date was two weeks off, but the challenge was a welcome one, because of the play. A set had been designed by the gifted Jan Scott. Walter Matthau agreed to play Moe Axelrod and Marty Ritt, the director, played Uncle Morty. We got Leo Fuchs to play Grandpa and Jack Lemmon's wife, Felicia Farr, to play Henny. The mother, which is a difficult role to cast, was Ruth Storey.

Ron Rifkin played Sam Feinshreiber, Ralphie was played by Robert Lipton and Milton Selzer, the father.

Awake and Sing was my first experience with multiple camera tape. I produced and directed the show, but the actual shots were called by an associate. For my first experience I didn't want to call the shots, because I found it very confusing; I wanted to watch the performances and I felt that if I had to watch all the monitors I would be only half-looking at performances. It's an interesting craft question, even as one gets better at calling the shots. There are people who have been in the business since the days of live television who find working in the booth very easy; they grew up with it — people like Delbert Mann, and George Schaefer. For those of us who came from the theatre and single-camera film, it's more difficult to master.

I was interested to learn that there was a time when it was thought that a director — after having directed the actors for a couple of weeks and after having laid out the shots and given them to the technical director to call — would do best to watch the on-the-line monitor, the shot that is going out to the audience, rather than watching all four monitors, plus the on-the-line monitor. There are those who subscribe to the view that the performance can best be judged by watching that one monitor. There is a Directors Guild ruling, however, that states the director is the one who calls the shots; obviously, directors will not give up their credit. So you have many of them calling shots when they might be better off judging performances.

PARKER: But if you're just watching the on-the-line monitor it's a fait accompli.

LLOYD: No, no. You have laid out the shots. But the technical director, who's doing the switching, calls your shots.

Blocking, for example, is done different ways: some directors sit in the booth and block, other directors like to be on the floor and block, to be close to the actors. I block on the floor. You have a monitor, and your production assistant is next to you with your shots. The shots are being punched up by the technical director in the booth, while you're on the floor looking at the monitor. The cameras are there, and so is the monitor. You can adjust the shot right there as it is being punched up by the technical director in the booth. You're not calling them — you're just setting them and the blocking. You can actually set the blocking and have personal and immediate communication with the cameramen. I resent the use of the PA system when talking to the actors. When you're recording the show, the associate director could call the shots, while the director watches the on-the-line monitor performance, which he has directed over a period of days or weeks. This is in the tradition of great directors in the theatre; Max Reinhardt didn't start with line one, page one. Preparation was done by many people before he came in to finish the work; it was done by his associates so that he could keep his eye on the ball. This approach is not permitted by the Directors Guild — because he who calls the shots is the director. You can share credit with such a person, but you cannot deprive him of credit.

The objection to my theory is that the timing of the shot is inherent in the quality of the production. I understand the beauty of that, particularly if you are a master of the booth, as some are. I would not deny that it has a value in the rhythm and the timing of the show.

PARKER: It's functioning as an editor.

LLOYD: Yes. It is my opinion that very often the director is more concerned with that and so misses elements of performance. He's looking at four different monitors; meanwhile, somebody may be hamming it up, or text eludes you — something else eludes you. Even with the production assistant watching text, values elude you. The director in film with a single camera does nothing but watch the performance. Here the director is obliged, as you say, to edit, and I know it's part of the skill of being a tape director; it's now been done for many, many years and will continue to be done. But I do think that the greatness of a director is in his communication with actors and his understanding of the story.

PARKER: I think you're absolutely right. Today with electronic editing, isolated cameras and the fact that you're going to edit anyway, why not?

LLOYD: I'll tell you what the objection to that is. If you used isolated cameras and rely on electronic editing to do a great deal of correction, you are losing — and I do agree with this — one of the chief values of multiple camera tape.

PARKER: That's a big issue.

LLOYD: Well, then they're not using tape correctly or to its fullest. The value it has is that while you're shooting and recording, you are taking away about eighty-five percent of the work you would ordinarily have to do in editing. Unless you take advantage of that, there's no point in using tape; that is the greatest value of tape.
 I know there's a lot of talk about acting for tape; actors do fifteen-page scenes, they get a run on it — and consequently they begin to approximate the rhythm, and the joys of acting in the theatre.

PARKER: Some of them play for audiences.

LLOYD: Yes. I remember in *Shadow of a Gunman*, which we did at PBS, we did a thirty-four-page take. On

other shows we've done takes approximating that — it
just went the whole act of a two-act play. You can do it if
you're well rehearsed and if you have luck with actors.
In this case, we had Jack McGowran, whose performance
in *Shadow of a Gunman* is one of the definitive performances of our time; it's the best performance of that part I've
ever seen. The actors began to approximate the rhythms
and the interplay of theatre, which is often broken up by
the shorter takes in film.

The chief value of tape is an economic one. You can
eliminate so much of your post-production time by correctly calling the shots with multiple cameras, so that
most of the job is done.

Awake and Sing was the start of my producer-director
relationship with *Hollywood Television Theatre* which went
on for about five years. At this time, Lewis Freedman,
who had been sent to KCET by the Ford Foundation, was
running *Hollywood Television Theatre* and I was producing
for him; in that capacity I did Arthur Laurent's *Invitation
to a March*, Lillian Hellman's *Another Part of the Forest*, and
Shadow of a Gunman by Sean O'Casey. *Another Part of the
Forest* ran about two hours and twenty minutes. I heard
that we offended Lillian Hellman by cutting it and she inquired, through a third party, about what we had had the
gall to take out. I sent word back that the version was the
one her own touring company had used, to put the play
into a single set.

I also produced and directed Jean Renoir's *Carola*,
which was an interesting undertaking. Leslie Caron and
Mel Ferrer starred in it; among the other actors were Anthony Zerbe and Albert Paulsen. Renoir wrote *Carola* as a
play, not as a film — although it had many cinematic
qualities. It had been his intention to direct it but he was
affected by his last illness and could not. I was accorded
the honor of being given the piece by Renoir. I don't
think anything he wrote was directed by anyone but himself up to that production.

It's a fascinating, very Renoir piece. Jean was still alive and we did make some cuts in Jim Bridges's adaptation, but it ran two hours and twenty minutes; we should have cut twenty minutes more. It would have been better at two hours. It is a mixture of drama, melodrama, and comedy that is so characteristic of Renoir.

The action of *Carola* takes place during the Nazi occupation of Paris and the play attempts to show a difference between the traditional German military man and the Nazis. I know there are those who don't think there is any difference — Ben Hecht said of the Germans after World War II, "They're only resting." The story is told from the point of view of an actress in the theatre, played by Caron, who tries to help her acting company live during the Nazi occupation. Truffaut saw *Carola* when I screened it for Renoir, and he has told Mrs. Renoir that the play influenced him in making *The Last Metro*, which has a similar subject.

The actress's former lover, a German general of noble family, sees her perform and comes backstage; he attempts to protect her. Meanwhile the French Gestapo—whom Renoir shows to be as bad as the German Gestapo—are looking for a young lieutenant of the Resistance, believed to be hiding in the theatre. This is the case; he could have escaped but he worships the actress and would not leave the theatre without first getting her autograph. This is very Renoir.

With the Gestapo looking for him, he finally reaches the actress's dressing room, where, in desperation, she hides him in the closet before both the French Gestapo and a Nazi colonel enter the room. When they have left and the lieutenant gets out of the closet, the German general is there; the general wants to save him. They get him out of a window but he is eventually caught.

The play has a sense of history about it. Strangely enough, it has never been done in the theatre in France. At the time we shot *Carola*, it wasn't fashionable to do plays about Nazis; it seemed to be something out of ancient history. Now, with the emergence of the Holocaust as a major historical phenomenon, there's a great deal of material being done on the horrors of that time.

Freedman went over to CBS and I was appointed executive producer of *Hollywood Television Theatre*. The first production I did was *Winesburg, Ohio* — the play based on the Sherwood Anderson stories. The production had Jean Peters coming out of retirement, which caused a great stir in the press; the other leading actors were William Windom and Joe Bottoms. The three played mother, father, and son.

Much to my amazement the play was very successful with the audience. This version of the material is a poor one because the adaptor introduced a great deal of material of his own; although it is based on *Winesburg, Ohio*, it is not authentic Sherwood Anderson. We reached into the heartland with that play. We had been accused of being elitist, but this was more down-to-earth.

There was difficulty at this time in getting new material. I regretted this, but I had to get shows on the air. We were still obtaining grants from the Ford Foundation but usually they came at the last minute, pushing us to have something on the air in two months. Rights to material, assuming I found something I wanted to do, weren't always so quickly obtained; one was fortunate to get rights and not be held up on production.

Besides my regret that we were not getting more original material, I had not clarified at that point what I wanted to do with the *Hollywood Television Theatre*. If I liked a piece of material I would do it. When I think about it, maybe that's enough to do in any theatre — you like it, you do it. We had thematic problems — it should have been new material, American material. But then I would say that *Shadow of a Gunman* was a hell of a play, so why not do it?

Shadow of a Gunman was in fact selected by Lewis Freedman, who, previous to my coming on the show, had done several European works — Beckett and Ionesco, among others.

Coming into my office one day, I found on the desk a play, published in paperback, called *Steambath*. I asked my secretary who had left it there; she replied that she didn't know, so we tried to find out who had done so and whether it was a submission. It remained a mystery. Nevertheless, I read the play and reacted with enthusiasm, and I set out to put this show on the air.

The first thing I realized was that the language might present a problem to the network, so I talked to Chuck Allen, program director of the station, about it. I learned that Robbie Lantz represented Bruce Jay Friedman, who wrote the play, and I called him in New York. He told me Bruce was at the Beverly Hills Hotel and that I should contact him there. When I did so, introducing myself and telling him what I wanted, we were off and running — that was all there was to it. We paid him the modest sum of three thousand dollars, for what is called four "uses," which had to be played over a period of three years. A "use" was any number of performances within a given time period, such as one week — then that was it, for the year. After the three years, all rights reverted to the author.

When *Steambath* was done Off-Broadway, it was only moderately successful. Bruce Friedman said that it was much better on television than in the theatre; it played better in terms of the play itself, than it had in the proscenium. If he had realized this when he was writing it, he said, he would have written it for television; he felt that the cutting of the multiple cameras gave it a pace, and the close-up gave a presence and an interest to the individual actor, more so than in the theatre. We had this experience with a later production, *Incident at Vichy* by Arthur Miller. Arthur, too, felt the material projected better on television — again because the cutting gave it a pace and consequently a vitality it did not have in the theatre.

There was an extraordinary reaction to *Steambath* when it played on television. The cast was an excellent one — Valerie Perrine, Bill Bixby, Herb Edelman, Stephen Elliott, Ken Mars, and Jose Perez. When the play had been done in the theatre, the part of the Puerto Rican attendant was created by Hector Elizondo, a rather large man, who had apparently played it like a bullfighter. Not to infer that his interpretation was wrong — but Bruce Friedman said he would like to see a different approach, playing it more casually; he came up with the idea of using Jose Perez. We had a difficult time finding him, but when we did, Bruce's hunch was absolutely right. He was superb.

This figure of God with a Puerto Rican accent offended many people all over the country. Of the approximately two hundred and eight stations on the PBS network, only twenty-eight initially played the show. To most of the stations the play was sacrilegious and its language and nudity unacceptable.

During rehearsals Valerie Perrine, who was never loath to exhibit her body, wandered around in two towels, one to cover her hips and the other to cover her breasts, which on occasion flopped out. While we were blocking, she'd sometimes fall asleep on the set. Work would stop all over the lot, in all the offices, because everyone was watching the monitors that were tuned in on our rehearsal; Valerie was giving the boys a great show. There was one scene where it was claimed that the nipples of her breasts were visible. I, a grown man, had to meet with the editor and electronically raise the frame of the picture to cover them — staring all the while to make certain there were no nipples. Then we had a little matter of pubic hair in connection with the two gay chorus boys who did a dance — a dance that is one of the great moments of modern television.

Tony Charmoli did a hilarious piece of choreography with the two dancers; it was one of the most brilliant immediate inspirations I have ever seen. We asked Tony to come to the office; he had read the script, and we talked about it. He was sitting on the sofa in the office when he got up and immediately did the whole dance. It scarcely changed when he choreographed it with the two dancers from what he had done in the office. It was perfect. The dancers' use of the towels was enormously skillful and on their exit they threw the towels away so you saw their bare asses. But just before they turned, Jim Loper, who was then the head of KCET, insisted pubic hair was visible. He came to me to request that these frames be taken out.

I removed the pubic hair. Nevertheless, the show was an utter scandal. The station's license was in jeopardy because of the production. Chuck Allen's job was on the line. He was in charge of programming for the station, and very brilliant he was at it; he had a great sense of the modern — of what went today. For two weeks he wouldn't talk to me and I would see his face going by — the manifestation of his fear that he was going to be hung from the highest yardarm. It was ironic — in view of the fact that it turned out to have been Chuck Allen who had put the play on my desk, a fact I didn't learn until months later. Apparently, he had first submitted it to Lewis Freedman who, according to Chuck, had virtually chased him out of the office. Lewis thought the play was an abomination and had wanted to throw things at him. So poor Chuck was feeling the brunt of his enthusiasm — and of my having done my job too well.

He rode out the storm. For the moment, we were the rage of show business. The production had the highest rating of any dramatic show on KCET until that time; there have been higher ratings subsequently, but not much. People found out about it and it was repeated many times; there are those who have watched it every time it played. It's a show you can see over and over again because it's so delicious, so funny and so moving.

The transmission of *Steambath* is a story in itself. We were castigated by ministries all over the country. There were places in Minnesota and Wisconsin where they would not play it until they heard that the one or two isolated stations who did play it on pledge night raised large sums of money for themselves. The very preachers who wanted us taken off the air began to play *Steambath* to raise money.

I was invited to a convocation of PBS in Washington, D.C. to be on a panel with Michael Straight, Carter Brown of the National Gallery, and others; Clifton Daniel of the *New York Times* and the whole PBS hierarchy were also present. Caspar Weinberger, then Secretary of Health and Welfare, spoke; there were many pronouncements that better things were needed on television, and so on. My panel was at the end of the day; it was a very proper and upright group.

"I find myself in a peculiar predicament," I told them. "You are talking about good things, unique things for public broadcasting that other networks don't play. We did a show called *Steambath*. Here we are in Washington, the home base of PBS — and you haven't played it in this town, a year after we did it." The head of PBS at that time was a gentleman who ran a station in Dallas; he was one of the station heads who had found that running *Steambath* brought in many pledges of money. "We should have discussed this in the morning," he said. It was then about five in the afternoon, and there was going to be a dance and festivities that evening. "This is the wrong time to discuss it; it is not something to get into right now."

He killed any discussion we might have had; I had wanted to make the point that when they had something of quality, they were reluctant to play it.

The KCET delegation refused to speak to me for the rest of the trip; they ignored me. I went to the festivities in the evening and was looked at very suspiciously by all and sundry. I felt very good about that; I'd had enough of the cant and fancy talk. We had to listen, during the evening, to William Buckley; it would have been interesting to see how he would have reacted to *Steambath*.

I think it's fair to say that *Steambath* has remained a classic in television drama. It is timeless in its concept.

Hollywood Television Theatre went, after the season of hour-and-a-half plays, to a season of one-hour plays, *Conflicts*.

We started with Shaw's *Man of Destiny*, with Stacy Keach and Samantha Eggar, followed by a new play by Gardner McKay, *Me*. Geraldine Fitzgerald and the then unknown Richard Dreyfuss played in it; it was about an autistic child, who turned out not to be autistic at all. I then directed a play of Steve Tesich's called *The Carpenters*, with Vince Gardenia. It was a very tough play, seemingly naturalistic but very much influenced by Gunter Grass, which became evident when the house started listing and flooding. We did *Incident at Vichy*, and then a play by Alfred Hayes, which he adapted from his long short story, *Gondola*. This was a three-character play based on the Scottsboro case.

A gondola is the name of the coal-carrying railroad car in which a prostitute said she was raped by three black boys. Al had the idea that the girl ran off when she was freed, after she saved herself by lying. She settles in an inner-city tenement in the Midwest, where she is found by a civil rights lawyer, a character who is from New York, is wealthy and successful, and who devotes some time each year to look for evidence which could lead to the release of the Scottsboro boys. He feels, now that she is no longer in the Southern town, he can appeal to the girl to tell the truth. The girl is traveling with a man who is a rather arrested character. When the lawyer makes his appeal to them on moral grounds, he is told off in no uncertain terms; the girl mocks his morality. Al points out that the lawyer had the luxury of morality; the girl didn't.

Sondra Locke played the girl in a beautiful performance — perhaps her best ever. Bo Hopkins was her companion, bringing danger and authority to the role. I played the lawyer. It was a very well-written piece, gloomy and down — but it was about something very real.

The final play of the season was a long one-act by Robert Anderson called *Double Solitaire* which Susan Clark and Richard Crenna did for us. It's the study of a break-up of a marriage, and it has been often used by psychologists, in classes and with patients. It was well done, particularly the last twenty-minute scene, and it has proved to be one of our most popular shows.

Although we worried about money, there was a source — the Ford Foundation. As a result of the success of *Conflicts'* first season, our funding was renewed.

We came up with three shows: Philip Hayes Dean's *Sty of the Blind Pig*; a Steve Tesich play which had been called *Baba Goya* in the theatre, but *Nourish the Beast* when he adapted it for television; and *The Lady's Not for Burning*, starring Richard Chamberlain and Eileen Atkins.

Sty of the Blind Pig, which had a black director, Ivan Dixon, and starred Mary Alice, who is a brilliant black actress, is a play I thought had amazing qualities — simple, curious qualities. It had an all-black cast, and a fine performance by Richard Ward. As well played as it was, our audience didn't like it. It included an extraordinary Pentecostal scene, played by Mary Alice, where she is possessed by voices — and I really believed she was possessed. The play dealt with black mysticism, blacks living in poverty with a sad life. It was a world from which there was no way out. The score was sung by Reverend Cleveland and his choir, one of the best gospel singing groups in America, and was written for them.

Quantities of English drama are bought by PBS because they are less expensive than the domestic product. If I had *Hollywood Television Theatre* to do again, I would not do *The Lady's Not for Burning*, even though it was a good production. Joe Hardy directed it; in addition to Eileen Atkins, who was superb, and Richard Chamberlain who was also very good, we had a fine supporting cast. They were solid classical actors. I had no fault to find at all with the production, and our audience loved it — the Pasadena audience thought it was supreme.

But for myself — other than that I had a charming conversation by long-distance phone with Christopher Fry — I didn't really know why I had done it. I realized I had fallen into the trap of Chamberlain's being a genuine television star, and he and Joe Hardy brought me the idea. This was really something for *Masterpiece Theatre*. Our task at *Hollywood Television Theatre* was to bring to life American writing.

I would not want to do another English work either. I did produce the brilliant *The Chinese Minister*, by Enid Bagnold. I am glad in retrospect that I did do it, contradictory as this may seem, because Judith Anderson's performance is recorded, on tape, in a style of acting for the theatre that no longer exists. She was one of the finest exponents of the grande dame leading lady, a style requiring a vast technical resource, one of great gestures; the vocal production is enormous. Lines are not delivered in a flat, naturalistic manner but in an almost Shakespearean cadence which is fascinating and gripping.

Judith Anderson filled our rehearsals with a vital sense of theatre. She created an atmosphere that one had imagined existed all through the theatre when first entering it. Regal, theatrical, larger than life. It was my then five-year-old granddaughter, Madeleine, who, upon visiting the set, informed Dame Judith that she, too, had been in a play. "You were, were you," observed Judith in a manner that has discouraged any subsequent theatrical activity on my granddaughter's part. And a good thing, too. Dame Judith, clearly, would brook no competition.

When Dame Judith declared she would not say the last line of *The Chinese Minister* on the air because it contained the word "fornicate," I wrote Enid Bagnold informing her of the situation, pointing out at the same time that I was not against fornication on or off the air. I was not allying myself with Judith in this matter. I had, by way of producer skullduggery, told Judith that I would blame it on the PBS network—it forbade the use of the word—which, of course, was not the case. But when it came to writing the letter I could not bring myself to do it, for which I am much relieved. Enid Bagnold was too fine a writer with whom to play these games. (She made it clear to me that she did not want to be called Dame Enid or Lady Jones or Miss Bagnold, but Enid Bagnold.) I did ask her if she would care to offer an alternative line if she deemed it fit. Back came a letter to Judith, bypassing me, not only urging her to say the line as written but also laying out the word "fornicate" on the page in such a way as to pronounce it gently and easily. It looked, as she broke up the word in syllables and accents, as it might be residing in a dictionary. She also mentioned casually that she had a new play in the works. Perhaps it was the latter that prompted Judith, in the end, to say the word, gently and easily.

I see the place now for what we were doing on *Hollywood Television Theatre*. For example, towards the end of our run I was beginning to move very much towards musical theatre. I thought audiences would like it — that they had had enough of problem plays. I was trying to move to a more imaginative area — not always successfully, but it was a way to go.

We did Oliver Hailey's lively play, *For the Use of the Hall*, which I think is the kind of project which should be done. Lee Grant directed with a good cast: Barbara Barrie, Susan Anspach, Joyce Van Patten, George Firth, and David Hedison. The play had been tried out at the Trinity Theatre in Providence, Rhode Island, but it needed new life — with revised writing, a new cast and director — in short, an advancement towards the play's realization. Rick Bennewitz called the camera shots for this production.

We followed it with *Ladies of the Corridor*, by Dorothy Parker and Arnaud D'Usseau. When it was first done on Broadway in the fifties, it did not do well; it was staged with a turntable moving the sets slowly around, and the changes between scenes were interminable. On television, it moved dynamically with cuts from room to room. Robert Stevens did a remarkable job as director, restructuring the piece and giving the work vitality. This impressed Arnaud D'Usseau so much that he thought this production superior to the original.

The play is a study of women growing old in a hotel, and what they do for interest — their loneliness, their dependence on their children. It worked as well when we did it, thematically, as when it was written, though it may have recently become too romantic.

We took another play which had flaws, but it was within the function of *Hollywood Television Theatre*: Faulkner's *Requiem for a Nun*. It had very interesting literary qualities; he started to write it as a play — then forgot it was a play and began to novelize it. He would pick it up as a play, then forget again and go back to writing it as a novel. Ruth Ford, who had appeared in it, worked with him to help make it into a theatre piece.

It's the kind of material that you bring to life again — virtually a new play, as few had seen it. For a program on PBS, it was ideal. Sarah Miles and Mary Alice were in it, and both were fascinating; it had a good reception.

I then received a play by a young English writer,
David Hare. *Knuckle* is a play like a film noir, written in
the style of Ross Macdonald. It is set in Brighton. One
of the characters wishes himself on the beach in Santa
Monica — so I got Hare's permission to adapt it to an
American situation, and we shot some of it on the beach
in Santa Monica. David Scott Milton did the adaptation
and we had an interesting cast — Michael Cristofer,
whose play *Shadow Box* won a Pulitzer Prize, Gretchen
Corbett, Jack Cassidy, and Eileen Brennan. They all gave
moving performances. It was a curious show. Like a
Ross Macdonald story, it was filled with detective novel
components, but they were not dramatized sufficiently.
There were good individual scenes but the plot was too
complicated and the audience got lost in a sea of facts.

Short Night

In 1978 I received a call from Hilton Green, then in the production department at Universal. We met for lunch and he informed me that Hitchcock had inquired if my services were available to work on *Short Night*. This, I am certain, was Hilton's diplomatic way of putting it. I have always suspected that it was his idea to have me work again with Hitchcock for a host of reasons. Hilton knew both of us well, having been assistant director on the television shows and later with Hitch on the features. Hitch was fond of him and trusted him.

Hitchcock was in trouble. His health was failing; the pain in his knees from arthritis was intolerable. *Short Night*, the story on which he was working from a book of the same name, which he had owned for some eleven years, was a potboiler, a poor story predictable in its second-rate style. But in all the pain and cares of age, there still operated the canniness of an old lion. He was determined to keep working on this project since there was no other. James Costigan had been hired to write the script but was removed from the assignment without writing a word. Now it seemed Hitch was ready to go with a script by Ernest Lehman. It had just been completed when I arrived on the scene. A board was put together by Newt Arnold. Robert Boyle, the production designer, and I were to go to London and Finland to select locations. Bob Boyle was a particular favorite of Hitch's, who always called him "Bobby" in a tone of warmth and affection. Bob, in his turn, adored Hitch and was intensely loyal to him.

My assignment was to help Hitch in all areas, particularly in regard to shooting the locations. One might call the assignment that of a second unit director but it was going to be more than that. There was no way Hitch was going to be able to get to Finland and shoot in the forests and on the lakes. The principals were involved in a major way at all these locations. Therefore, I was going to shoot with the principals those sequences which would have added up to at least half the picture. The plan was that these sequences would be shot and brought back to Universal, where the interiors would be shot by Hitch.

Bob and I, with a member of the Universal production office, went to London, Helsinki, and outlying regions where we temporarily selected locations, photographs of which were taken by Bob, a first rate photographer, to show to Hitch.

We returned to find that Hitch had rejected the script and was requiring a rewrite. The weather being a major factor in shooting the Finnish locations, Hitch's decision to get a rewrite precluded shooting on the dates already determined. Indeed, because of the weather, it meant a postponement of a year.

Not too keen about the property and in intense physical pain, he once said he would never make the picture. When I protested and asked why, he replied, "Because it's not necessary."

Thus he had, or so he thought, staved off things for a time. He did not want to make the picture, but he did like the idea of preparing it, writing it, having Bob Boyle and myself around, secretaries, Peggy Robertson (his production assistant) — the entire retinue.

He decided to do a new continuity, thus abandoning Lehman's script. Meanwhile, his behavior grew more erratic, his drinking more frequent to ease his pain. At home there was Alma, his wife, bedridden, desperately ill. Hanging over the entire situation was his great fear of death, which would bring on crying spells. For me, to whom this man was a king, it was an awkward and painful situation.

In addition, Hitch, for whatever reason, became irrational about Peggy Robertson, who had worked with him for some twenty years. He wanted to fire her. When Sue, his devoted secretary of an almost equal time, defended Peggy, Hitch wanted to fire both ladies. But he wouldn't do it himself. He insisted the studio do it and until they would, he refused to go to his office on the lot.

Thus it was that we worked on the continuity at Hitch's home with a new secretary present. I went to Herman Citron and discussed the situation but in his wise way he decided to wait it out. Soon Peggy Robertson was laid off and Sue was transferred to another office at Universal.

Meanwhile, we continued working. Hitch had flashes of brilliance but one had to wait for them as they emerged from the miasma of nostalgia in which he seemed to be immersed. One day, when we were about two-thirds of the way through the new continuity, Hitch declared we were ready to go into screenplay. I suggested that we ought to complete the continuity. But Hitch insisted. I then asked who would write this screenplay. Hitch replied, "You." I had a knee jerk reaction. Without a pause, I said, "Not me."

Forever after I have regretted this decision, although I know it was the right one. Hitch is reputed to have said to Pat, his daughter, "After all I've done for him." True. But I knew we were going nowhere with the film. Hitch didn't want to make it and I had no desire to play games. Certainly, had I stayed, I would have been blamed for the fiasco. That's the way it is.

Hitch's immediate reaction was to freeze me out. I couldn't get to see him for two days despite my requests, for I had had second thoughts and decided I would work with him on the screenplay. Finally, I just walked in on him in his office and found him working alone on the script. I offered my services but Hitch, a proud man, said he would do the script himself.

That was the end. He did get the studio to pay for another writer, which he had doubted he could do, but the script that resulted was never shot.

To this day I wish I had bitten my tongue when he said he wanted me to write the script and taken my beating like a man. There are times when the work is secondary to the human relationship and I loved this man with whom I had been friends over a period of thirty-eight years.

St. Elsewhere

There followed *Tales of the Unexpected*. Some episodes I produced over a three-year period, two I directed. It was while producing this series that I attended a party at Bruce Paltrow's home at which he suddenly got the idea that I should be in *St. Elsewhere*, his new series. I didn't discourage him. And so the following six years were a rich experience during which time I played Dr. Daniel Auschlander on the series. My admiration is unbounded for Bruce Paltrow, the executive producer, whose courage was the foundation on which the show rested.

There are many rewards in doing a series of quality such as *St. Elsewhere*. Money, of course. And then there's the fame. It was Brecht who once said to me, "An artist needs fame." Recently, going through customs in Holland with my grandson, Jesse, whose father is my dear son, Michael, we were about to get in line to show our passports. "Ah, Dr. Auschlander!" cried the customs official, "Please go through." And so I did, not daring to look at those waiting in line but, at the same time, whispering to my treasured grandson, "Remember that, Jesse." Without a weekly television series, such fame would have been denied me.

St. Elsewhere was a demanding, exasperating and rewarding show from the director's point-of-view. After looking at the first three or four days rushes of the pilot, Paltrow decided that the show was too "pretty," too smooth, that what it needed was "roughing up," particularly in camera work. Thus evolved the "St. Else-where" style — grainy, thrown away, hand-held (Panavision) and, in general, close to a documentary feel-ing where possible. And fast.

Now most directors bring a rather settled style to their television assignments in the interest of self-preservation, considering the front office schedule demands. At the back of each TV director's mind as he shoots the script is the next job. In a series, his awareness is even greater considering the multiple opportunities that present them-selves.

But this safe style did not work for *St. Elsewhere* and directors were hired and forgotten in large numbers. In addition, there was the situation with the actors, par-ticularly as the series settled in for its run. The principal actors had, over a period of time, evolved characters who were now recognized and accepted by the public. The actors, most of whom came from the theatre, took great pride in their characterizations.

Thus, woe betide the director who sought to meddle by attempting "to work with the actors," a much over-rated and suspicious phrase that has become a cliché and cop-out for many so-called directors.

This is my fifty-seventh year in show business and one of the things that *St. Elsewhere* impressed upon me is the change in the style of acting from when I started at Eva Le Gallienne's Civic Repertory Theatre in 1932 to the present day. The Stanislavsky system, advanced by The Group Theatre in this country, was the major force in bringing acting to a recognizable reality from the pseudo-English drawing room style that reigned, as well as the declamatory style. Nowadays, good actors speak to one another and listen to one another in a scene, radiating their presences in simple terms — a far cry from the "chin up" theatre (to project to the second balcony) and "tennis anyone" acting which was prevalent in the '30s. These changes over the years served the film and television mediums particularly well. The danger lies in performances becoming an imitation of naturalism rather than being natural. Here is where the director must perceive the difference and remedy matters, always remembering that two of his functions vis-à-vis the actor are to preserve the performer's ego and show a constant interest in the performance.

Dead Poets Society

One day I was called by my agent and asked to test for a picture with the intriguing title of "Dead Poets Society." No matter how long one is in this business, there are always surprises. This time it was in the form of the test. Not the usual appearance on the set with camera and crew but a visit to the casting director's office where a small tape camera was set up and one did a scene from the screenplay. The result was a cassette mailed to the director, a long cry from the days when he sat in the projection room and judged the performance on a screen in standard ratio rather than VCR.

In my case, the cassette was sent from Burbank to New York where Peter Weir, the director, was based while looking for locations in the Eastern states. Eventually he settled on Delaware.

Peter viewed the cassette, decided I had the "right attack" on the part and I signed, although I was not happy with billing or the money. Nonetheless, there followed one of the most rewarding experiences that I have had in pictures. And all because of Peter Weir.

Peter is a man of special charm, perhaps one might call it Australian. He has the face of a Shakespearean clown, a smile that ignites the set and a firm grip on the center of things.

It was, for me, as if a leap had occurred from the days of Chaplin, Hitchcock and Renoir. Now again, one was operating on a plane that made the profession worthwhile.

What are his special qualities, apart from his technical facility? Peter is serious in the way an artist is serious.

He is totally concentrated and committed, attributes which carry over and inspire cast and crew without Peter having to make demands of them. His demeanor on the set is patient, dignified and filled with humor. His cinematic sense is strong, and, with his enormously gifted cameraman, John Seale, they make a combination that is reflected in an outstanding body of work.

His method, so to speak, was to convey to the actors in a particular scene what the story meant at that point, what he was looking for, relating it at all times to the overall story. He would, of course, get more specific with the individual actor, speaking more or less in result terms colored by Weir's special poetic strength.

If the scene suggested it, he would improvise with the actors, on occasion incorporating things that emerged from the improvisation into the text. With Robin Williams and the boys in *Dead Poets*, a great rapport was created through this method and many discoveries were made.

Music played an important part in rehearsal. Peter would have a "ghetto blaster" on the set and would play what he deemed to be appropriate tapes before or during the rehearsal of a scene. Two of the classical pieces of music used in this manner ended up in the score of the picture—the second movement of Beethoven's Piano Concerto no. 5 and the "Ode to Joy" from Beethoven's Ninth Symphony. Sometimes, Peter would use the score of a previously made film; Morricone's music from *The Mission* was a major musical influence for the latter stages of *Dead Poets* and, indeed, affected Maurice Jarre's eventual treatment of those scenes. Often, Peter would play the music between takes. He created an atmosphere for the actors to help them retain the emotion they had produced during the take, aiding them in their concentration.

Then, at dailies, Peter would bring his tapes and ghetto blaster and, as a given scene came on, play the music he had selected. Thus, in effect, the dailies were "scored."

At all times, there was a feeling of emotion which was contagious and preserved. One perceived through it Peter's strong visual sense.

It was a dazzling time when one thought all the dazzling times must be in the past. It was a youthful time still filled with aspirations.

For the present, I shall stop writing. There's still much more to do on the stages — as director, actor and producer. So — show me the stage and point me in its direction. On we go.

Norman Lloyd:
A Professional Chronology

1932   **Actor**. Apprentice, Eva Le Gallienne's Civic Repertory Theatre, New York City; productions: *Liliom*, directed by Eva Le Gallienne, starring Le Gallienne and Joseph Schildkraut; *Alice in Wonderland*, directed by Eva Le Gallienne, starring Josephine Hutchinson.

1933   **Actor**. The Apprentice Theatre, May Sarton, artistic director; productions at The New School for Social Research, New York City: *A Secret Life*, written by H. R. Lenormand; *The Childrens' Tragedy*, written by Karl Schonherr; *Naked*, written by Luigi Pirandello; *Fear*, written by Alexander Afinogenov; *The Armored Train*, written by Vsevolod Ivanov; *The Call of Life*, written by Arthur Schnitzler; *The Sowers*, written by Jean Giono.

1934   **Actor**. The ILGWU Theatre, Forest Park, Pennsylvania; Summer Stock: *A Bride For The Unicorn*, directed by Joseph Losey, written by Denis Johnston, music by Virgil Thomson for the Harvard dramatic club.

1935   **Actor**. Longacre Theatre, Broadway: *Noah*, (role of Japhet), starring Pierre Fresnay, written by

Andre Obey. The Associated Actors, Boston; May Sarton, artistic director; productions: *Dr. Knock*, (role of Knock), written by Jules Romains; *Gallery Gods*, adapted from German by John Houseman and Henrietta Malkiel; *Gods of the Lightning*, (role of Macready), written by Maxwell Anderson and Harold Hickerson, directed by Joseph Losey. The Peterborough Players, Peterborough, New Hampshire, Summer Stock: *School for Wives*, written by Molière.

1936   **Actor**. The Theatre of Action, New York City: *Crime*, written by Michael Blankfort, directed by Elia Kazan. The Federal Theatre (The Living Newspaper), New York City: *Triple "A" Plowed Under*, directed by Joseph Losey; *Injunction Granted*, (role of the Clown), directed by J. Losey; *Power*, (role of the Consumer—Angus Button-cooper), directed by Brett Warren.

1937   **Actor**. Deertrees Theatre, Harrison, Maine; Summer Stock: *The Queen's Husband*, *Officer 666*, *Romance*.

1937- **Actor**. The Mercury Theatre, New York City; John
1938   Houseman and Orson Welles, producers; productions: *Julius Caesar*, (role of Cinna the Poet), directed by Orson Welles; *The Shoemaker's Holiday*, (role of Hodges), directed by Orson Welles.

1938   **Actor**. Columbia Workshop Radio Show (CBS): "I've Got the Tune," (role of Private Schnook), written by Marc Blitzstein, directed by Irving Reis. National Theatre, New York City: *Everywhere I Roam*, (role of Johnny Appleseed), written by Arnold Sundgaard and Marc Connelly, directed by Marc Connelly, sets by Robert Edmond Jones.

1939   **Actor.** The Group Theatre, New York City: *Quiet City,* (role of David), directed by Elia Kazan, written by Irwin Shaw, music by Aaron Copland.

1940   **Actor.** Broadway: *Medicine Show,* directed by Jules Dassin. Henry Miller Theatre, New York City: *Village Green,* directed by Felix Jacoves. Dock Street Theatre, Charleston, South Carolina: *Pigeons and People,* written by George M. Cohan.

1941   **Actor.** Theatre Guild, New York City: *Liberty Jones,* directed by John Houseman, written by Philip Barry, music by Paul Bowles. Pre-Broadway run, Boston and New Haven: *Twelfth Night,* (role of Sir Andrew Aguecheek), starring Helen Hayes and Maurice Evans. Paramount: *The Forgotten Man,* a short film, with Robert Benchley, directed by Leslie Roush.

1942   **Actor.** Universal: *Saboteur,* (role of Fry), directed by Alfred Hitchcock.

1943   **Actor.** Biltmore Theatre, Broadway: *Ask My Friend, Sandy,* (role of Sandy), produced and directed by Alfred de Liagre Jr., written by Stanley Young.

1944   **Actor.** Paramount: *The Unseen,* directed by Lewis Allen.

1945   **Actor.** David O. Selznick Productions: *Spellbound,* directed by Alfred Hitchcock. United Artists: *The Southerner,* directed by Jean Renoir; Lewis Milestone Productions: *A Walk in the Sun,* directed by Lewis Milestone; MGM: *A Letter to Evie,* directed by Jules Dassin.

1946   **Actor**. MGM: *The Green Years,* directed by Victor Saville. The Actors Lab, Los Angeles: *Volpone,* (role of Mosca), directed by Morris Carnovsky.

1947   **Actor**. MGM: *The Beginning or the End,* directed by Norman Taurog. United Artists: *Young Widow,* directed by Edwin L. Marin, produced by Hunt Stromberg Sr.

          Co-manager, with John Houseman, Coronet Theatre; Pelican Productions: *The Skin of Our Teeth,* directed by Paul Guilfoyle; *Galileo,* directed by Joseph Losey; *No Exit,* directed by Tamara Geva; *Dark of the Moon,* directed by Paul Guilfoyle; *The House of Bernarda Alba,* directed by Vladimir Sokoloff.

1948   **Director**. La Jolla Playhouse: *The Road to Rome.* Coronet Theatre: *The Stone Jungle,* written by Paul Peters.

          Associate to the Director, Lewis Milestone; production: *Arch of Triumph.*

          Actor. Enterprise Productions: *No Minor Vices,* directed by Lewis Milestone.

          Co-manager, with John Houseman, Coronet Theatre, Pelican Productions.

1949   **Actor**. Walter Wanger Productions: *Black Book,* directed by Anthony Mann. Universal: *Calamity Jane and Sam Bass,* directed by George Sherman. MGM: *Scene of the Crime,* directed by Roy Rowland.

Assistant to the Producer. Republic: *The Red Pony*, directed by Lewis Milestone.

1950   **Actor**. Warner Bros.: *The Flame and the Arrow*, directed by Jacques Tourneur, produced by Hecht-Lancaster. Universal: *Buccaneer's Girl*, directed by Fred de Cordova.

1951   **Actor**. Columbia: *M*, directed by Joseph Losey, produced by Nebenzal-Nero-Superior; *The Flame of Stamboul*, directed Ray Nazarro. United Artists: *He Ran All the Way*, directed by John Berry. MGM: *The Light Touch*, directed by Richard Brooks. National Theatre, New York City: *King Lear*, (role of Fool), directed by John Houseman, starring Louis Calhern, music by Marc Blitzstein.

   Director. La Jolla Playhouse: *The Cocktail Party*.

1952   **Actor**. United Artists: *Limelight*, (role of Bodalink), directed by Charles Chaplin.

   Director. La Jolla Playhouse: *The Lady's Not for Burning*. MCA Revue Productions; *Chevron Theatre*: "That's My Pop," "Annual Honeymoon," "Bacular Clock," "Mungahra," "Survey Man," "Meet the Little Woman," "The Reluctant Burglar," "One Thing Leads to Another"; *Gruen Theatre*: "Dream Man," "A Boy With a Gun," "Bird of Prey," "For Life." Hal Roach Productions: "You're Just My Type." *Omnibus*: "Mr. Lincoln," five half-hour films written by James Agee, produced by Richard de Rochemont for the Ford Foundation, released to CBS.

1953   **Director**. La Jolla Playhouse: *I Am a Camera, You Never Can Tell, Dial M for Murder, The Postman Al-*

ways Rings Twice. Phoenix Theatre, New York City: *The Golden Apple*.

Actor/Co-Director. Phoenix Theatre, New York City: *Madam, Will You Walk* (role of Dockweiler), directed with Hume Cronyn, written by Sidney Howard.

1954   **Director**. La Jolla Playhouse: *The Winslow Boy, Anniversary Waltz, Sabrina Fair, The Seven Year Itch, The Vacant Lot*.

1954-   **Director**. Industrial Films: *A Word to the Wives,*
1955   *The Right Touch, Room for Improvement*.

1955   **Director**. La Jolla Playhouse: *The Rainmaker, Native Uprising, Billy Budd, The Time of the Cuckoo*.

        Actor. La Jolla Playhouse: *Don Juan in Hell,* (role of the Devil), written by George Bernard Shaw.

1956   **Director**. The American Shakespeare Festival, Stratford, Connecticut, and Phoenix Theatre, New York City: *The Taming of the Shrew*.

        Actor. The American Shakespeare Festival, Stratford, Connecticut, and the Phoenix Theatre, New York City: *Measure for Measure,* (role of Lucio), directed by John Houseman and Jack Landau, music by Virgil Thomson. *On Trial* (TV series): "The Jewels of the Tower of London," directed by Harry Horner.

1957-   **Associate Producer**. *Alfred Hitchcock Presents*.
1962

1957-   **Associate Producer.** *Suspicion.*
1958

1958   **Director.** *Alfred Hitchcock Presents*: "$2,000,000 Defense," "Six People, No Music," "Safety for the Witness."

      Actor. *Alfred Hitchcock Presents*: "Design for Loving," directed by Robert Stevens.

1959   **Director.** *Alfred Hitchcock Presents*: "Your Witness," "Human Interest Story," "No Pain," "Anniversary Gift," "Special Delivery," "Man From the South," "Day of the Bullet."

      Actor. *Alcoa Hour*: "ESP," directed by John Newland.

1960   **Director.** *Alfred Hitchcock Presents*: "Hooked," "Very Moral Theft," "Contest for Aaron Gold," "O Youth! O Beauty,!"

      Actor. *Alfred Hitchcock Presents:* "The Little Man Who Wasn't There," directed by George Stevens Jr.

1961   **Director.** *Alfred Hitchcock Presents*: "Incident in a Small Jail," "I Spy," "You Can't Be a Little Girl All Your Life," "Strange Miracle," "The Faith of Aaron Menefee."

      Actor. *Alfred Hitchcock Hour:* "Maria," directed by Boris Sagal, written by John Collier.

1962   **Director.** *Alcoa Premier*: "The Jail", by Ray Bradbury; *Columbo* episode; *Alfred Hitchcock Hour*: "Final Vow."

1962-   **Producer**. *Alfred Hitchcock Hour*.
1963

1963-   **Executive Producer**. *Alfred Hitchcock Hour*.
1965

1964   **Director**. *Alfred Hitchcock Hour*: "The Jar," "The
        Lifework of Juan Diaz."

1968   **Executive   Producer**. Twentieth   Century-Fox:
        Journey to the Unknown.

        Producer. Universal: *The Bravos*, two-hour pilot;
        What's A Nice Girl Like You ..., film for ABC.

        Director/Producer. Universal: *The   Smugglers*,
        world   premiere   film   for   NBC; *Companions   in
        Nightmare*, world premiere film for NBC.

1969   **Actor**. Universal: *Night Gallery*, directed by Jean-
        not Swarcz.

1970   **Actor**. PBS: *The Scarecrow*, directed by Boris
        Sagal.

1971   **Actor**. PBS: *Gondola*, directed by Paul Stanley,
        written by Alfred Hayes. *Kojak* episode.

1972   **Producer/Director**. PBS: *Carola*, written by Jean
        Renoir, adapted by James Bridges.

1972-   **Executive   Producer**. PBS, *Hollywood   Television
1976   Theatre*: "Man of Destiny," written by George Ber-
        nard Shaw; "Double Solitaire," written by Robert
        Anderson; "Gondola," written by Alfred Hayes;
        "Me," written by Gardner McKay; "Winesburg,
        Ohio," from Sherwood Anderson stories; "Steam-
        bath," written by Bruce Jay Friedman; "Incident at

Vichy," written by Arthur Miller; "The Chinese Prime Minister," written by Enid Bagnold; "For the Use of the Hall," written by Oliver Hailey; "Ladies of the Corridor," written by Dorothy Parker and Arnaud D' Usseau; "Requiem for a Nun," written by William Faulkner; "The Hemingway Play," written by Frederic Hunter; "The Lady's Not for Burning," written by Christopher Fry; "Sty of the Blind Pig," written by Philip Dean Hayes; "The Last of Mrs. Lincoln," written by James Prideaux; "The Ashes of Mrs. Reasoner," written by Enid Ruddt; "Six Characters in Search of an Author," written by Luigi Pirandello; "And the Soul Shall Dance," written by Wakako Yamauchi.

Executive Producer/Director. PBS, *Hollywood Television Theatre:* "Nourish the Beast," script by Steve Tesich; "Knuckle," by David Hare, adapted by David Scott Milton; "Ascent of Mount Fuji," script by Aitmatov and Mukhamedzhanov; "The Fatal Weakness," written by George Kelly; "Philemon," written by Tom Jones and Harvey Schmidt; "Actor," written by Jerome Lawrence and Robert Lee.

Director/Producer. PBS, *Hollywood Television Theatre:* "The Carpenters," written by Steve Tesich; "Awake and Sing," by Clifford Odets.

Producer. PBS, *Hollywood Television Theatre:* "Shadow of a Gunman," written by Sean O' Casey; "Invitation to a March," written by Arthur Laurents; "Another Part of the Forest," written by Lillian Hellman.

1974   **Actor**. Mark Taper Forum Theatre, Los Angeles: *Major Barbara*, (role of Undershaft), written by George Bernard Shaw.

1976   **Actor.** United Artists: *Audrey Rose*, directed by Robert Wise.

1978   **Actor.** Universal: *FM*, directed by John Alonso; *Harvest Home*, five-hour TV film directed by Leo Penn for CBS.

1980- **Producer.** *Tales of the Unexpected* (American
1982   episodes), syndicated.

       Producer/Director. *Tales of the Unexpected*, "Youth From Vienna," script by John Collier; "Wet Saturday," script by John Collier.

1980   **Actor.** Universal: *The Nude Bomb*, directed by Clive Donner; United Artists: *King Cobra*.

1982- **Actor.** NBC: *St. Elsewhere*, (role of Dr. Daniel
1988   Auschlander).

1989   **Actor.** Touchstone Pictures: *Dead Poets Society*, directed by Peter Weir.

Index

A

B

Miles, Sarah, 223

Milestone Corporation, The, 99

Milestone, Lewis, 85, 91-92, 94-95, 99-101, 104-111, 113-114, 121, 126, 137, 143

Milhaud, Darius, 123

Milland, Ray, 85

Miller, Arthur, 215

Miller, Gilbert, 194

Milton, David Scott, 173, 224

Mission, The, 234

Mitchell, Thomas, 206

Mitchum, Robert, 112

Modern Times, 36, 134

Monroe, Marilyn, 139, 151

Montgomery, Douglas, 156

Moon Over the Yellow River, 20

Moorehead, Agnes, 66, 206

Morley, Robert, 181-182

Morosco Theatre, New York, 7

Moross, Jerome, 33, 165

Moscow Art Theatre, 20, 62

Moscow Rehearsals, 162

Mostel, Zero, 84

Mother Courage, 119

Mother, The, 33

Movie of the Weekend, 206

Mowbray, Alan, 152

Mozart, Wolfgang

Amadeus, 16

Muhl, Edward, 190-192

Muni, Paul, 37, 162

Murfin, Jane, 58

Museum of Modern Art, 49, 120

Music Corporation of America (MCA), 150-153, 179, 186, 188, 190

Mussolini, Benito, 33, 42, 47

My Fair Lady, 165, 167

N

Naish, J. Carrol, 89

Name of the Game, 177, 197-198, 200-201, 206

National Association of Broadcast Employees and Technicians (NABET), 196

National Theatre, 52, 140

Native Son, 40, 54

Native Uprising, The, 157

Nazimova, Alla, 14, 16

Neal, Patricia, 156-157, 161

Neighborhood Playhouse, 26

Nelson, Portia, 165

Nelson, Ruth, 60, 99

New School for Social Research, 17-18

New Theatre League, 30

New York Daily News, The,

Wolfe, Ian, 73

Women Have Their Way, The, 5

Wood, Audrey, 164

Woodward, Joanne, 141, 146

Woolrich, Cornell, 187

Works Progress Administration, 29, 32, 34

Wright, Teresa, 157

Writers Guild of America, 105

Wyatt, Jane, 29, 106, 120

Wyler, Tali, 114

Wyler, William, 95, 114-117, 162

Wynn, Keenan, 120

Wynter, Dana, 195

Y

Yarrow, William, 17

Yates, Herb, 152

Yeats, William Butler, 21

Yiddish Art Theatre, 20, 163

You Never Can Tell, 156, 158

Young Go First, The, 28

Young Widow, 99

Young, Gig, 195

Yurka, Blanche, 89, 120

Z

Zanuck, Darryl, 98

Zerbe, Anthony, 212

Ziegfeld, Florenz, 16

Zinnemann, Fred, 117

Zoot Suit, 32